JANE AUSTEN: SIX NOVELS AND THEIR METHODS

JANE AUSTEN: SIX NOVELS AND THEIR METHODS

Michael Williams

MACMILLAN

First published 1986
Reprinted 1990

Published by
MACMILLAN ACADEMIC AND PROFESSIONAL LTD
Houndmills, Basingstoke, Hampshire RG21 2XS
and London
Companies and representatives
throughout the world

Printed in Great Britain by
The Ipswich Book Company Ltd
Ipswich, Suffolk

British Library Cataloguing in Publication Data
Williams, Michael
Jane Austen: six novels and their methods.
1. Austen, Jane – Criticism and interpretation
I. Title
823'.7   PR4037
ISBN 0–333–38495–4

9.7.90(D)

Contents

Acknowledgements

I owe a particular debt of gratitude to R. T. Jones, for his advice, criticism and encouragement. Others whom I should like to thank for their help at various stages of the project are Timothy Webb, Jenny Bailey, Ruth Pulik, Ann Shiel, and my wife, Merle.

Some parts of Chapters 3 and 5 appeared originally in 1983, in an article in *Unisa English Studies*, and I should like to thank the editor, Professor S. G. Kossick, for permission to reproduce this material in an adapted form.

Note on References

Reference is made to the following works by Jane Austen:

The Novels of Jane Austen, 5 vols, 3rd edn, ed. R. W. Chapman,
with revisions by Mary Lascelles (London, 1932–4);
Minor Works, 1st edn, ed. R. W. Chapman, with revisions by B. C.
Southam (London, 1954);
Plan of a Novel, ed. R. W. Chapman (London, 1926);
Jane Austen's Letters, 2nd edn, ed. R. W. Chapman (London,
1952) – hereafter referred to as *Letters*.

Page references to the novels and other writings of Jane Austen
are, where appropriate, given in the text. The same applies to
secondary, critical works cited, with reference by (at least)
surname of author, date of work and page number. Further
references, in the same style as in the text, are included in the
Notes, which also embraces page references to primary works
not by Austen. The Bibliography should be consulted for fuller
information. Where two dates are given in a reference, the first is
the date of original publication, the second that of the edition
cited.

1 Introduction: Fictional Methods and their Effects

> *. . . but All the Good will be unexceptionable in every respect –*
> *and there will be no foibles or weaknesses but with the Wicked,*
> *who will be completely depraved & infamous, hardly a resem-*
> *blance of Humanity left in them. (Plan of a Novel)*

It is no longer necessary to defend Jane Austen from the charge that she achieved her art unconsciously, and that in Henry James's celebrated phrase she was not much more than 'instinctive and charming'. It is, though, worth recording just how fully she knew, artistically, what she was about, and also how soon the knowledge came to her.[1] Among even the earliest surviving pages of the juvenilia, the spirited imitation of fictional devices is often more than a mockery of the clumsy or the improbable or the excessively stylised, on the surface. It is also a critical and amused questioning of some of the more fundamental aspects of the techniques and conventions available to a novelist for shaping a novel, and for helping to determine a relationship with a possible reader.

Take the example of the first pages of 'Jack & Alice'. Some of the burlesque looks to the methods and motives of characterisation, as in the portrait of the dazzlingly flawless hero exaggerated into the nonsensical, or the sets of supposed antitheses that are no more than jangling synonyms. Other elements go deeper still, and the opening of 'Jack & Alice' is also a joke about the workings of openings in general, and the problem of entering *in medias res*. Jane Austen starts her 'novel' by describing a masquerade, but instead of using the opportunity, as so many of her predecessors did, to introduce low scheming and thuggery, or an elevated disquisition on truth and its disguises, her masquerade is regarded from the first as a novelistic problem. She interrupts her account of it in order to describe the people who will be

1

attending, but does so with such thoroughness that the account of the masquerade, when resumed, is largely unnecessary. Even when they are masked, we know who everyone is, so that the 'never failing genius' of the hero, demonstrated in the speed with which he penetrates the masks, becomes a joke about the elaborate contrivances needed to convey this 'genius', a joke also about the dubious nature of the 'genius' itself.[2]

This strain of complex burlesque is also to be found, at least intermittently, in each of the six novels Austen wrote in adult life. Here it has become part of the novelist's pervasive effort to investigate the methods by which she establishes, orders and tests her material. It is of course true that any study of Austen's novels is in some way an examination of the narrative techniques they employ. The attempt to locate Austen in a literary–historical context, or to relate her achievement to the intellectual and moral preoccupations of her contemporaries and predecessors; the working-out of a consciously ideological argument about what W. H. Auden called her interest in 'the amorous effects of "brass"'; the drawing-out of 'education' as a significant theme in the novels; the consideration of these novels in relation to a general description or theory of what novels can or should 'do': all will have occasion, in one way or another, to examine the effect of the dialogue, for example, or the functioning of the authorial irony.[3] But then such attempts are at best limited, at worst entirely predetermined, in what they reveal of the novels and their methods, by the particular nature of the approach being followed. To look at techniques in a more than oblique or incidental way, there must be a greater concentration on how individual techniques work and what they achieve. One way of doing this is to examine, on the one hand, the means employed by the novelist to shape the material of the novel, and, on the other, the interrelated but separate question of the kinds of response which the reader makes to the novel.

The bond and the discrepancies between 'text' and 'response' have been central issues for literary theorists in recent decades. Positions adopted have ranged from vigorous defences of the authority of the 'text' to equally vigorous declarations of the rights and freedoms of the 'reader'. My purpose is to adopt one of the less extreme positions, and I would cite what Wolfgang Iser (1976; 1978, p. x) has described as a 'dialectic relationship between text, reader, and their interaction'. As the term 'dialectic' indicates, such a position allows vital force both to 'text' and to 'reader'. The 'text' initiates and controls – but partially, never wholly – the response in the 'reader'; and the 'reader', in responding to the 'text', produces an 'interaction' that is more than the 'text', or at least in some respects different from it.[4]

It must at once be said, though, that my interest in this theoretical position is a specific and limited one. My focus is on the six Austen novels, their kinds of 'interaction' with 'readers', more specifically still on how some of these 'interactions' become possible. It is not, therefore, my intention either to provide a large-scale testing and demonstration of Iser's theories, or to provide rival accounts of the novel as a form, or of reading as a process. In short, my interest is in practical applications, rather than in theoretical implications. So, for example, though Iser and others have developed the notion of the 'implied reader' – the reader that the novelist has in mind when writing the novel, the reader created or projected by the novel – this is not a notion that I shall be seeking to apply. I do not doubt its use in other contexts, but it allows more predicative force to the novelist than the problems I examine in Austen's novels seem to suggest.

A focus on narrative techniques, in one way or another, is of course not new to Austen studies; but it would be fair to say that the emphasis has hitherto been on the shaping hand of the author alone, rather than on any concept of a 'dialectic'. The practice has also been to treat the narrative techniques as separate units that can be abstracted from the novels and then analysed and classified. As a method, it has naturally led to valuable insights, but it has limitations, some that are particularly telling for Austen's novels. The more completely we analyse the techniques as 'units', the less we can usefully say about the complex variousness of their interaction, or about the way they function within each novel as a whole. In order to establish general rules, exceptions are flattened out, variations are simplified, and the subtlety with which the techniques are used, on particular occasions, is blurred.

But it would be foolish to overlook what the approach has achieved. Mary Lascelles has lastingly enriched our understanding of the novels, in *Jane Austen and her Art* (1939), with the consideration of Austen's mastery of tone and of dialogue, and the use she makes of her 'communicative' style (pp. 90–102); of the ways in which the novelist 'chooses to fashion and control, by the limitations she imposes on her subject, both its shape and its substance' (p. 133); of the analysis of the characteristics of Austen's comedy (pp. 139–46); or of the investigation of the relationship between narrator and reader (pp. 173–200). In all this there is valuable thinking about the general principles involved, but it is constrained by the fact that it can do only a little more than generalise. It is true, for instance that the link between reader and character depends on a sympathy that is 'compounded of liking and compassion in varying proportions' (p. 215), but we need more than this very general rule if we are to consider how, in particular, for one character, the link is forged, or the way its composition and strength vary through the course of the novel.

Some years later, in *Jane Austen's Novels: A Study in Structure* (1953; 1962), Andrew H. Wright offered an analysis of the complex variations of point of view in the six novels: 'it is sly, often intentionally misleading – or at least very delicately subtle: quite unobtrusive transitions carry the reader from one viewpoint to another, and only the closest attention will enable him to ferret out the real intention of the passage in question' (p. 46). Wright goes on to acknowledge that 'to separate is to do violence both to the unity of each novel and to the contextual harmony of the passages examined', yet he still prefers to categorise the 'six characteristic points of view' – ranging from 'objective account' to 'interior disclosures' – and he confidently assures us that his method 'clears a hundred ambiguities and misapprehensions; it makes plainer the intention' (p. 47). Of course his approach makes for some clarification, but the limitations, which he himself acknowledges, cannot be overlooked.

Much more recently, Karl Kroeber's *Styles in Fictional Structure* (1971) offers an examination of Austen's novels – and also those of Charlotte Brontë and George Eliot – in order to attempt an account of the concept of 'style' and its inherent difficulties, and to describe the merits of 'systematized studies of fictional structures'. As that suggests, he too looks for the general rule, whether in regard to 'vocabulary', or 'character', or 'point of view', or the way a novelist can develop stylistically, or the use of 'imagery', or the 'romance–novel distinction', or the different ways in which larger or smaller parts of a novel are linked to and reflect the whole (pp. 8–9). Lloyd W. Brown's *Bits of Ivory* (1973) concentrates specifically on Austen's methods. Interestingly, he argues for a move 'beyond the familiar categorization of the various components of the novelist's style. The full significance of each unit can only be grasped when it is analysed in relation to the themes and forms of each novel' (p. 5). That sounds promising enough, until we discover that his aim is actually to substitute for the old 'categorization' a new one of his own devising: thus his units – and they are treated very much as units – are 'verbal disputes', 'imagery', 'symbolism', 'conversation', 'letter writing', 'dialogue' and 'parody'. That does not quite prevent him from treating the 'units' as intimately connected with the novels as wholes, but the degree to which the classification is successful is also the degree to which this other aim is frustrated.

In *A Reading of Jane Austen* (1975) Barbara Hardy has also taken up questions relating to Austen's techniques. She is much less concerned with explicit categorising, but she still reflects different general approaches to the novels, in terms of 'the feelings and the passions', 'storytellers', 'social groups', 'properties and possessions'. Most usefully, perhaps, she examines what she calls Austen's 'flexible medium, a capacity to glide easily from sympathy to detachment, from one mind to many minds, from solitary scenes to social gatherings' (p. 14). Much of the preliminary mapping of this notion was done by Mary Lascelles, and it fits exactly the ground covered by Andrew Wright; but it is a measure of how far the thinking has advanced that the stress is now on the fluid movement from one position to another, rather than on defining the boundaries of each position. Even so, Hardy's remains an account of how, in general, the movement happens, and what in general are its effects.

More recently still, there is John Odmark's *An Understanding of Jane Austen's Novels* (1981). This seems at first to be promisingly asking some of the questions which earlier approaches omitted, since it claims its theoretical framework in a 'theory of reception' that is concerned with the 'relations among the component factors in the reading process: the *author*, the *text* and the *reader*' (p. xii). But unfortunately, this turns out, at least in Odmark's hands, to be among the least satisfactory of the attempts to deal with Austen's techniques. Like earlier approaches, it works by generalising: in his first two chapters, for instance, he takes up questions of 'irony' and 'point of view', but only to reach conclusions that were often anticipated, often indeed overtaken, by Mary Lascelles forty years earlier. He is equally inadequate when showing what it is exactly, in the novels, that calls for the application of his theory, since he always seizes on some commonplace and then sets that up as if it *were* the novel. Assuming that *Northanger Abbey* is weakly constructed (p. 4), or asserting that in *Sense and Sensibility* there is 'a schematic presentation of character' (p. 6) are not achievements that either illuminate the novels or vindicate the theory. Even less fortunate is the way that, though he evidently conceives of reading as a very active process, Odmark is so preoccupied with accounting for authorial control and guidance that the reader seems, almost invariably, to be being led passively to preordained conclusions (pp. 43–5, 52–4, 182–3, for instance). It is hardly necessary to suggest that readers seem usually to find the experience of reading Austen's novels somewhat less lifeless and rather more ambivalent.

It is the aim of this study to break with the tendency to generalise, and to examine the techniques of the novels as *techniques at work*, to see each novel in terms of the way it is put together, the questions it considers, the means it finds for exploring its material, and the 'dialectical' responses the reader can make. Where general principles and patterns are revealed they will be commented on, but it is not my primary purpose to examine the techniques in order to look for the general principles from which they derive, or the set of rules which their general functioning constitutes. And, once we view the techniques in terms of the specific effects they have at particular points in the novels, and the problems and pleasures of reading from page to page, then we shall find it more and more difficult, especially with these six novels, to see anything beyond a quite elementary usefulness in trying to establish the general rules. It is obvious that the novels have a common basis in ways of thinking and seeing the world, and in ways of deploying this understanding; equally it is true that the novels represent a significant chronological development, in terms both of what they deal in, and of how they do it. But it is as much the case that each novel has its own 'questions' to ask, and finds its own ways of asking them. Each, in short, has its own way of being a novel.

Another consequence of approaching the novels in this way, as we shall see, is that we shall find that there is an unusual degree to which the novels do *not* deal in truths and certainties, but are rather the means of investigating and testing propositions and situations. That is not, somewhat anachronistically, to wish on Austen a heady relativism, and there is no particular sense in which she was not possessed of the certainties and the doubts of her own age: but it is what she did with these that is striking, and it is this that can be missed if we search too impetuously for a theme or a pattern in the novels. What are often taken as the conclusions towards which the novels work will thus begin to look more like the premises from which they start their investigations. It is not, for example, that Austen leads us to some conclusion, however elaborate and sophisticated, about the ways in which 'prejudice' and 'pride' can limit or pervert the understanding, in *Pride and Prejudice*: this is the assumption from which she starts, and in considering some of the difficulties and complexities of these concepts, she asks the reader what if, in a particular set of circumstances . . . ?

This takes us to the matter of existing criticism of the novels, by now a substantial body. As a record of previous readings of the novels, itself stimulating to later readers, and as an indication of those areas in the novels that have been most stimulating, or challenging, or rich, or difficult, or unpalatable, this substantial body is of crucial importance to an account of the novels that is also specifically and consciously an account of the reading of the novels. Therefore, the account offered here of the functioning of each novel will incorporate an account of its past treatment by the critics. That is not to suggest, though, that this is merely an attempt to provide a synthesis of established opinion; indeed we shall find that such a synthesising would be surprisingly difficult. It is of course to be expected, and it is necessary, that a novel worth the effort of reading should be susceptible to different, even divergent, readings, but, once that allowance is made, then the divergence associated with these novels is still surprisingly large – a consequence, no doubt at least in part, of the striking unresolvedness already noted. It is easy enough to find a consensus among the critics about the novels, but this is only possible in the broadest and least cutting of terms; if we try to be more specific and incisive, we must embark upon a particular 'interpretation', one which may borrow some credence from the novel, but which, as the product of an interaction between novel and reader, is at once more and less than the novel. We can all agree that *Sense and Sensibility* is 'about' the dangers of sensibility and the advantages of sense, or that *Emma* is 'about' the limitations of

imagination: any move beyond these placid and obvious generalities is a move towards the vitalised particularity and also the
limitations of a specific 'interpretation'.

One means of focusing on particular instances of methods or
meanings in the novels will be by way of comparisons with
examples from the work of other writers. These contrasts will
primarily be critical in nature, and will point to similarities and
differences in the workings of a method, the solution of a technical problem or the achieving of a particular effect. Examples will
come for the most part but not entirely from the eighteenth
century, and for the most part but not entirely from novels.
Thus, while this study makes no claim to offer a full literary
history, even in sketch form, even in the end notes, it will imply
some broad patterns of development, and some specific lines of
descent: it will suggest ways in which Austen was influenced by
her predecessors, or herself influenced her successors. But the
chief purpose of these contrasts will be to illuminate the six
novels and their workings.

Similarly, there will be occasion to consider more closely
something of the social and historical context of the novels, the
events and ideas out of which they grew, or which at any rate
were a large part of the world in which they grew. Obviously, no
amount of reading background or sources will make us see things
quite as Austen and her contemporaries did; obviously there is a
real sense in which it is much more important to establish her
significance in the last decades of the twentieth century than to
estimate her significance in the first decades of the nineteenth.
But what she means now also incorporates, however vaguely or
imperfectly, what she meant then. So, while making no pretence
to a comprehensive account of 'background', and determined
only by the exigencies of a particular problem in a particular
novel, the questions formulated by the novels, and the means of
dealing with them, will sometimes be examined in relation to the
times of the novels. Everyone can see, for instance, that *Mansfield
Park* is 'about morality' in some sense: whether or not that
morality is to be associated with the Evangelicals or some other
contemporary group is a question that, in the end, only *Mansfield
Park* can answer. But it is an answer that we can only perceive if
we already know something of the views and influences of
contemporary moralists.

There are some obvious objections to the approach I am

embarking upon: it could be said, for example, that there is a certain rather carefree eclecticism about the diversity of ways I adopt in approaching the novels; or that I am somewhat ineffectually attempting to provide a hold-all for saying all I wish to say about the novels. Certainly, I have been suggesting that there are different means of considering them, and that some of these should be adopted simultaneously. But the different means all spring directly from the problems that arise when one attempts to consider the workings of Austen's novels, and· their effects. And I make no pretence to having made use of all such possible approaches, or even to having made exhaustive use of the approaches I do follow. This connects with what must be the more serious charge that, while I imply that there are limitations to the act of 'interpretation', and that I have found a means of passing beyond those limitations, I offer accounts of the novels that are themselves 'interpretations'. But that is both inevitable and obvious. Any attempt to make a coherent statement about a novel must, if it tries to move beyond the obvious generalities, be an attempt at interpretation, and all I can say of mine is that they are offered in the knowledge of the limitations by which any act of 'interpretation' is beset. I do not claim to have analysed every last and least possibility of meaning, or to have catalogued all the ways of Austen's ambiguity. All I claim is that by considering the workings of the novels, and the different ways in which these can be responded to, I have shed some light on what *are* the ambiguities, and what *are* the possibilities of interpretation, for these novels.

There is only one way of organising such a study, and that is to order the accounts of the novels chronologically, novel by novel. There is of course a special difficulty with Austen here, since the chronology of the first three novels remains uncertain. But, since our interest is, in the first place, in the novels as they have come to us, rather than in the process by which they actually reached that condition, the date of first publication effectively orders all but one of the novels. *Northanger Abbey* remains a problem because that would place it last, jointly with *Persuasion*, and yet it was, at least in an earlier version, the first to be sold to a publisher. I have therefore followed the modern convention of treating it as 'first', but always with the reservation that this may not be entirely accurate since the possibility of late revisions can never be discounted.

2 *Northanger Abbey*: Some Problems of Engagement

'Oh! I am delighted with the book! I should like to spend my whole life in reading it. I assure you, if it had not been to meet you, I would not have come away from it for all the world.'
(Catherine Morland on *The Mysteries of Udolpho*)

Everybody knows that *Northanger Abbey* is a parody of the Gothic novel. Everyone sees that it is also, to borrow the sub-title of Fanny Burney's *Evelina*, the 'history of a young lady's entrance into the world'. And a well-established tradition insists that these two aspects of the novel are incompatible, even that the existence of each one is an active threat to the functioning of the other. Of course, the novel is also about reading and pleasure, reading and instruction. Does this help to heal the fracture?

The novel was probably first drafted after the earliest versions of what were to become *Sense and Sensibility* and *Pride and Prejudice*. In 1803 the manuscript was sold to a publisher, but never published by him, and Austen repurchased it thirteen years later. After 1803, she probably revised it at least once, but the nature of the revisions can only be guessed at, and in the last months of her life she wrote of having laid it aside in an apparently unsatisfactory condition: it was published posthumously. All of this seems to suggest that the novel is both 'early' and 'unfinished'; that it is a not-quite-successful experiment by a novelist who was yet to achieve the coherence of maturity; and that it is not much more than a bridge between the vigorous and percipient parodies of the juvenilia, and the substantial achievements of the later novels.[1]

The novel has, of course, never lacked defenders: but if their attempts are regarded successively, then they can still seem in fact to be revealing an incoherence in the novel. Unifying patterns are perceived, but only by including some and not all of the novel's facets. What is omitted is then often criticised as being crude or irrelevant. A sophisticated account of the problem has been given by A. Walton Litz (1965, pp. 59, 62, 68–9). He suggests that the chapters primarily concerned with parody – the first two, and the five concerned with Catherine's Gothic fantasies at the Abbey – 'form detachable units'. He concedes that 'the Gothic elements are a brilliant commentary on Catherine's general character and behaviour', and he argues that Catherine is at once the anti-heroine, created in reaction to the Gothic conventions, and a heroine being educated 'into reality'. Yet he also insists that the expression of the novel's main themes is 'hampered by lapses in tone and curious shifts in narrative method', and he concludes that 'Jane Austen was experimenting in *Northanger Abbey* with several narrative methods she had not fully mastered, and the result is a lack in consistency of viewpoint'. In other words, the reader is prevented from engaging fully with the text.

Others have tried to perceive a unity in just this diversity of method. Katrin Ristkok Burlin (1975, p. 89) insists that the novel is a 'single, complex treatment of the theme of fiction', in which the reader is exposed to four different kinds of fiction. These are 'the absurd extravagance of sentimental Gothic fictions', 'the satiric, educative fictions of Henry Tilney', 'the manipulative, egotistical fictions of the Thorpes', and 'the satiric and realistic fiction of *Northanger Abbey* itself'. But surely the novel is not only about reading and fictionalising, in the way that this categorising suggests? Jan Fergus (1983, pp. 11, 16, 19–20) concedes that 'the novel is about writing novels', but her interest is largely confined to the elements of burlesque; and, though she also claims that the processes of education are important in the novel, this is only as far as they affect the reader, since for Fergus the heroine is deliberately excluded from such processes. Eric Rothstein (1974, p. 14) takes a significantly larger view of the question of education, in developing his argument about how 'the strength of *Northanger Abbey*, and its theme, emerge from the connections between Catherine's education and ours, and between the social and literary modes of her experience'. But, since his is a sophisticated extension of the contrast between high-flown Gothic improbabilities, and the ordinariness of the everyday, he is silent on the important non-Gothic literary links with the novel. Frank J. Kearful (1965, pp. 514–17, 527) claims that the unity of the novel resides in a complicated interplay of satire and serious novel: but he has to redefine the parody in the first two chapters to make it into satire and thus a part of his formulation. Kearful also exemplifies the danger of making too much of the novel as a many-faceted thing. For him, Austen

> is writing what is not simply a novel or a satire, a burlesque or a parody, a comedy or a tragedy, a romance or an anti-romance. She is, rather, combining elements of all these in such a fashion as to make us aware of the paradoxical nature of all illusion – even those illusions by which we master illusion.

But that begins to read like Polonius's recommendation of the Players; certainly it is more than Kearful's argument actually supports. Then, too, he assumes that the differing 'methods' exist as large and sequential blocks of chapters, but this leaves him insufficient scope for dealing with the way that there can be a shift of 'method' from sentence to sentence, or even within one sentence.

It begins therefore to seem that the novel is indeed attempting to pose important and difficult questions about the links between fictional and actual worlds. But, if we are not to conclude that the questions are muddled, we must find a form in which the different elements of parody, satire and education novel can each take their due part. This means in turn that we must establish a way in which the reader is able to respond simultaneously in different ways to the different elements, when they combine. Perhaps we need to think in terms of a continuum, one that will enable us to perceive a diversity of positions, and the complex interchange between the different positions that are reflected in the novel. At one end, there are accounts of Gothic, some so broad as to be pastiche, or even simple imitation, rather than parody; there are the occasions of genuine and cutting parody of the Gothic, and there are the significant echoes, often parodic, of non-Gothic literature; there is the shading of parody of novels into satire on the reading of novels, and that satire into a different but related satire on the social life of Bath, where art is the stylised representation of life, and life can seem to be an imitation of the imitation; there is the more straightforward reading of books for entertainment and education, and there are other means of acquiring education to be tried out, as a means of preparing for and coping with the exigencies and the common-places of everyday life. If the novelist touches frequently on different points along this continuum, singly and in combination, then it will be possible for the reader to see the Gothic and the anti-Gothic elements mingling, but also in contrast. Catherine Morland is a heroine in everyday ordinary unheroineliness; she avidly follows the careers of 'genuine' heroines in the books she reads: but she can also – on occasion – quite naturally become a comic approximation to the specifications of the high Gothic. None of these possibilities is complete in itself; each exists and functions in combination with the others.

That begins to hint at the complexities of the dialectic rela-tionship between the reader and *this* text. But it is not merely that *Northanger Abbey* presents a complex combination of elements with which the reader can engage in a correspondingly complex dialectic relationship. The artful playing with possibili-ties and combinations that constitutes the text suggests that Austen is in some special sense aware of the potential that exists in the resulting dialectic. One could say that she is inviting the reader to share a joke with her about the nature of that dialectic. One could say that she is playing a 'game' with the reader in which she seeks to outwit him (and the reader who does not fully perceive the 'game' will still help to create a dialectic but will do so with what is significantly less than the text). Either way, this implies a large, conscious, ironic awareness on the part of both author and reader of the relationship between text and reader.

This is not to turn Austen into a daringly experimental twentieth-century novelist. Fielding and Sterne had already variously demonstrated how far a novelist could go in not dealing directly with his readers, but in teasing and mystifying, in digressing and explaining, and in arguing with his readers about the way the novel should develop. If *Northanger Abbey* is a direct descendant of these novels then we should expect it to declare its ancestry nowhere more clearly than in the opening pages, because, when a novel is self-consciously concerned with its existence as a novel, and its relations with its readers, the opening will of course be the ground for the first skirmishings with the reader. The obvious example of this must be the first pages of *Tristram Shandy*; but, for the purposes of *Northanger Abbey*, *Tom Jones* is probably more instructive. Fielding's interest in opening chapters turns out to be an elaborate joke at the expense of the reader. Authors, his narrator argues, should provide a 'bill of fare' before inviting readers to partake. The irony behind the seemingly reasonable suggestion becomes obvious when he tells us that his own bill of fare is 'no other than HUMAN NATURE', since this, he admits, is 'the subject of all the romances, novels, plays and poems, with which the stalls abound'. But what counts, he says, is 'the author's skill in well dressing it up'. And in extending his metaphor he is soon parodying the use of metaphor, so that we can smile with him while knowing that he is laughing at us. All he offers is the broadest of declarations – that at first his will be the 'more plain and simple manner' and that he will later add 'all the high French and Italian seasoning'. But then, in not answering the questions he sets himself, Fielding's narrator has actually demonstrated something significant about the way he intends to handle his material, and the kind of relationship he is seeking with his reader.

At the opening of *Northanger Abbey* Austen, like Fielding, sets out to play on her reader's expectations, and to reveal something of her narrator's functioning. But we are left less sure of what that functioning is, and of how her narrator stands, exactly, in relation to the material of the novel. If Fielding's narrator is ambiguous, he is at least a recognisable force, constantly and insistently drawing attention to his actuality and his opinions. Austen's is puzzlingly demure.

No one who had ever seen Catherine Morland in her infancy, would have supposed her born to be an heroine. Her situation in life, the character of her father and mother, her own person and disposition, were all equally against her. Her father was a clergyman, without being neglected, or poor, and a very respectable man, though his name was Richard – and he had never been handsome. He had a considerable independence, besides two good livings – and he was not in the least addicted to locking up his daughters. Her mother was a woman of useful plain sense, with a good temper, and, what is more remarkable, with a good constitution. She had three sons before Catherine was born; and instead of dying in bringing the latter into the world, as any body might expect, she still lived on – lived to have six children more – to see them growing up around her, and to enjoy excellent health herself. A family of ten children will be always called a fine family, where there are heads and arms and legs enough for the number; but the Morlands had little other right to the word, for they were in general very plain, and Catherine, for many years of her life, as plain as any.

And so we move on through the list of all the ways in which Catherine Morland is not a heroine. The effect, though, is to threaten any attempt by the reader to find a secure basis for his understanding. The opening sentence appears to have behind it the authority of the axiom, yet it carries no actual endorsement from the narrator, and is no more than an appeal to the consensus that is yet to be established. The ambiguity centres on the word 'heroine', and if we glance down the page then it seems at first as if there is just a simple irony at work: Catherine is a straightforward inversion of some of the more hackneyed conventions of the popular novel. But such a formulation soon fails to contain the problem, because, if Catherine is not a typical heroine, then what *is* she?

We are faced with the engaging puzzle of finding a way of being interested in a heroine who is 'ordinary' and thus 'realistic', but also not 'real'; is necessarily a heroine, even if a dull one, whose dimensions and functions can only be communicated to us by way of the dangerous and confusing and ridiculed literary conventions. Nor is it only that the realistic account of the education of an ordinary girl is beset by complicated jokes and questions about the way novels are written and the way they are read. The biographical details of this seemingly unsuccessful heroine are themselves a tangled string of paradoxes and ironies, each requiring a slightly different kind of unravelling from the one that precedes it, each weakening a little our grasp of what has already been revealed. A 'family of ten children' is 'fine', at least in the everyday conversational sense, but then this loose usage is criticised by the application of serious and good sense; serious, that is, until we realise that it is heads, as well as arms and legs that must be counted. Then we are told that the Morlands are 'in general very plain', so the word 'fine' is entirely inappropriate except in the already discredited conversational sense.

Later, it is revealed that Catherine's abilities are 'extraordinary', and the narrator seems to be operating with fairly simple reversals, since it is clear that Catherine is 'extraordinary' only because she is ordinary. It is natural therefore that she 'never

could learn or understand anything before she was taught', since
this places her in direct opposition to the absurd literary convention by which heroines acquire extraordinary knowledge and
abilities unaided. But then we are told that Catherine is also
'often inattentive, and occasionally stupid', and here no simple
reversal seems possible: 'ordinary' may mean 'life-like' but it is
also rather dull. Yet of course it is a well established (though not
quite universal) convention that a heroine be beautiful: and it *is*
a universal convention that a heroine be interesting in some way.
It is only at the very end of the long first paragraph, when we are
told of her love of 'rolling down the green slope at the back of the
house', that we can properly disentangle the ambiguities. It is
the vividness, the particularity of this small detail, given osten-
sibly in Catherine's favour but apparently operating against her,
that has on reinterpretation to be seen to work for her, that fixes
some secure basis for our interest in Catherine. If she is ordinary,
then she is also refreshingly natural, and she possesses the
natural vitality of a ten-year-old child.

   This security, though, is also momentary. The second paragraph informs us, with a telling irony, that Catherine becomes
'almost pretty'; the third that she has lost her tomboyish ways
and is 'in training for a heroine'. So she stocks her memory with
quotations that will comfort and sustain her through the 'vicissi-
tudes' of heroineship. The quotations themselves are not surprising, given that this is a family in which *Sir Charles Grandison* is
read (a favourite, incidentally, of Austen herself), but 'new
books' are not easily obtained (*Northanger Abbey*, p. 41). Yet they
present us with a very complex irony. Catherine, the vital
'person' who once enjoyed rolling down banks, and who even
now has only a vague apprehension of what it is to be a heroine,
is nevertheless *the* heroine of this novel, one who attempts to
study the habits and functions of other heroines. Her eager
response to *Twelfth Night*, which the narrator argues is proof that
she is a promising apprentice heroine, is also evidence of the
naïve literalness with which Catherine sometimes approaches
literature. And this is a quality that will actively determine her
career as the heroine of *this* novel. To Catherine, 'a young
woman in love always looks – "like Patience on a monument /
Smiling at Grief"'.

In many ways, the opening chapters of *Northanger Abbey* are the most challenging and disconcerting for the reader. Elsewhere the separate workings of the parody, the satire and the education novel, and the different ways in which they combine, can be as complicated and surprising (can even surprise because we have lapsed into a false security): but the later chapters tend to be a more thorough exploring of possibilities that have already been sketched. In this respect, the range of literary reference in the opening pages is interesting. It is usually assumed that this is confined to the Gothic, but, as the questions about beautiful and interesting heroines suggest, the range is actually much wider. And in this breadth there is an important clue to the functioning of the literary allusions and the parody in the rest of the novel, and to the connections between this and other elements in the novel.

The Mysteries of Udolpho (1794), much discussed in the novel, is obviously one source, but it is not the only Gothic source. Further, Mary Lascelles has shown that the signally unaccomplished Catherine Morland of the first chapters is much more like the opposite of Charlotte Smith's *Emmeline* (1788) than anything in the Radcliffe novels: she adds the wise proviso that there is 'great similarity among the heroines of that age'. This takes us away from the purely Gothic, since *Emmeline*, though it has distinct Gothic touches, is also a quite respectable daughter of a Fanny Burney novel.[2] The range of reference extends even beyond this point: being locked up by one's father is an almost indispensable part of a Gothic heroine's career, yet it is also a practice common to the fathers of Sophia Western and Clarissa Harlowe. And, when we are told that Catherine is so unheroinely as to prefer cricket 'not merely to dolls, but to the more heroic enjoyments of infancy, nursing a dormouse, feeding a canary-bird, or watering a rose-bush', we have moved to the area of the then current children's literature, and the pages of Thomas Day's *Sandford and Merton* (1783–9), or – even more likely – Sarah Trimmer's *Fabulous Histories* (1786): teaching children to be kind to animals was a part of Day's function and it was central to Trimmer's; both were also eager to offer practical instruction in natural history.[3]

This widening of the range of reference operates as yet another means of undermining our attempts to find a simple and coherent pattern. There is, though, another significant consequence:

Austen is not merely warning us that a too-literal application of fictional conventions can be dangerous; she is also deliberately invoking and examining the literary tradition within which such warnings were given. In eighteenth-century writing, the omnivorous tradition that charts an excessive preoccupation with reading, and demonstrates its consequences for characters whose expectations of reality are too much governed by the conventions of literature, became, itself, a stock part of the literary landscape, so that it could be established by a few hints. In *The Rivals* (1775) Sheridan's Lydia Languish illustrates the point exactly: we know precisely what to make of her as soon as we know of her voracious delight in novels; it becomes natural that she should have 'very singular taste'. We can anticipate that she would hugely enjoy an elopement; we can even guess the terms in which she would understand the experience: '– so becoming a disguise! – so amiable a ladder of Ropes! – Conscious Moon – four horses – Scotch parson'.[4]

Northanger Abbey has been connected by the critics with a particular strand within the tradition. This is made up of the many rigid imitators of *Don Quixote*, for whom the delusions generated by popular literature are *the* theme, rather than merely *a* theme, and who borrow Cervantes's shape to suit their own narrowly didactic purposes.[5] Thus Charlotte Lennox's *The Female Quixote* (1752) looks to the heroic French romance of the previous century; Richard Graves treats Methodism and John Wesley in *The Spiritual Quixote* (1773); Maria Edgeworth's tale *Angelina: or, L'Amie Inconnue* (1801) is aimed at the excesses of the sentimental novel. And Eaton Stannard Barrett's *The Heroine* (1813) is directed at the Gothic novel, but also includes references to works as diverse as *Sir Charles Grandison*, Johnson's *Lives of the Poets*, and Madame de Staël's *Corinne*. Austen herself responded with 'very high' pleasure to *The Female Quixote*, and she thought *The Heroine* a 'delightful burlesque' (*Letters*, pp. 173, 377). Something of this can be glimpsed if we consider a passage from *The Heroine*. Cherry Wilkinson is convinced that she is a 'Heroine', and that her real name must be Cherubina de Willoughby; so her father, a mere farmer, cannot be her father.

'What!' cried I, 'can nothing move thee to confess thy crimes? Then hear me. Ere Aurora with rosy fingers shall unbar the eastern gate – '

'My child, my child, my dear darling daughter!' exclaimed this accomplished crocodile, bursting into tears, and snatching me to his bosom, 'what have they done to you? What phantom, what horrid disorder is distracting my treasure?'

'Unhand me, guileful adulator,' cried I, 'and try thy powers of tragedy elsewhere, for – *I know thee!*' I spoke, and extricated myself from his embrace.

'Dreadful, dreadful!' muttered he. 'Her sweet senses are lost.' . . .

I relate the several conversations, in a dramatic manner, and word for word, as well as I can recollect them, since I remark that all heroines do the same. Indeed I cannot enough admire the fortitude of these charming creatures, who, while they are in momentary expectation of losing their lives, or their honours, or both, sit down with the utmost unconcern, and indite the wittiest letters in the world.[6]

Barrett's version is of particular interest in relation to *Northanger Abbey*, because of the way it does not confine its attention to a single kind of literature. But it must also be clear that this kind of parody can only work in superficial and crude ways, and in this respect Barrett is typical of this strand of the tradition. There is a certain lack of skill and confidence, an uneasy interaction between 'fancy' and 'reality': in the passage from *The Heroine*, for instance, the joke about heroines writing elegant accounts of horrible experiences is apt, but only if we are not made – as we are – to think too closely of Cherubina actually sitting down to write this account. So, in general, the frequent and earnest reminders of the realism of the setting are self-defeating, and require as frequent explanations of the elaborate mechanisms at work in sustaining the illusions of the central character. That means, inevitably, that the sustained illusion will become progressively less likely, less interesting, less entertaining. Similarly, there is an over-eagerness in emphasising the moral: usually there is a solemn invocation of Cervantes, and the moral lesson he can teach; usually too there appears a worthy and wordy doctor of divinity, at the end of the novel, to lecture the character into a proper understanding of himself, and to ensure that the reader also gets the point.[7]

It is worth noting, by contrast, that Cervantes himself never allows these problems to obtrude in *Don Quixote*. He relies, rather, on the degree to which he can control our sympathetic laughter, and he trusts to the workings of the burlesque. There is none of the muddling preoccupation with the problems of realism: the Don sees giants, we *know* they are windmills. Consequently, also, Cervantes shows no felt need to preach illusions out of the reader, can afford even to suggest that religious discourse is an ineffectual means of curing the Don: it is turned into the joke about a 'great and pleasant Inquisition' of the Don's books; quickly becomes parody, in the pedantic debate of the merits of each book; then becomes a satire on the careless zeal of such Inquisitions, when the priest loses interest and the books are indiscriminately burned.[8]

While it would be perfectly correct to argue that Austen has a share in this tradition, it is surely wrong to suggest that *Northanger Abbey* is a significant reflection of that share. It is in the juvenilia, in works such as 'Love and Freindship', that there is the single-minded burlesquing of the Lennox or Barrett kind. Even here Austen shows herself, unlike them, to be free from the distracting preoccupation with the need to ensure that the picture is 'real' and the character 'deluded', and like Cervantes she turns the moralising into a target for more burlesque. When Sophia dies – she is 'carried . . . off' by 'a galloping Consumption', the result of fainting on damp ground – it is as one *heroine* speaking to another, not as someone cured by her desperate plight of the fanciful illusions generated by novels, that she utters her last words to her friend: 'Beware of swoons Dear Laura. . . . A frenzy fit is not one quarter so pernicious; it is an exercise to the Body & if not too violent, is I dare say conducive to Health in its consequences – Run mad as often as you chuse; but do not faint –' (*Minor Works*, p. 102).

But there is another strand of the tradition that links Cervantes with Austen, one that will occasionally borrow something from the more simple burlesquers, but is much more broadly interested in the relationship between fiction and truth. Fielding acknowledged his debt to Cervantes on the title page of *Joseph Andrews*, and in that novel he made what he had borrowed into something that is very much his own. Smollett and Sterne are both under the influence of the same tradition, and Scott connects interestingly with it when, at the start of *Waverley*, he explains how Edward Waverley's reading has coloured his mind: Scott deliberately repudiates any link between his novel and the simple burlesques in imitation of *Don Quixote*, and the contrast he draws with Cervantes is put in terms which could be applied, almost exactly, to Catherine Morland. His subject, he says, is not

> such total perversion of intellect as misconstrues the objects actually presented to the senses, but that more common aberration from sound judgement, which apprehends occurrences indeed in their reality, but communicates to them a tincture of its own romantic tone and colouring.[9]

It is after all the mere sight of the furnishings of Mrs Tilney's room that destroys Catherine's most fervid Gothic imaginings (*Northanger Abbey*, pp. 193–4). Henry's subsequent lecture merely helps to fix that lesson. So, in making its own distinctive contribution to this more elevated strand of the tradition, *Northanger Abbey* is also showing how it fulfils the promise of its opening chapters. Catherine is the 'heroine' deluded by reading who must be brought to her senses, and yet she is also, more broadly and subtly, the young girl who has been somewhat confused by the difference between appropriate and inappropriate ways of understanding the world. She is put right by the pedagogically inclined 'hero': but Henry, while he can be pedantic, can also at times be possessed of a narrator-like irony, and he can be a young man who is rather too partial to his own wit. Further, he can teach her so well, and she be so effectively taught, not only for the sound literary reason that he is the wise hero and she the erring heroine, but because they are, albeit unequally, in love. There is also a final twist: we can see the way parody shades into satire, and the way both are intimately bound up with the education novel, but the parody is also a parody of parody, and Henry, the exhorting clergyman who has just come back from attending to affairs in his parish when he finds Catherine outside his mother's room, is also Austen's mocking echo of the wordy divine who so often dogs the closing pages of the lesser burlesques.

That should alert us to the way that the relation between *Northanger Abbey* and its sources and targets is constantly varying. Eric Rothstein (1974, p. 20) argues that there is a pattern in the variation of treatment from character to character: 'Mrs Allen is the null version of the chaperone. Isabella is a genuine but corrupt confidante, and her brother a shrunken but certainly genuine unwelcome suitor. The General, finally, is a reasonable facsimile, within a social world, of a Montoni or Schedoni.' But this only partially holds. Isabella is a 'confidante', but she also sees herself as a 'heroine', and is a much closer and more consistent approximation to the Gothic model than Catherine herself. John Thorpe is the 'unwanted suitor' but he also comes close, on occasion, to displacing the General as 'villain'; and the General's 'villainy' is modified by the fact that he is the dupe of John Thorpe. Even Mrs Allen is not always merely the 'null version of the chaperone': it is clear that she in no way fits the Gothic requirements of her role, and it is as clear that she cannot properly fulfil ordinary everyday expectations about chaperones, since she is incapable of giving Catherine almost any useful guidance.[10] But there are occasions when she much more actively inverts her role. Catherine's entrance to Bath's Upper Rooms is delayed until Mrs Allen, herself, is provided with 'a dress of the newest fashion'; they enter late because it is Mrs Allen who is 'so long in dressing'; and then Mrs Allen does so with 'more care for the safety of her new gown than for the comfort of her protegée' (*Northanger Abbey*, pp. 20–1).

The range of variation in the use of literary devices is most obvious with Catherine herself. After her first meeting with Henry, for example, she is puzzled by his apparent disappearance from Bath: 'This sort of mysteriousness, which is always so becoming in a hero, threw a fresh grace in Catherine's imagination around his person and manners . . .' (pp. 35–6). A perfectly understandable response, but one which does not allow for the actual and perfectly ordinary explanation, yet also begins to suggest the excitement that a genuine Gothic heroine could have wrung from the situation. Conversely, when John Thorpe carries her off in a carriage, away from the interesting Tilneys, and towards the delightful horrors of Blaize Castle, the parody seems obvious enough, especially when we realise that, though Catherine thinks it genuine, Blaize is sham Gothic; especially when John Thorpe's bluster ('But Mr Thorpe only laughed, smacked his whip, encouraged his horse, made odd noises, and drove on' – p. 87) is the caricature of a typical Gothic villain. In fact the moment brings together a rich diversity of literary and social patterns. The business of the heroine being abducted in a carriage is a familiar enough Gothic cliché, but a famous non-

Gothic literary abduction (one that Catherine herself would have known of) occurs in the exemplary pages of *Sir Charles Grandison*. And in *Northanger Abbey* part of the force and part of the comedy derives from the fact that Catherine is, on this occasion at least, entirely unresponsive to literary parallels, whether Richardsonian or Gothic, and sensibly and volubly insists on regarding John Thorpe's behaviour as being no more than rude and deceitful.

The practice of writing and reading novels is of course also openly debated by the narrator. The most obvious instance, outside the opening and closing chapters, is the 'defence of the novel' (pp. 37–8) and, here as elsewhere, what might appear plain and simple turns out to be difficult and divergent. As the appeal for sisterly support from other heroines suggests, a criticism of silly improbable novels and dull over-literal readers is not a rejection of the novel as a form – a point that none of the simpler burlesques make with any conviction. It is also an energetic assertion of the 'genius, wit and taste' that can be found in novels. But the narrator becomes increasingly enthusiastic in defending novels, and begins to take up the role of a too-consciously partisan novelist, defending her art a little too vehemently: the polemic seems at once to be serious and a self-parody. The novel is, we are told, 'only some work in which the greatest powers of the mind are displayed, in which the most thorough knowledge of human nature, the happiest delineation of its varieties, the liveliest effusions of wit and humour are conveyed to the world in the best chosen language'. The real ground for the defence of the novel must lie a little lower than the heights of these superlatives. Then, too, there is the implied need for some means of discriminating between novels: *Cecilia* can perhaps be more enlightening and more substantially entertaining than, say, *The Castle of Wolfenbach*. But on what basis, exactly, do we judge this? How, more particularly, does the naïve reader learn to make the judgement?

For there is Catherine, herself a 'heroine', and one known to 'take up a novel'. Though the 'defence' has all the appearance of a digression into generalities, it is sandwiched between the first mention of the fact that Catherine and Isabella read novels, and an account of their pleasure in reading *The Mysteries of Udolpho*, and it is fair to ask how far the 'defence' connects with Catherine. In fact, she is something of an embarrassment to it: true, she does not scorn novels, true she does derive a great deal of the promised pleasure from reading them; but what of the high claims about 'the most thorough knowledge of human nature'? All Catherine herself claims, even for *Sir Charles Grandison*, is that it is 'very entertaining' (*Northanger Abbey*, p. 42), and it is doubtful that the novels of Burney and Edgeworth, so eagerly praised by the narrator, would necessarily elicit a wider response from Catherine. Yet of course Catherine does take instruction from *some* novels: as with her means of finding entertainment in novels, though, she does it rather indiscriminately. Thus she rather credulously acquires a 'great store of information' (p. 16) about the ways of love, and the contours of French and Italian landscape, and the behaviour to be found in abbeys. But there is another complication, because, though she sometimes assumes that life is like literature, she has a firm-enough grasp, if not fully consciously, of the idea that literature is not like life. Her intense delight in 'Laurentina's skeleton', her insistence that she should not be told what is 'behind the black veil' (pp. 39–40), both show that she clearly considers them to belong to the province of fiction and not reality. Similarly, when Henry offers for her terror and delight a pastiche Gothic novel (pp. 157–60) it is clear that she at least half understands what he is about. And, when Isabella declares that, 'were I mistress of the whole world, your brother would be my only choice', we are told that Catherine is as much struck by the 'novelty' of this utterance, as she is by the way it reminds her of 'all the heroines of her acquaintance' (p. 119). What this seems most cogently to suggest is a need to consider the ways in which these complex half-perceptions can be made whole, and Catherine can become more fully aware of the confusing border between fiction and life – a border that has been teasing and perplexing the reader since the start of the novel.

So we return to *Northanger Abbey* as an education novel. This too is an incomplete form, and we have to take it in conjunction with the other forms. We are told that Catherine 'never could learn or understand anything before she was taught' and this has already been noted as the pillorying of a popular fictional convention. But it is also a statement of the empiricist contention that experience is the prime source of all knowledge, summed up in

John Locke's famous notion of the *tabula rasa*. This notion underlies much of the novel.[11] It is obvious that Catherine is handicapped by a lack of experience, and that, as her experience, direct and indirect, widens, so she begins to build, sometimes usefully and sometimes not, on her understanding. Isabella introduces her to the pleasure of *Udolpho*, a pleasure which she at first assumes to be universal. John Thorpe's brash and muddled assertions about novels persuade her to revise this assumption, and so she hesitates to mention this favourite topic to Henry because 'gentlemen read better books' (*Northanger Abbey*, p. 106). Henry's response, though she does not fully understand it, persuades her to make yet another assessment.

But, then, the empiricist pattern, like all the others, does not hold completely, and Catherine is often moving, not always unprofitably, beyond the realms of her experience. Were she no more than the application of Lockean principles then there might be more justification than actually exists for those critics who find her 'dull', or who claim that her mind is a 'somewhat implausible blank' (Butler, 1975, p. 178), because then the development of her understanding could be a steady and mechanical progression, as experience widens and knowledge grows.[12] But no such orderly structure exists. Catherine's relationship with Isabella is illuminating, here, because Isabella is four years older than Catherine, and 'at least four years better informed' – at least in the matter of balls, fashions, flirtations and quizzes (p. 33). It is hardly necessary to warn the reader of the selfishness, the false intensification, the constant reliance on trick and deception, that make up Isabella's behaviour; but it is interesting to notice how the 'naïve' Catherine responds. We might expect that she would tend to accept Isabella's version of the world, at least until experience proved it false, but in fact what happens is more complicated and less predictable. In their first long conversation in the Pump Room (pp. 39–43), she sometimes does respond unquestioningly, but at other times she is more critical, even if the criticism is not always quite consciously made. At some points, she rejects what Isabella says for reasons that are firmly based on her own experience, as when she questions Isabella's opinion of *Sir Charles Grandison* because she has herself read it. At others, though her criticisms are no less appropriate, they are much less the result of anything that she has experienced. This is most apparent when the talk turns to the interesting subject of young men. Henry Tilney's name is mentioned and Isabella offers some sisterly support but Catherine is able to reach something rather more profound than Isabella's gushing.

> 'Where the heart is really attached, I know very well how little one can be pleased with the attention of any body else. Every thing is so insipid, so uninteresting, that does not relate to the beloved object! I can perfectly comprehend your feelings.'
> 'But you should not persuade me that I think so very much about Mr Tilney, for perhaps I may never see him again.'
>   (*Northanger Abbey*, p. 41)

We know already that Catherine has been toying fancifully with the fact of Henry's absence, and this indicates the quite precise limits that she actually sets herself. And, though her only experience, in this area, comes from novels, she is not using that experience or she would more readily assume the inevitability of a happy ending. Even Harriet Byron, despite her much-prolonged doubts, does finally become Lady Grandison.

The arrival of John Thorpe brings another combinaton of possibilities and difficulties. It is easy not to like him, but it is worth noting how far Catherine moves towards an active dislike of him, since, as the narrator observes, she does not 'understand the propensities of a rattle' (p. 65). Then, and it is another reminder of her vulnerability, her dislike is bought off by the fact that he is James's friend and Isabella's brother, and that he has offered himself as a partner for the evening, so there is a complex interaction of 'friendship' and 'flattery', of 'diffidence' and 'youth' (p. 50).

With Henry, the links and the contrasts are most various. For Catherine, he is the desirable suitor, who is also a useful instructor, as well as being a habitual and sometimes puzzling wit. His delight in his own wit is frequently at odds with his functioning as a teacher, and both are sometimes complicated and compromised as he becomes increasingly a lover: there are also times when, though he seems to be reaching the heights of a narrator-like detachment, he is himself firmly under the ironic scrutiny of the narrator. Inevitably, critics have tended to see this either as further evidence of the incoherence of the novel, or else have tried to regularise and simplify his functioning.[13] But he is actually an integral part of the process by which different patterns are made to exist simultaneously.

Catherine herself is not merely the ingenuous admirer of Henry. After their first dance, she finds him 'as agreeable as she had already given him credit for being. He talked with fluency and spirit – and there was an archness and pleasantry in his manner which interested, though it was hardly understood by her' (p. 25). This is entirely predictable from an open, good-natured and ignorant girl of seventeen: we need, it seems, only pause to note how similarly Catherine is quickly delighted with Isabella's friendship, and so to record how vulnerable this tendency makes her. Yet there is more. The distance between Henry and Catherine is never greater than when he gently but pointedly satirises the ways of Bath, which she is just beginning tentatively to understand, and uses a way of thinking and talking that is quite beyond the reaches of her experience (pp. 26–7, 65–6). But she still perceives a good deal of his meaning, and, though she is uncertain, her impulse is to laugh with him. When he exercises his wit on a subject so well known to her as Mrs Allen, she can even wonder whether 'he indulged himself a little too much with the foibles of others' (p. 29), a view that is not entirely without justification, but is also probably coloured by the fear (not, perhaps, fully thought out) that, just as the quite unwitting Mrs Allen is being teased, so might she herself have been unwittingly amusing him. It is only later, when she is completely enthralled by him, that she more confidently, if a little confusedly, assumes that 'Henry Tilney could never be wrong. His manner might sometimes surprize, but his meaning must always be just: – and what she did not understand, she was almost as ready to admire, as what she did' (p. 114). And, having thus discovered the beauty of his perfection, it is by an ironic reversal of the conventional love story that she is able, later still, to admit to herself the possibility, at least in theory, that he may have some minor flaws (p. 200).

In himself, Henry stands for a succession of differing possibilities. In the early encounters with Catherine, he is obviously charmed by her frankness and innocence, but he is also highly amused by her, and will laugh secretly at her, for example, when he talks of the country dance as an emblem for marriage, and she insistently refuses to see an emblem as an emblem (pp. 76–8). But later at least some of the laughs are against him: on the walk round Beechen Cliff, for instance, the narrator dwells pointedly on the advantages to a young woman, at least if she is 'good-looking', of being ignorant, and then goes on to describe one of Henry's more serious attempts to lessen that ignorance by way of a lecture on the picturesque, 'in which his instructions were so clear that she soon began to see beauty in every thing admired by him, and her attention was so earnest, that he became perfectly satisfied of her having a great deal of natural taste' (p. 111). Clearly each is, to a degree, unwittingly duping the other and the self. Yet it is also uncertain, at least for Henry, whether this is more than a momentary lapse, since he soon appears to be complete master of the conversation again, and he presides with a narrator-like amusement over the confusion generated by Catherine's vision of the unreal Gothic horror, and Eleanor's knowledge of the real violence of the Gordon riots or the Reign of Terror.[14] Later still, just at the point when he begins to find her 'irresistible' (p. 131), the ironist in him is muted and may even be silent: when Captain Tilney asks Isabella to dance, and Catherine assumes that he is motivated only by kindness, Henry tells her that she is 'superior in good nature . . . to all the rest of the world' (p. 133), and it is not certain whether this is a very gentle reminder of his satirising powers, or whether these are the words of a young man who is beginning to be decidedly in love.

All of which suggests that the events at the Abbey, far from being a tiresome interruption, are a natural, indeed crucial, part of a complex whole, as the novel works to its conclusion. It is entirely appropriate to his diverse functions that Henry, who on the way to the Abbey delightedly fuels Catherine's Gothic expectations, should also be the one to ask her, insistently, what 'ideas' she has 'been admitting' (p. 198) when she subsequently takes things ludicrously too far. Catherine enters the Abbey in ignorance, but with high literary expectations, and at first assumes an easy access to the superficial trappings of the Gothic – bloody daggers and lost manuscripts. When that proves illusory, she makes the second but much more interesting mistake of actually trying to apply the psychology of the Gothic to the person of the General. She treats the Abbey as if it *were* something in a novel; her excited 'terrors' are much more like those induced by 'Laurentina's skeleton' than anything she would actually feel if Northanger really were the place she imagines it to be. So, when the 'visions of romance' are over, when she is 'awakened' (p.

199), she has at last a firm hold on much that has previously been close to her understanding, but has never before been properly in perspective, about life and about novels. In this way she takes the decisive step into adulthood.

Or so it would seem. Certainly there is a lesson clearly learned, but how exactly is Catherine transformed? The novel does not, in point of fact, resolve its complexities quite so easily. Catherine sees through Isabella's letter (p. 218) and this might suggest an advance in her understanding, but it is one that is all but forced upon her by the fact that she already knows James's side of the story. And there is the moment when Catherine, having resisted all the Gothic blandishments of a stormy night, a late, noisy and unexpected arrival at the Abbey, and mysterious noises outside her bedroom door (p. 222–3), finds that Eleanor has come to tell her that she must precipitously leave the Abbey, in what looks like the best Gothic tradition. Is this an intrusion of the Gothic as it might actually be found in real social life? We could then say that, though Catherine was wrong to think that the General had murdered his wife, she had actually fastened on to something ugly in his nature. But this will not quite do, since her ideas about him are based only subliminally on what could have been the useful evidence of the discomfort she feels in his presence, a discomfort which seems also to be felt by his children. Her thoughts derive much more from nonsensical pseudo-literary speculations about the General's relationship with his wife ('He did not love her walk: – could he therefore have loved her?' – p. 180). Equally, it is possible to argue that the General exhibits no more than the social vice – about which there is nothing especially Gothic – of rudeness. If we believe that he is the dupe of John Thorpe, then the General will regard Catherine, such is the irony, as a kind of Isabella (p. 246); and, given that he is irascible and forceful, his treatment of Catherine could *almost* be said to be reasonable.[15] And there is Catherine's solitary journey home, which, since she survives unscathed, could be said to point to her newly acquired maturity, except that she seems too stunned by the suddenness of her departure to worry about its consequences (p. 230), and the thing seems to point as much to the ordinariness of the everyday, or even to be an opportunity for the narrator, while seeming to apologise for the unnovelistic nature of the event, to make jokes about a 'heroine in a hack post-chaise' (p. 232).

And so the matter of the exact change in Catherine finally evades us and comes to be something that we can merely speculate about, something that is still to be negotiated with a future that is outside the pages of this novel. The novel has examined ways of understanding the world, and the links between these ways as they exist in fiction and in reality, but it will not resolve itself into a too-easy aphorism about moral or psychological or social development that Catherine's progress could be said to demonstrate, and the reader who needs such a thing must devise his own. So, too, this novel about an ordinary unheroinely heroine ends, fully in the spirit of the opening pages, with the narrator deliberately reminding us that this is, itself, a novel shaped by art; it is not 'life'. The resolution of the difficulties of heroine and hero is so contrived as to be a joke about the clumsy unreality and the necessity of endings in fiction. Likewise there is a claim, for the 'perfect' future happiness of the hero and heroine, that can only belong to the fictional world. As a final joke at the expense of the reader, in the closing words of the novel's last sentence a spurious debate is initiated about what this novel can be said to 'recommend'.

3 *Sense and Sensibility*: Ideas and Arguments

'At my time of life opinions are tolerably fixed. It is not likely that I should now see or hear anything to change them.'
(Marianne Dashwood on first attachments)

Sense and Sensibility is a very different enterprise from *Northanger Abbey*. It is much less obviously comic, and, though there are fleeting similarities between Catherine Morland and Marianne Dashwood, each represents a very different way of being seventeen. Even more significantly, *Sense and Sensibility* offers none of the playing with different kinds of novel that makes for the entertaining and puzzling openness in *Northanger Abbey*. Rather, it is a sustained exploration of the scope of one kind of novel: the novel as intellectual argument.

For some critics, indeed, the novel asserts only one argument, and does it too firmly, too particularly. For them, the reader's opinions are soon, like Marianne's, 'tolerably fixed'; unlike hers, they will remain so. These critics claim that there is an unyielding schematic antithesis, declared in the title and made too explicit in the persons of the two central characters, and that the novel always demonstrates the superiority of Elinor's Augustan sense over Marianne's Romantic sensibility, so that it does not really make use of the dynamics inherent in an antithesis. Inevitably, therefore, such critics are not convinced by what they take to be the novel's arguments. For them Elinor is sensible but dull and conforming, while Marianne's capacities are too easily undermined. Austen is accused of laboriously employing a mechanism that she works much more competently and convincingly in *Pride and Prejudice*. If all this is valid then the possibilities of a dialectic relationship between the reader and this text must be limited indeed: the reader will either passively accept or blankly reject what the text offers.[1]

31

Certainly, some patterns in the novel are insistently drawn. Edward Ferrars and Willoughby are very neatly balanced in their links with the sisters, and in the way they themselves embody the distinction between sense and sensibility. These situations are bluntly and consistently matched, right down to the fact that both depend for their fortunes on the whim of an elderly and irascible female relative. And, as with the sisters, the preference we seem obliged to feel, however unsatisfactorily, is for the honourable if confused Edward, rather than the charming and selfish Willoughby. Even the smallest details echo and reinforce the similarity and the contrast. Two incidents involve locks of hair and each time the sisters draw reasonable but mistaken conclusions. Willoughby acquires a lock of Marianne's hair, but this is not, as she and Elinor assume, a binding token of his love (*Sense and Sensibility*, p. 60). Edward has a lock of hair set in a ring; the sisters both conclude that it is Elinor's and take it as a proof of his love: in fact the lock is Lucy Steele's (pp. 98–9, 135).[2]

But then such careful thoroughness is not necessarily rigid and stultifying. And anyway it is only on the most superficial level that the novel functions as a simple antithesis, for Elinor and against Marianne. If we consider Marianne's attitudes and actions, only the most devotedly ingenuous defender of Romantic practices would find her hectic and uncritical insistence on her own feelings to be wholly admirable; would not immediately see, when her response to what she understands to be no more than a temporary parting from Willoughby is strained to the utmost (p. 83), that she must grow in maturity and curb this dangerous abuse of feeling. It is because of this abuse that she is quite defenceless against the debased and opportunistic sense pretending to be sensibility that, by his own admission, is Willoughby (pp. 319–30). The point is surely so obvious that it can hardly be said to constitute a 'lesson' that Austen would impart to the reader, and beyond this point it is very difficult to see the novel as being didactic in any straightforward way. Certainly it is not didactic in the way that, for example, Hannah More's *Coelebs in Search of a Wife* (1808) is – a sermon masquerading as a novel which animadverts upon deviations from its own narrow principles. Even the example of Richardson's instructive moral debates can be considered only with marked circumspection, as tending rather too decisively to particular conclusions.[3]

Indeed, once we recognise Marianne's extreme position it is hard to perceive the workings of an antithesis through the whole of the novel. Some critics still insist – not very convincingly – that the novel is merely didactic, relentlessly separating admirable sense from dangerous sensibility, but there has long been a growing trend that recognises a synthesis as much as an antithesis. The case has probably been most fully stated by Ruth apRoberts (1975), and for her the novel works thus:

> Historically, it appears to use and to criticise the abstract intellection of the Enlightenment, and at the same time anticipates the novelistic realism of the nineteenth century. Austen would have us beat our dichotomies into pluralities, as more closely adapted to what will be felt to be the variety of reality, the relativistic view of life.

And she argues that Austen 'takes her contraries or antitheses not as ends, but as means, to a kind of progression or education'. But even this is not so much a decisive move beyond the limitations of the antithetical mode, as an elaborated and modified series of antitheses, tightly argued and sharply juxtaposed; apRoberts also writes of the 'mathematical kind of thoroughness in the way Austen wrings each aspect of the irony from the dialogue' (pp. 357, 355). Though seeking nineteenth-century contents, the argument is much more about eighteenth-century machinery. Yet it is as easy to go too far in the other direction. Tony Tanner (1969, pp. 7–9) has noted the widespread use of antithesis in eighteenth-century writing and its tendency to 'produce polarized abstractions, the confrontation of stereotypes, and the automatic opposition of extremes'. But, he insists, *Sense and Sensibility* does not quite work in this way: 'Marianne has plenty of sense and Elinor is by no means devoid of sensibility'. The novel he says is nineteenth-century in its preoccupation with the 'tensions between the potential instability of the individual and the required stabilities of society', and with sickness. However, in rejecting the conception of the novel as 'an eighteenth-century matrix containing . . . the embryo of a nineteenth-century novel which struggles but fails to be born', Tanner pays too little attention to the 'eighteenth-century matrix'.[4]

In any event the notion that there is mixture of sense and

sensibility in both the sisters is not the conclusion toward which
the novel moves, but the point from which, explicitly, it departs
(p. 6). And, throughout the novel, when antitheses are stated
they mark what is no more than the beginning in an argument
that then moves beyond the confines of the antitheses. It is as
though Austen assumes that the reader already knows the workings of the argument by antithesis as a method for contrasting
and defining ideas and can at least begin to see beyond this
stage, to the point where the ideas are actively integrated again
as 'working' abstractions. The novel is a complex debate that
ranges over a territory in which the two most prominent features, connected and yet separate, are 'sense' and 'sensibility':
features which are perceived in terms of morality, economics,
aesthetics, psychology. What we are presented with is a succession of more and less coherent statements and disputes about the
nature of the world of the novel, in terms of these ideas. And,
while the successive adjustments make for some resolution, this
is never complete.

Unlike *Northanger Abbey*, then, where the space between novel
and reader is consistently mediated by questions about the
novel, as a novel, *Sense and Sensibility* cuts straight across this
area. But it does not actually reveal its significance to the reader
any more straightforwardly. We find ourselves continually being
offered the opportunity of adopting revisions of the argument,
and its terms, only to find that the revisions have themselves to
be adjusted and changed, from the simplest antithetical distinction to the most elaborate combination of unity and opposition.
To establish a 'reading' of the novel is to arrive at a position
where the earlier versions are in perspective, and where we can
be said to have a much surer grasp of the questions it poses; it is
not to have reached a solution, in the way that one could be said
to have solved a mathematical equation.

The opening of the novel is no less telling than *Northanger
Abbey*, though much less obviously so, in revealing the characteristics of its own distinctive way of engaging and also of
confounding our interest. No other Austen novel opens so quietly
and unironically, or proceeds with such seeming directness of
purpose to an unadorned account of its background. Where the
orderly surface of the narration is broken by an irony, the effect
seems at first to be localised: old Mr Dashwood's will, 'like
almost every other will, gave as much disappointment as plea-

sure'. The example of Fielding's *Amelia* is useful here. The reader who approaches it after *Joseph Andrews* or *Tom Jones* is likely to be struck by a significant change in tone. Most noticeably, Fielding's narrator is much less in evidence. It is not that the novel is without paradoxes and ironies, but that these are often presented directly and without much intermediate commentary. Even the first chapter, though it is given over entirely to the narrator, has nothing like the boisterous satirising of Richardson and Colley Cibber at the start of *Joseph Andrews*; and there is none of the obvious and deliberate playing with the reader's expectations, as in *Tom Jones*. Consider the first sentence: 'The various accidents which befel a very worthy couple after their uniting in the state of matrimony will be the subject of the following history.' This leads to the quiet revelation that the couple's distresses were 'exquisite' and the causes 'extraordinary', then to the general reflection that 'Fortune' is often blamed for what is the consequence of purely human strengths and weaknesses. But an uncertainty has already been introduced: if 'Fortune' is not to be blamed for their misfortunes, then must we blame this 'very worthy couple'? Once we know the couple better, another kind of doubt is introduced, since worthiness is found unequally in them. Amelia's merits are rather passive, but cannot be seriously questioned; her husband is often recklessly unthinking.[5] To determine the cause of their unhappiness one has therefore to evaluate the effect both of his impetuosities and of the viciousness of others. Fielding's narrator is less obtrusive, but not more direct.

Something similar happens in *Sense and Sensibility*. In the brisk account of the separating of the Dashwood women from the family estate there is a series of pervasive ironies that are no less telling because they are concealed to an unusual degree. There is, for instance, the 'interest' which directs the 'constant attention' bestowed on old Mr Dashwood. It is, admittedly, 'interest' of the most honourable kind, and Henry Dashwood, the old man's heir, desires the estate principally for the security it will bring his family. Still, there is 'interest', 'interest' that is thwarted by the reading of the will. Questions of money and property loom unusually large in this novel, and they are constantly argued and schemed over in terms of 'interest', 'competence' and 'independence', of 'will' and 'duty'. Henry Dashwood's 'interest' is at one end of a line of graded contrasts that includes every character in the novel, and has at the other end the figures of Mrs Ferrars and Lucy Steele. Indeed, the line begins to become visible as soon as the narrator argues that, because John Dashwood is rich in his own right, and richer still by his wife's, 'the succession to the Norland estate was not really so important as to his sisters'. This is a view that his father, Henry, must take, but it is almost entirely contrary to the view John Dashwood actually takes, as his notorious debate with his wife, in the second chapter, shows.

And what of the old man's will? The narrator seems to be rather partisanly endorsing the opinions of Henry Dashwood – the old man denies the claims of affection, and the needs of the Dashwood women; indeed he perverts the principle of affection into a senile doting on that infrequent visitor, the infant son of John Dashwood. But there is irony of more than one kind in the novel's opening sentence: the most likely explanation of the will lies in the principle of primogeniture, a principle which, it is implied, ensured that the 'family of Dashwood had long been settled in Sussex', and which (fairly or unfairly) makes the hold of Mrs Dashwood and her daughters on the estate a slender one.

These possibilities are held only momentarily before us. The fourth paragraph shows the 'cheerful and sanguine' Henry Dashwood hoping that time and large profits from the estate will improve his fortune. This pleasing opportunity is itself peremptorily removed by the fact of his death; and the question of his daughters' fortunes is left in the hands of John Dashwood, a man who 'had not the strong feelings of the rest of the family'. But the antithesis this implies begins to soften and change as soon as it is made. John Dashwood is 'not an ill-disposed young man', but equally he is 'rather cold hearted, and rather selfish'; yet he also conducts 'himself with propriety in the discharge of his ordinary duties'. In the end it is his wife, that 'strong caricature of himself', who most determines the exact scope of his nature; and, even when they seem together to be at their worst, as in the debate in the second chapter, they cannot simply be read as cyphers on a chart of antitheses. Rather, they embody slightly different combinations of corrupted sense and debilitated sensibility.

At the same time, the 'strong feelings' which he does not possess, and which are to be found in his stepmother and her daughters, are themselves under close and critical scrutiny

within a page, when the unfeeling assertiveness of Mrs John
Dashwood tempts her mother-in-law to an extreme and rigid
response: for 'in *her* mind there was a sense of honour so keen, a
generosity so romantic, that any offence of the kind . . . was to
her the source of immoveable disgust'. It is Elinor who restrains
her mother, and this leads naturally to the statement about the
mixtures of sense and sensibility in the sisters. Elinor has the
remarkable 'strength of understanding, and coolness of judgement', and the markedly 'strong' feelings which 'she knew how
to govern'. Marianne is 'sensible and clever; but eager in every
thing; her sorrows, her joys, could have no moderation'. The
abstract distinctions have already been made, and we must now
see what happens to these abstractions, in differing combinations, and in practice.

Thus the novel invites us to join an argument about how sense
and sensibility can be combined, how they can be separated.
Fully to appreciate the terms of this invitation, though, we have
to put it in the context of some arguments that ranged through
the eighteenth century. Most obviously, perhaps, 'sense' and
'sensibility' invoke the distinction between Augustan and Romantic ways of viewing the world. This is not to force a crudely
chronological separation – 'sense' for the Augustans, 'sensibility' for the Romantics – but rather to suggest the ways in which
combinations of the two qualities, and differences between them,
existed and developed throughout the eighteenth century. It is
for example as much a matter of distinguishing between Pope
and Wordsworth as it is between Locke and Shaftesbury, or
Johnson and Rousseau.

Consider the concept of 'taste'. It is an inevitable meeting-
ground for concepts such as sense and sensibility, often it is a
battleground. Taste is an important concept in all of Austen's
novels: one remembers the question of Catherine Morland's
'great deal of natural taste' on Beechen Cliff and elsewhere; in
the later novels it is probably *Persuasion* that treats the concept
most sustainedly. In *Sense and Sensibility* it is a key term for Elinor
and Marianne in themselves, and in their dealings with others.
Almost everyone in the novel is judged in terms of taste, and
often it is the particular conception of taste underlying the
judgement, as much as the judgement itself, that is of interest.[6]

One useful starting-point for a consideration of Austen and taste is to be found in two essays by David Hume. There is no evidence that she actually read them, though a filtered version of their contents could doubtless have reached her; but their relevance here is not as sources, but as a useful analogy in terms of means and conclusions. Hume's first essay, 'Of the Delicacy of Taste and Passion' (1741),[7] argues that this extra-sensitivity 'enlarges the sphere both of our happiness and misery'. He notes that the 'good or ill accidents of life are very little at our disposal; but we are pretty much masters what books we shall read, what diversions we shall partake of, and what company we shall keep'. He goes on to suggest that delicacy of taste 'improves our sensibility for all the tender and agreeable passions; at the same time that it renders the mind incapable of the rougher and more boistrous emotions'. Delicacy of taste is, for him, as much a matter of 'strong sense' as it is of 'sensibility of temper'. By way of concluding, he notes that a delicacy of taste must make one more discriminating about other people. In almost all of this, Hume could be speaking for Elinor Dashwood; just as, at almost every point, Marianne Dashwood contradicts him, either by her stated principles or by the effects of their practice. The only point on which *Sense and Sensibility*, as a whole, is at odds with Hume's speculations, and here it is inclined to be more pessimistic, is on the question of the degree of choice open to the individual, and in the necessary efficacy of these pursuits. It is significant that it is of Elinor that we are told – and the phrasing is telling – that her 'mind was inevitably at liberty; her thoughts could not be chained elsewhere' (p. 105), and, despite the elegant and available occupations of reading and drawing, she cannot always resist musings that are sad, fretful and pointless.

In his later essay 'Of the Standard of Taste' (1757)[8], Hume enters fully into the difficulties of the concept. There is the 'great variety of Taste' that exists: for him, general aesthetic or moral principles can be stated with general assent, but particular instances will be a matter of individual variation and preference. He argues that time is the best test of an object's value, since time will expose it to the taste of many: for the individual, the exercise of taste can very easily be rendered false, since it requires a 'perfect serenity of mind, a recollection of thought, a due attention to the object'; a '*delicacy* of imagination' in order to 'convey a sensibility of those finer emotions', and a 'delicacy of taste' if we are to perceive every detail and measure every proportion. It is hardly surprising that he comes to the conclusion that few individuals, if any, can satisfy on all or most of these point, since

> though the principles of taste be universal, and nearly, if not entirely, the same in all men; yet few are qualified to give judgement on any work of art, or establish their own sentiment as the standard of beauty. The organs of internal sensation are seldom so perfect as to allow the general principles their full play, and produce a feeling correspondent to those principles.

And these are very close to the standards, and the difficulties, marked out by the dramatised debate between the sisters in *Sense and Sensibility*, particularly when they argue about their own standards of taste, and those of Edward, Willoughby and Brandon. Hume and Austen are not, of course, embarking on exactly the same enterprise: Hume argues for at least the theoretical possibility of a universal principle, which is probably more than Austen actually commits herself to; Hume offers a comprehensive account of a general concept, while Austen considers how aspects of the concept are likely to occur in particular sets of circumstances. But they are at one in resisting the temptation to seek a partisan and over-simplifying theory, and in trying thoroughly to survey the difficulties and confusions which the concept engenders in practice.

The similarities in their approaches are the more marked when we consider how pervasive was the tendency to reduce the problem to a too-easy theory. In 1759, for example, two years after Hume's later essay was published, Edmund Burke brought out a second edition of his *Philosophical Enquiry into the Origin of our Ideas of the Sublime and Beautiful*, and he added an introductory essay 'On Taste',[9] at least partly, it would seem, in response to Hume. Burke argues that 'the standard both of reason and taste is the same in all human creatures', and for him what is usually called a 'difference in taste' is actually a 'difference in knowledge'. Burke simply reiterates Lockean principles, and declares that, since all is founded in sensory perception, this is ultimately the basis for a general standard of taste. Joshua Reynolds, too, rejects the idea that it is simply 'intuitive'; he too looks for a

Lockean model. Taste, he stipulates, has to be 'cultivated', and must 'on every occasion' be founded on reason.[10]

But others were much less decisively in favour of reason and a universal standard, much more ready to push the claims of feeling. Hugh Blair – whom Henry Tilney was fond of quoting – turns Burke's formula inside out. For him, taste is 'ultimately founded on a certain natural and instinctive sensibility to beauty', and in matters of taste 'reasonings appeal always, in the last resort, to feeling'. And Archibald Alison actually treats taste simply as an emotion, his object being to establish how its functions differ from 'every other Emotion of Pleasure'.[11]

In the midst of this rush to take sides on different aspects of this complex debate, therefore, Austen clearly stands for something rather different. For her, it is not, finally, a matter of asserting that taste is founded, entirely or in some relative way, on reason; entirely or in some relative way, on feeling: what she offers her readers is the chance of joining a debate about whether and how reason and feeling can be held to equally and simultaneously. This does not mean that, as a concept, taste has been made, as it were, to disappear, that it is really no more than the expression of a happy blend and contrast of sensibility and sense. Taste becomes one of the significant expressions of an unending struggle, one that does not only denote the always-felt tension between sense and sensibility, or even this tension as it is given dramatic meaning in terms of the harmony and discord between the needs of the individual and the needs of society. Taste is also to be perceived as the perpetual, more or less successful attempts by individuals to balance the risks of a response to the world, or to one of its features, that is personal to the point that it is inanely idiosyncratic, with those of a merely second-hand effusion: to find a middle ground between the declarations of a sluggishly reasoned piece of indulgence, and the sterilities of a too-reasoned abstraction. What the novel offers, in a sense, is a sequence of such attempts.

If, though, this is novel as intellectual argument, why does it seem to many readers to be one-sided? Even the most articulate and sensitive accounts of the novel tend to some kind of bias: Stuart M. Tave, for example (1973, pp. 96–8), insists that the novel is Elinor's; while Tony Tanner (1969, p. 27), though he writes convincingly of 'the loving tension' between the sisters, still writes more convincingly about Marianne. This may perhaps be saying no more than that every reader will in the end take up his own position in the debate: but the question is not so much about the bias or the conclusions of particular readers; it is whether the novel is sufficiently open and balanced in itself.

One of the difficulties in seeing the sisters equally lies in the way that Elinor, without doing it as obviously or self-consciously as Henry Tilney does in *Northanger Abbey*, often fulfils the narrator's function. With Elinor the problem is actually compounded because it is also much less obvious than with Henry Tilney that she is herself subject to the narrator's irony. Consider her assessment of Mr Palmer:

> Elinor was not inclined, after a little observation, to give him credit for being so genuinely and unaffectedly ill-natured or ill-bred as he wished to appear. His temper might perhaps be a little soured by finding, like many others of his sex, that through some unaccountable bias in favour of beauty, he was the husband of a very silly woman, – but she knew that this kind of blunder was too common for any sensible man to be lastingly hurt by it. – It was rather a wish of distinction she believed, which produced his contemptuous treatment of every body, and his general abuse of every thing before him.
>
> (*Sense and Sensibility*, p. 112)

This analysis remains wholly within Elinor's consciousness; it is later modified, both by her better understanding of her subject, and by the changes in his behaviour, in London (p. 279) and at Cleveland (pp. 304–5). But, in moving from the simple contrast between Mr Palmer and his wife to a much fuller and subtler account of the man, Elinor uses methods and terms of analysis that could almost be said to have been borrowed from the narrator. Even the more sophisticated readers can incline to the view that this endorses Elinor's status: Tave's argument about the centrality and the rightness of Elinor rests heavily on the fact that much of Marianne's story is contained within Elinor's, and told as Elinor sees it (1973, p. 97).

Yet of course such an arrangement need not commit us wholly to a view of the primacy or the perfection of Elinor. Once we grasp the obvious point that Elinor has made the necessary adjustment to adult life which Marianne has yet to make, once we know something of Elinor's impressive sense, Elinor becomes an obvious and useful part-narrator. Clearly, we should learn almost nothing about Elinor from Marianne (the point is emphasised by the occasional glimpses we do have of Marianne's view of things). And, clearly, Elinor as part-narrator is not simply an illustration of the workings of sense: Edmund Wilson (1944; 1950, pp. 202–3) was surely right to claim that the 'most passionate thing in Jane Austen' is not Marianne's love for Willoughby, but 'the emotion of Elinor as she witnesses her sister's disaster'. Some of the recent criticism of the novel has actually begun to look at Elinor's limitations, but the novel seems to allow rather more than has yet been assumed. It is not sufficient or even accurate to claim, as Mansell (1973, pp. 65–6) does, that Elinor functions as a crude parallel to her sister, learning the value of sensibility at Cleveland, just at the point when Marianne's illness forces her toward sense: Elinor may discover a little about sensibility while at Cleveland, but she has always known its value. Susan Morgan (1976, p. 200) suggests that Elinor is 'a flawed heroine, not in the simpler sense of Marianne, through making mistakes and learning to see them, but in the more interesting sense of using an awareness of her own failings as a factor in maintaining a continuing and flexible process of judgement'. This is exactly what we can see exemplified in the way Elinor's opinion of Mr Palmer adjusts, in the course of the novel; but it is hardly the striking thing that Morgan's claim suggests, and is in reality no more than we might expect from any character not over-confident or omniscient. It is surely much more interesting that there are occasions, unobtrusive but not infrequent, when Elinor does not quite see her own failings and limitations, and, though she appears to be doing no more than maintain the balance between thinking and feeling, both are actually awry.

How does the novelist accomplish this? Samuel Richardson, who always portrayed the virtuous individual rather more thoroughly than Austen, himself shows an awareness of the problem.[12] In *Sir Charles Grandison* (1753–4) he establishes a copiously detailed portrait of Harriet Byron's virtue, wit, intelligence, as equalled only by the good Sir Charles. Yet, as this ideal marriage comes slowly to take place, we can detect that there is some strain and inconsistency. As Harriet becomes increasingly

sure of her love for the hero, and increasingly unsure of its being
returned, her letters betray a fretfulness, some strongly marked
(and strongly curbed) jealousy, and a recurring wish to terminate the connection with him.

> But, dear Lucy, have you any spite in you? Are you capable of
> malice – *deadly* malice? – If you are, sit down, and wish the
> person you hate, to be in Love with a man (I must, it seems,
> speak out) whom she thinks, and every-body knows, to be
> superior to herself, in every quality, in every endowment, both
> of mind and fortune; and be doubtful (far, far worse is *doubtful*
> than *sure!*) among some faint glimmerings of hope, whether his
> affections are engaged; and if they are not, whether he can
> return – Ah, Lucy! you know what I mean – don't let me
> speak out.
>   But one word more – Don't you think the Doctor's compli-
> ment at the beginning of his Letter, a little particular –
> 'Delight of EVERY-ONE who is so happy as to know you.'
> Charming words! – But are they, or are they not, officiously
> inserted? – Am I the delight of Sir Charles Grandison's heart?
> Does *he* not know *me*? – Weak, silly, vain, humble, low, yet
> proud Harriet Byron! – [13]

In allowing this minor distortion to the picture of virtue,
Richardson has actually fleshed out the life of the thing; has
made those moments when Harriet is able to accept the doubts,
can even pity her 'rival', the more striking. The distortion has
become a useful adjustment.

Richardson, though, relies on a single aberration from the
pattern to make the pattern clearer: Austen goes further, since
the limitations in Elinor and in what she represents are rather
more substantial. A contrast between Richardson and Defoe is
useful here. In *Moll Flanders* (1722) Defoe's problem, as he partly
acknowledges in his Preface, is to maintain our sympathetic
interest in this woman, and 'all her vicious Practises'.[14] The
difficulty lies of course in retaining the vivacity without becoming merely salacious, in achieving a sharp moral focus without
moralising. The solution lies in the way Moll tells her story: she
is frank but also ingenuously self-revealing and not entirely
trustworthy. Thus, the 'Felony' which places her mother in
Newgate, where Moll is born, is 'a certain petty Theft scarce

worth naming, (*viz.*) Having an opportunity of borrowing three Pieces of fine *Holland*, of a certain Draper in *Cheapside*'.[15] Yet we cannot criticise Moll without also criticising the society in which she is placed. In so clearly revealing Moll's faults, Defoe does not make judgement any simpler for the reader, or moral sense any easier to establish. What he allows for is that the reader will be able to acquire a fuller understanding of the nature of the problem.

If Richardson does not go far enough for Austen's purposes, though, then perhaps Defoe goes too far. The doubts and incompatibilities of Elinor's 'system' are certainly in frequent danger of revealing themselves; and they do invite the reader to make, not a quick judgement, but an attempt to understand the circumstances that make them inevitable. However, the weaknesses are so quietly stated that they can easily be missed in a way that the much more obvious and substantial faults of Moll and of her society cannot. In an early discussion with Marianne, for example, about whether or not Edward is sufficiently endowed with taste, Elinor offers what appears to be a detached assessment, but it ends thus:

> At first sight, his address is certainly not striking; and his person can hardly be called handsome, till the expression of his eyes, which are uncommonly good, and the general sweetness of his countenance, is perceived. At present, I know him so well, that I think him really handsome; or, at least, almost so.   (*Sense and Sensibility*, p. 20)

And this is the language of sense being momentarily and unwittingly overtaken by the energies of sensibility, with the attempt, only in the hesitation of the last words, to regain control. What is more, Marianne – like her mother – denies any distinction between liking, esteeming and loving, so there is irony in the way that even this very high praise is no more than the decidedly moderate recommendation that Marianne could herself bestow. There is also the real ambiguity in Edward, perceived by Elinor (p. 22), which makes her feel that she ought to restrain the emotional aspect of her attitude to him until it is satisfactorily resolved, while also revealing that this restraint is perhaps already beyond her. In such circumstances, sense alone cannot suffice.

Indeed, it is surely not merely by accident or mistake that some characters in the novel – Edward, Willoughby, Colonel Brandon – are rather more potent as ideas in the minds of others, and especially in the minds of the sisters, than they are in the flesh.[16] With Edward, this is particularly appropriate. Once we properly understand his position, caught between the demands of his mother and of Lucy Steele, further entangled by an unexpected love for Elinor which seems unfulfillable (a love as unwilled and unreasoned as hers is for him – p. 368), it is easy to see why he should so often appear sadly and mutely static. There is more to him than this: when he visits Barton Cottage, his 'low spirits' (p. 96) alternate with a quite lively cheerfulness, as when he joins spiritedly with Marianne in the debate about the picturesque (pp. 96–8), and his mocking depreciation of his own ignorance of the terms and objects of picturesque taste actually shows him possessed of an effective skill in parodying them. Even the dichotomy between Edward and Marianne is not a clear one: when he admires the beauty of the countryside, but also notices a 'very dirty lane' (p. 88), much to her astonishment, we cannot assume that he is merely opting for tidiness and sense. Marianne's favourite William Cowper himself recorded a preference for a 'cleanlier road' over 'miry ways' (*The Task*, III: 17, 4). The difference between Edward and Marianne is perhaps best contained in the resolution achieved by Wordsworth in 'Tintern Abbey'. It is with Marianne that we associate the first stage of the poet's experience, when

> like a roe
> I bounded o'er the mountains, by the sides
> Of the deep rivers, and the lonely streams,
> Wherever nature led
>
> (lines 67–70)

while Edward, in sympathy with the maturer vision, is more able to value

> These plots of cottage-ground, these orchard-tufts,
> Which at this season, with their unripe fruits,
> Are clad in one green hue, and lose themselves
> 'Mid groves and copses.
>
> (lines 11–14)

For, however differently they do it, they are admiring the same landscape.[17]

But, if this helps to illumine, for us, the nature of Elinor's attraction to him, then it also makes her understanding of his inconsistencies the more perplexing. Given that Elinor does not yet know of the secret engagement, we cannot blame her for judging incorrectly, but the insufficiency of her judgement is interesting nevertheless, for she places all the blame on the unknown Mrs Ferrars (pp. 101–2), rather too easily as the narrator points out, and in doing so she momentarily borrows a way of thinking from her mother. Thus she simplifies the question to one, put with uncharacteristic vehemence, of the 'old well established grievance of duty against will, parent against child'. She plainly finds this an unsatisfactory explanation, yet it is not surprising that she does not fully acknowledge this, since this would admit the possibility that her love will never be fulfilled. Thus she feels no conscious wish to state the obvious criticism of Edward, that he is temporising and doing nothing to establish his independence. Paradoxically it is Mrs Dashwood who thinks rather like her daughter on this occasion, and points directly to the practical solution of his difficulties, by suggesting that he needs a profession. But this too founders before long, because Mrs Dashwood too eagerly puts the argument in her own terms, arguing that 'patience' can easily be called 'hope', and concluding with an excessively optimistic account of what she takes to be Mrs Ferrars' 'will', 'duty' and 'happiness' (pp. 102–3).

Once Elinor is made to share Lucy Steele's confidence, we can test her sense further. She seeks to treat both Lucy and Edward fairly, even in the face of Lucy's dishonourable strategies, but the degree to which she succeeds is questionable: there is a considerable sharpening of her judgement and her sense of her own intellectual and moral superiority over Lucy ('illiterate, artful and selfish' – p. 140); and, in clinging (understandably, though too tightly) to the assumption of Edward's love for herself, she relies perhaps too much and too uncritically on the opinions of people whom she would never normally trust – her mother, Marianne, even her ill-natured sister-in-law (p. 139). Then, the way she subsequently takes up the matter with Lucy is really nothing but unbalanced sensibility and misguided sense. She is of course trapped by Lucy, and cannot either speak or remain silent without playing the 'game' according to Lucy's terms: but to find that she cannot 'deny herself of endeavouring to convince Lucy that her heart was unwounded' (p. 142) is to ignore the jealousy which she already knows to be motivating Lucy, and which will leave Lucy unconvinced. The encounter itself is productive only of an awkward and edgy duelling that tends to provoke, in each, 'an unsuitable increase of ease and unreserve' (p. 150).[18]

Similarly, when there is an embarrassing encounter in London – Lucy has just come to boast of Mrs Ferrars' amiability to herself, when Edward arrives — Elinor's successful struggle to keep her composure appears as a complete vindication of her 'system', and yet . . .

> Her exertions did not stop here; for she soon afterwards felt herself so heroically disposed as to determine, under the pretence of fetching Marianne, to leave the others by themselves: and she really did it, and *that* in the handsomest manner, for she loitered away several minutes on the landing-place, with the most high-minded fortitude, before she went to her sister. (pp. 241–2)

This 'high-minded' loitering has little to do with the operations of sense, and the fetching of Marianne, so very obviously a pretext, produces all the embarrassment which Elinor would, in a cooler moment, have foreseen and avoided. Marianne is enthusiastic, even in the midst of her own grief, over what she not unnaturally takes to be her sister's happiness, and eagerly welcomes Edward as if he were engaged to Elinor, while treating Lucy as an insignificant acquaintance. She is even indifferent to a spiteful remark from Lucy (it is Elinor who is 'very angry'), and insists on praising Edward, quite unaware of the irony, for being 'most scrupulous in performing every engagement however minute, and however it may make against his interest or pleasure' (pp. 243–4).

And there are the events at Cleveland when fever, that preeminently Romantic condition, brings Marianne un-Romantically to sense, and at the same time threatens to overthrow the sense of everybody around her. Her 'infection', with its 'putrid tendency' (p. 307), so taints the air that the silly Mrs Palmer actually stops laughing, and rushes away with her baby; Mrs

Jennings, for all her kindness and practical usefulness, entertains
a luridly tragic vision of Marianne's impending death, and she
infects Colonel Brandon, made partial by his love, with her
forebodings: even Elinor, calm at first, comes to dread the worst
during the night of crisis, a night 'of almost equal suffering to
both' sisters (p. 312). As soon as Marianne begins to recover,
Willoughby appears, and Elinor finds yet more unexpected ways
in which her sensibilities are worked, even against the inclinations of her sense, and in which her judgement must admit
adjustment. Then, at the end of the novel, there is the violent
burst of 'tears of joy' with which she greets the unexpected news
that Lucy has married Robert Ferrars, and by which she turns
the implications of that event into a statement of fact. There is
nothing in all these incidents that is unnatural, little that is
culpable: but it has become clear that her combination of sense
and sensibility is by its nature always struggling with the world,
always trying to establish and maintain a shifting set of com-
promises; and that it is seldom more than partially successful.

And Marianne? Is she simply someone whose single, gross
error is the worse because the world actually consists of complex
shadings of grey rather than the single line between black and
white that she sees? One can as easily put her case less pejoratively by arguing that Marianne is naturally given to intensity,
whatever the form its expression takes, rather than that she
simply and recklessly puts strong feeling above everthing else:
that while Elinor constantly struggles to hold to the middle
ground, Marianne tries always to push to the outer limits. At the
start she is intensely mourning the death of her father, soon she
is intensely in love, and then she grieves as intensely at parting.
She is intensely shocked, when betrayed, and her almost over-
whelming pain becomes mixed with some intense regrets when
she learns that Elinor's private sufferings have almost matched
her more public ones: 'Marianne was quite subdued. – "Oh!
Elinor," she cried, "you have made me hate myself for ever. –
How barbarous have I been to you! – you, who have been my
only comfort . . . " '(p. 264). That is another way of saying that,
except by her own extraordinary standards, she was not subdued
at all. This mixture of intensities becomes the 'pain of continual
self-reproach' (p. 270), and turns to 'moments of precious, of
invaluable misery' (p. 303); soon she is so intensely sick as to
make her, for a while, intensely passive, then intensely penitent.

The promise at the end of the novel is that, having inevitably acquired a little of the moderation of maturity, she marries Brandon, 'and her whole heart became, in time, as much devoted to her husband, as it had once been to Willoughby' (p. 379). One could wish that this last stage were no merely dry assertion, but the sequence as a whole convinces.

Then too there is a deep vein of comedy in the novel that qualifies its tragic potential. In the awkward encounter in London between Elinor, Lucy and Edward, for example, when Elinor leaves the room 'under pretence of fetching Marianne' (p. 242), we admire her self-control, but we also smile at her. This, though, is as nothing to what happens when Marianne enters and, at once the maker of comedy and one of its targets, works with her usual forthrightness, and by the light of an untruth which she not unreasonably takes to be true, to illuminate, dazzlingly and unwittingly, the untruths and less-than-truths by which the other three, with more or less compliance, have been operating.[19]

Marianne engages and disengages our sympathetic interest, and, just as there is a conflicting urge to laugh at and to censure her extremes, so we can also find ourselves pitying her, and sympathetic to some of her attitudes. Her selfishness can often be the result of ignorance, as much as self-regard, and ignorance that is also sometimes unavoidable. When she is generous (that of course means *very* generous) it is not always misapplied. On Edward's arrival at Barton Cottage (pp. 86–7) she turns instantly from a bitter disappointment – she assumed at first that he was the returning Willoughby – to a heartfelt happiness on her sister's behalf, and a 'warmth of regard' for Edward that, contrasting with his coolness, points directly to the as yet unexplained deficiency in him.

What is more, in a novel where feelings are so often suppressed, corrupted or entirely absent, Marianne offers a significant reminder of their importance and power. If one line of the argument demonstrates that feelings in isolation and excess can be dangerous, then another suggests that there can also be too much suppression. Even Elinor, who so sensibly contains and yet expresses her feelings, who often in fact feels it necessary additionally to restrain her own feelings just because her sister is so immoderate, can suppress too much. In her dealings with Lucy Steele, for example, she can become so entangled as to be

in a position that is all but false. Elinor teases her sister about the
rapidity with which she and Willoughby become acquainted: we
can recognise the force of Elinor's comment, and we shall
discover, exactly, the risks of Marianne's impetuousness, when
we see that Willoughby can seem to be sharing her taste while
merely mimicking it (and that the quiet but genuinely apprecia-
tive Colonel Brandon is dismissed by Marianne as being without, among other things, 'genius, taste, nor spirit' – p. 51). But
her reply to Elinor's teasings also has its own resonance.

> 'Elinor,' cried Marianne, 'is this fair? is this just? are my ideas
> so scanty? But I see what you mean. I have been too much at
> my ease, too happy, too frank. I have erred against every
> common-place notion of decorum; I have been open and
> sincere where I ought to have been reserved, spiritless, dull,
> and deceitful . . . .'   (pp. 47–8)

But above all we should not overlook her youth. That Marianne at seventeen, under the occasionally unreasonable influence of her mother, is the possessor of some ill-judged notions
should not surprise us, should indeed partly charm and amuse
us. It is Colonel Brandon, whom it is only too easy to see as
Marianne does, who is, ironically, most aware of this view of
Marianne, and it is this that makes him decisively more than
Marianne's estimate. He gives early expression to his delight in
the 'prejudices of a young mind' (p. 56): Elinor is understandably much less enthusiastic, but then she also sounds a little
like an impatient elder sister. And Brandon is right, to a point, to
value even the 'prejudices', as an expression of the remarkable
energy that Marianne cannot quite contain, an energy which, he
knows, must change in time, and which can all too easily be
transformed into the unpleasant or the ugly. For Brandon,
though he exemplifies that abomination, the second attachment, and though as readers we might feel that his story could
have been better, and better told, is still the man who has lived
in the fullness, though not the fulfilment of his sensibility. His
tale of the two Elizas (pp. 204-11), while it has all the marks of a
careless borrowing from a sub-Richardsonian novel, still has a
significance because it is the breaking-out of an inner passion
and confusion in which the concerned interest in Marianne is
mixed with painful memories of his past; in which every power-

ful reason and feeling that works towards revealing the story is countered by its opposite.

And there is one other point about Marianne. Whatever her faults, it is her openness in a society that will not deal openly that exposes her; it is the duplicity of Willoughby that betrays her. And Willoughby? If by Brandon's account he is a Richardsonian villain, a scaled-down Lovelace, then by his own he is to be considered as much less designing and much more feeble, caught between his mercenary urgings and the feelings he is surprised to find that he possesses: to be censured, certainly, but also to be a little pitied. Elinor herself finds his account of himself moving and persuasive, without being convinced on every point.

It is easy to deduce from the fact that a work is 'early' the conclusion that it is inferior. *Sense and Sensibility* has some obvious defects, but on the whole they are slight. Even if he is more than he at first seems, Brandon remains a figure that has only roughly been sketched out, so that the way Marianne is despatched into his arms is unconvincing. Other defects are less serious. Some of the plot mechanisms, such as Willoughby's visit to Cleveland, are unnecessarily clumsy. Sometimes the narrator's irony is a little too easy and achieves a blunted effect. Sir John is delighted that the sisters will visit London: 'for to a man, whose prevailing anxiety was the dread of being alone, the acquisition of two, to the inhabitants in London, was something' (p. 157); of course he is indiscriminate in his friendships, but even he would acknowledge the difference between the number of inhabitants of London and the number of his acquaintances there. And the dialogue, even in passages where it is brightest and wittiest, has the occasional dead phrase. Elinor offers a lively defence of Brandon, but also observes that he is 'capable of giving me much information on various subjects' (p. 51).

D. W. Harding (1970, pp. 1–4) has noted the blemish in Elinor's defence of Brandon and he points out that much of the dialogue in *Sense and Sensibility* is 'stilted and unnatural', the characters exchanging 'little oral essays'. There is clearly some ground for this charge, but there is also a certain appropriateness, for this novel, even in the 'little oral essays'. It might be that in the other novels the ideas are more fully incorporated, but we must also allow for a deliberate choice that the ideas should be out in the open. The novel examines conceptions of head and heart, the bonds and the distinctions between them. Soon the argument becomes complicated by mediation through such notions as taste: and we find a succession of differing versions of the ideas in terms of wealth and occupation, of honesty and propriety, of will and duty, of selflessness. If *Northanger Abbey* is, in some ways, a testing of the different ways in which a novel can function, then *Sense and Sensibility* is a testing of the different ways in which some of these functionings can engage with ideas.

4   *Pride and Prejudice*: Informal Arguments

'. . . *but intricate characters are the most amusing. They have at least that advantage.*' (Elizabeth Bennet)

Pride and Prejudice is closer to *Sense and Sensibility* than to *Northanger Abbey* in its methods, but it is still radically unlike either. It does not present us with competing narrative structures, nor does it explore some of the formal links between ideas in the abstract and ideas in practice. To connect Darcy simply with 'pride' or Elizabeth with 'prejudice' is to be very reductive: to seek a useful antithesis or synthesis in the title is to be mistaken.

This novel deals in informal argument. Elizabeth's preference for 'intricate' characters is one that the reader is invited to endorse, but the kind of intricacy with which this novel deals is much more apprehendable in terms of what is internal rather than external to the novel. The argument invokes neither the history of the novel as a form, nor the history of a concept such as 'sensibility', but tends to work in its own terms, as revealed in the everyday occurrences of dinners and walks and disputes and card parties and dances that make up the plot. The novel starts with a disagreement among the Bennet family, but this does not provide an access to the literature or the thought of the eighteenth century. Instead we have to recognise its context in *this* novel, for it is already in progress at the start of the novel, and has indeed been under way for some twenty-three years. We might feel that by the end of the first chapter we can at least form some understanding of Mrs Bennet, but even in her case the form of her folly remains successively in doubt throughout the novel: and she, it is clear, is in no way intricate.

This comparative lack of formality is also reflected in the critical debate about the novel, and agreement is significantly less easy to achieve. As with *Sense and Sensibility*, we might look for a key in the title, but each individual critic has tended to find his own individual key. Some, such as Marilyn Butler (1975, p. 206), find a single meaning and a specific context: 'The subject of *Pride and Prejudice* is what the title indicates: the sin of pride, obnoxious to the Christian, which takes the form of a complacency about the self and a correspondingly lower opinion, or prejudice, about others.' But this simple austerity is denied by almost every usage in the novel. Others have preferred an approximation or a variation or an inversion of the statement offered by Everett Zimmerman (1968, pp. 65–6): pride is 'a detachment from other human beings', in which the self is seen as 'superior to them, as unconcerned'; and with prejudice, 'the self is completely involved with others, and everything is interpreted as it affects the self'. Yet others, such as Lloyd Brown, (1973, p. 32), attend to the sheer variety of possible meanings.

Even more bewildering is the range of suggested connections between 'pride' and 'prejudice', and other patterns of ideas that give significance to the novel. Samuel Kliger (1947, pp. 357–70) suggests the antithesis between 'art' and 'nature'. Marvin Mudrick (1952, pp. 94–108) stresses the distinction between simple and intricate people. Donald Greene (1953, p. 1028) argues for the rise of the middle class, and its conflict with the upper class. Dorothy Van Ghent (1953; 1967, p. 125) finds the irrational behind the rational in the novel, and she emphasises the 'reconciliation of the sensitively developed individual with the terms of his social existence'. Tony Tanner (1972, pp. 11–12) detects two significant oppositions: impressions and ideas; Enlightenment and Romanticism. Marilyn Butler (1975, p. 212) insists that the important distinction is between 'sceptical intelligence', and 'charity' and 'humility'; between 'satire' and 'candour'. Susan Morgan (1975, pp. 54–68) sees the novel as a 'study of the links between intelligence and freedom', in which the importance of intelligence, functioning with rather than without emotional involvement, is stressed.

This outline is not meant simply as a tribute to critical ingenuity. Any novel as rich and as written about as this one will inevitably attract a wide variety of interpretations. But in this case we are confronting a central area of difficulty with *Pride and Prejudice*: we can all agree that most, if not all, of these terms and distinctions are of significant relevance to the novel; the problem is in adequately accommodating the whole range of terms. As

Walton Litz acknowledges: 'The first two volumes of *Pride and Prejudice* are so complex that no one set of antitheses can define the positions of the hero and heroine, and any attempt to establish rigid patterns leads to absurdity' (1965, pp. 105–6). And, though we can turn to philosophy or theology or psychology or philology for amplification of its meanings, it is in the novel itself, and as the terms appear in it, in their everyday practical garb, that they matter most.

Consider the way that a concept as important as 'pride' is treated. It enters the novel in the mouths of Meryton, at the assembly, when Darcy is discovered to be 'the proudest, most disagreeable man in the world' (*Pride and Prejudice*, p. 11): and Mrs Bennet, part maker and part transmitter of Meryton opinion, next day reduces the account of his behaviour to the statement that 'every body says that he is ate up with pride' (p. 19). This is, ironically, the only point in the novel at which there is an easy and unqualified agreement between Elizabeth and her mother. Charlotte Lucas offers some defence of Darcy's 'pride', since he is 'so very fine a young man, with family, fortune, every thing in his favour'. Elizabeth answers Charlotte by asserting, 'I could easily forgive *his* pride, if he had not mortified *mine*.' Here of course 'pride' has two distinct meanings, neither of which approximates to Charlotte's, since by her own Elizabeth means a natural self-esteem, and by his she means, as she later tells him, 'your arrogance, your conceit, and your selfish disdain of the feelings of others' (p. 193).

Equally, Charlotte's pragmatic view becomes questionable once she shows herself willing to marry a complete fool, merely for the sake of the establishment he is able, by the grace of Lady Catherine de Bourgh, to provide. We might feel safe in dismissing her as a merely heartless materialist; but Charlotte's defence of Darcy is the one plain statement of a set of principles that underlie a great deal that is said and thought in the novel; thus she can be seen, not so much as a materialist, but rather as the clear spokesman for the crass materialism in her society. Mrs Bennet offers her own stupidly literal version of it at the start of the novel, when she declares of the new tenant of Netherfield, 'A single man of large fortune; four or five thousand a year. What a fine thing for our girls!' (pp. 3–4). The first impression created by Darcy at the Meryton assembly, before his 'fault' is discovered, depends as much on the striking largeness of his fortune as it does on the striking handsomeness of his appearance (p. 10). These are the principles that mark the only agreement between that otherwise ill-matched pair, Darcy and Caroline Bingley, and it is this that makes them act together in separating Bingley from Jane (p. 198). And of course it is a part of Darcy's thinking about Elizabeth: even Elizabeth herself, so often the spirited rejecter of these values, comes to be much less certain that her own views are anything more than personal when she understands her own potential for loving Darcy (p. 361). We might feel that Charlotte is being too uncritical of what she sees, but she is also the one to see it plainly.

What is more, this early debate does nothing to 'fix' important meanings of the concept of 'pride', and there is merely a canvassing of possibilities. The argument between Charlotte and Elizabeth, rather than pointing towards useful conclusions, tails off and is lost in the general and increasingly trivialising chatter. Mary Bennet, 'who piqued herself upon the solidity of her reflections', offers an entertaining instance of yet another form of pride, when she solemnly remarks that pride is 'very common indeed', and explains why 'vanity and pride are different things'. This is both simplistic and ponderous; and Elizabeth's reaction to Darcy has already implied that the distinction can be more apparent than real. The debate ends in the childish wrangling with Mrs Bennet that ensues when 'a young Lucas' claims that to be proud is to be rich and to 'keep a pack of foxhounds, and drink a bottle of wine every day.'

It is not therefore merely that the argument is especially enclosed, but also that there is an unusually large degree of uncertainty and incompleteness in it. In some ways the uncertainty is reminiscent of one of the kinds of imcompleteness in which Laurence Sterne deals, somewhat more thoroughly, in *Tristram Shandy* (1759–67). The major dislocation there is of course a temporal-spatial one, and the reader has consistently to suspend the usual processes of response and interpretation, in working through a succession of digressions and circumstantial details; we never arrive at a point where the picture is complete if fragmented. One kind of disordering used by Sterne can illuminate what Austen is doing. Tristram sometimes attempts to cut a path through the incompleteness and the unfixity, just in order to fix a limited fragment in the reader's mind. Thus he makes several attempts to 'explain' his father. He considers, at length, why Mr Shandy should entertain the odd idea that names 'irresistibly impressed upon our characters and conduct'; or the fact that he 'would see nothing in the light in which others placed it'.[1] These explanations themselves have continually to jostle with other digressions, and they are never quite capable of containing Walter Shandy. The sudden arrival of Dr Slop on the night of Tristram's birth, for instance, sets off a series of comments, randomly and at cross-purposes, which lead Toby into an extremely lengthy and detailed discourse on the 'science of fortification'. We know that he is wont to turn any topic in this direction, and we know that his brother finds the habit tiresome, but nothing that Tristram has already told us about them can quite prepare us for what happens. Toby is now well into his subject:

> By the mother who bore us! – brother Toby, quoth my father, not able to hold out any longer, – you would provoke a saint; – here have you got us, I know not how, not only souse into the middle of the old subject again: – But so full is your head of these confounded works, that though my wife is this moment in the pains of labour, – and you hear her cry out, – yet nothing will serve you but to carry off the man-midwife. – *Accoucheur*, – if you please, quoth Dr Slop. – With all my heart, replied my father, I don't care what they call you, – but I wish the whole science of fortification, with all its inventors, at the devil; – it has been the death of thousands, – and it will be mine, in the end. . . .
> My uncle Toby was a man patient of injuries; – not from want of courage, – I have told you in the fifth chapter of this second book, 'That he was a man of courage:' . . . nor did this arise from any insensibility or obtuseness of his intellectual parts; – for he felt this insult of my father's as feelingly as a man could do; – but he was of a peaceful, placid nature, – no jarring element in it, – all was mixed up so kindly within him; ny uncle Toby had scarce a heart to retaliate upon a fly.[2]

The violence of Walter's interruption, the quibbling aside to Dr Slop, the striking gentleness of Toby's response, the speedy reconciliation that ensues, the way Toby then immediately reverts to the dangerous subject of Stevinus (dangerous because it had first led him into his discourse on fortification) 'but my

uncle Toby had no resentment in his heart, and he went on with
the subject, to shew my father that he had none':[3] all this leaves
Tristram explaining after the event, and he is too dependent on
chance observation, chance mood, chance association; but the
brothers also represent more than can be covered by any single
explanation. Tristram is doubly at the mercy of his subject.

By contrast, the world of *Pride and Prejudice* appears to be
precisely defined and ordered. It would be more accurate to say
that it is a world with strict and clearly defined limits, yet one
which demonstrates the difficulties of establishing order, even
within such limits. Too often, like Tristram, we can explain
safely only after the event. Thus there are significant inadequac-
ies and contradictions even in the witty and intelligent Elizabeth
Bennet.[4] Of course much of the novel (and its best comedy)
works to demonstrate the ways in which a clever heroine's
understanding is less complete than she realises; but the discrepancy is larger than this. When Elizabeth passionately disapproves of Charlotte's marriage, and rightly (p. 122) assumes that
Charlotte's motives must be mercenary, her reasoning appears
to be incontestable. Discussing the matter with Jane, she concludes, 'You shall not, for the sake of one individual, change the
meaning of principle and integrity, nor endeavour to persuade
yourself or me, that selfishness is prudence, and insensibility of
danger, security for happiness' (pp. 135–6). But is this quite
fair? In seeking a balance between friendship and principle.
Elizabeth blinds herself to the difference in age, beauty and
wealth between her friend and herself that make it much less
easy for Charlotte to do anything but accept Mr Collins.[5] When
we see something of Elizabeth's easy and unquestioning delight
in the company of Wickham, it comes to seem that she is as
extreme in her disregard of questions of prudence as Charlotte is
in her concern for them. Yet, even when her posture is least
moderate, her argument has considerable force. Though she
acknowledges the practical difficulties of an 'imprudent' match
with Wickham, she also says,

> but since we see every day that where there is affection, young
> people are seldom withheld by immediate want of fortune, from
> entering into engagements with each other, how can I promise
> to be wiser than so many of my fellow creatures if I am
> tempted, or how am I even to know that it would be wisdom to
> resist?   (p. 145)

Elizabeth can also be more actively inconsistent, as when she tries to explain Wickham's defection to Miss King, the young lady who is rendered suddenly attractive by the 'acquisition of ten thousand pounds'. Elizabeth now suspends the principle so resoundingly stated in Charlotte's case, and she justifies Wickham's action in terms that could much more fairly be applied to Charlotte, who has none of Wickham's advantages, and is most disadvantaged by her sex: 'handsome young men', Elizabeth tells her aunt, 'must have something to live on, as well as the plain'. There is an elaborate logic that compels her to this conclusion, but one which compounds the inconsistencies of her position, because the realisation that she was never really in love with Wickham combines with a flattering proposition that rests entirely on the fact of his mercenary interest: 'her vanity was satisfied with believing that *she* would have been his only choice, had fortune permitted it' (pp. 149–50).

Equally, when Elizabeth and Charlotte talk about Jane and Bingley, and the degree to which a woman ought to make her feelings plain to a man (pp. 21–3), it seems that Elizabeth's is the juster case in principle, but that Charlotte's is more apt in practice. But this formulation itself looks more and more frail when we see how far the novel goes to question and invert both sides of the argument, point by point. Elizabeth's is a partial account, since it is founded on a sisterly concern, and, while she is clearly right to suggest that Jane and Bingley must also have time to develop a mutual understanding, she is muddled also, since the feelings which she claims are obvious to Bingley are just feelings which, half a page later, she suggests Jane herself is uncertain about. Charlotte's is an equally partial account because, although she admirably understands the conditions of their meetings, where levels of noise and standards of coquetry make expressed feelings rather more significant than feelings themselves, where candid and quiet charm may not suffice, she is intent on the process by which Jane could secure Bingley's attention, and denies the relevance of any mutual understanding.

Elizabeth assumes that the Bingley sister's liking for Jane shows the 'influence of their brother's admiration' (p. 21); the narrator has already suggested (p. 17) that the reverse is more likely. Even Bingley's 'generally evident' (p. 21) admiration for Jane can seem, as Mrs Gardiner later shows, to be no more than a passing infatuation (pp. 140–1). And Elizabeth is certainly unwise to be pleased that Jane's feelings will be secret, both for the reason that Charlotte advances, and because Jane does not have the protection her sister envisages: the 'match' is, from the start, the talk of Meryton and the boast of Mrs Bennet. Charlotte's remarks might seem to be an exact foreshadowing of what happens to Jane and Bingley, but here too the reader can detect important discrepancies. Bingley is soon strongly attached to Jane, without any of the encouragement that Charlotte feels he needs; and, though he underestimates the extent of Jane's love for him, it is Darcy who persuades him that it is minimal (pp. 198–9). And Bingley does have 'great natural modesty', an essential part of what makes him attractive to Jane, but a quality that also lays him open, to an unusual degree, to the arguments of his friends. To the 'gratitude or vanity' which Charlotte finds in 'almost every attachment' must be added 'diffidence', at least for this particular one.

Further, while we might join Elizabeth in doubting the merits of Charlotte's 'plan' for getting a husband, we have to notice that Elizabeth herself is prepared to use it in order to secure a desired attachment. When she prepares for the Netherfield ball, she is preoccupied with Wickham. 'She had dressed with more than usual care, and prepared in the highest spirits for the conquest of all that remained unsubdued of his heart, trusting that it was not more than might be won in the course of the evening, (p. 89). Finally, there is the ironical fact that the man Charlotte does marry is one for whom such a 'plan' is strictly unnecessary, because for him all social and personal considerations are contained in pompous and inane gestures.

In other words, what the novel contains is too complex and diverse for the terms of the argument between the two friends, not just because the terms are limited, but also because of the very nature of the complexity and diversity. Of course, this characteristic of the novel has not hitherto gone quite unnoticed; but the attention it has received has been tangential, or at best selective. Reuben Brower (1951; 1962, pp. 167–75) shows that, while the dialogue is vitally dramatic, it is also complicatedly novelistic..'No speaking voice could possibly represent the variety of tones conveyed to the reader by such interplay of dialogue and comment.' Yet Brower finds a too-easy resolution: the 'sense of variability is balanced by a vigorous and positive belief'. Brower seems to be confusing beginnings with endings, since, surely, the novel starts in 'vigorous and positive belief' and then sets out to test how this functions in practice, how far it must be modified and adapted. On the other hand, Everett Zimmerman (1968, pp. 68–9) goes perhaps too far when he suggests that in parts of the novel 'judgement is impossible; only amused spectatorship is possible', and the reader 'must constantly skip from attitude to attitude just as the participants do'.

Meir Sternberg (1978, pp. 129–58) has offered a fuller account of the problem, arguing that the novel is a 'complex, thematically and normatively polyphonic exploration of human fallibility from a number of complementary viewpoints – in terms of its constant and variable causes, manifestations, and effects on the character', and he points to the ways in which the reader is actively involved in this exploration. Even so, he still sees the questions too simply, and too simply in terms of Elizabeth. Too often, also, it is his system of classification rather than the novel that determines his reading; too often he has the advantage, without acknowledging it, of a second reading. It is not enough to claim that the first chapter contains a 'striking cluster of . . . explicit or generalized warnings' to the reader against 'failures of insight'. The failures of insight are so largely Mrs Bennet's that we are really only being shown what is obvious: stupid people are not perceptive – something that will, if anything, lull rather than alert the reader. Similarly, while it is obvious that Elizabeth is better at detecting prejudice in others than in herself (who is not?), it is perversely over-insistent to argue that her first impression of Bingley's sisters is compounded equally of objective judgement and prejudice, because she is '*too* *un*assailed by *any* attention' to herself (Sternberg's italics).

The most comprehensive account of the problem has been offered by Karl Kroeber (1975, pp. 144–55), who notes that the novel's terms are very much its own, and that it has a large dependence for its effect on the reader's imaginative response. We have, he says, to attend to the 'moving balances' between 'patterns of language', and 'representations of reality'. And he argues that the 'complicating, amplifying, and intensifying of originating disequilibria set up in the reader's mind', from the first sentence, allows the novel to offer us an 'enrichment of our apprehensive powers'. But, though this is an explanation of why the novel continues to excite interest, it indicates more about what we do with the novel than how we do it. And Kroeber's is sometimes a considerable underestimation of the complications contained by the 'moving balances', since he too easily finds a 'tidiness' in the novel's 'fictional structuring'. To assert, for instance, that, 'from the time of Darcy's letter, the reader has been sure that Darcy and Elizabeth will meet again', is to claim more than any *careful* reader will affirm, since expectations of this kind are frequently and variously frustrated in the six novels: a novelistic convention of this sort is something Austen is only too apt to laugh at.

What emerges, therefore, is that these several attempts to account for the problem are actually dealing with aspects or consequences of the problem, rather than with the problem itself. In order to see, more exactly and completely, the various ways in which the novel generates and contains these uncertainties, we must scrutinise its workings and its context a little more carefully.

We can usefully begin with some of the questions provoked by the marriage of Elizabeth and Darcy: this has an obvious centrality in the novel, and it also touches on matters that are of significance in all six novels, matters that could even confuse some of her contemporary readers, and are the more confusing to us because of our remoteness from Austen's times. Everybody knows that Walter Scott's account of *Pride and Prejudice* contains a misreading:

> The lady . . . hurt at the contempt of her connections, which the lover does not even attempt to suppress, and prejudiced against him on other accounts, refuses the hand which he ungraciously offers, and does not perceive that she has done a foolish thing until she accidentally visits a very handsome seat and grounds belonging to her admirer. They chance to meet exactly as her prudence had begun to subdue her prejudice . . . .[6]

This actually makes it very difficult to perceive how Elizabeth has 'done a foolish thing', and the events of the novel give the lie to such a narrowly prudential account of the way her 'prejudice' is subdued. Still, Elizabeth's initial response to Pemberley is curious; she is 'delighted', she entertains the thought that 'to be mistress of Pemberley might be something!', and she feels a 'something like regret' (pp. 245–6). Perhaps Scott was not, after all, so very wrong.

Once again, though, the reader is drawn not to make any simple distinctions, but to order a picture of increasing complexity and obscurity. Whatever the material significance of Pemberley, Elizabeth's response to it is also partly and powerfully an aesthetic response, one she shares with her uncle and aunt. Then, too, whatever are Elizabeth's unconscious wishes, *consciously* she approaches Pemberley believing Darcy to be absent, believing also that neither her feelings nor his would permit any renewal of the acquaintance. All we can perhaps say, in the end, is that, while Elizabeth is aware of the material significance of Pemberley – how could she not be? – there is no evidence to suggest that this plays any real part in making her wish to marry its owner. Indeed it is the material substantiality of Pemberley that actually represents the greatest obstacle to what would otherwise be a well-suited match.

But why is Darcy so very rich? There is an obvious point in making the contrast between Darcy and Elizabeth partly in terms of the fact that he is great in the eyes of the world, but the purpose would easily have been served with rather less greatness, for with £10,000 a year, Darcy is decidedly richer than every other major character in the six novels. In *Sense and Sensibility* Marianne fixes her monetary 'competence' at £2000 a year, just the size of income Willoughby aspires to, and Brandon actually receives; Elinor thinks in terms of something less than £1000, and this too most accurately foretells their income when she and Edward marry (p. 91). But Darcy is five times as rich as Brandon, and more than ten times richer than Edward Ferrars. The point is even more striking if we look to a contemporary source of comparison outside the novels. G. E. Mingay (1963, pp. 19–26) provides figures for 1790, rather early for our purposes but still offering the means for useful distinctions: by Mingay's figures, Darcy is within the 'top' category of 400 families who constitute the 'great landlords', while Edward Ferrars is decidedly amongst the lowest of the gentry.[7]

Does this mean that Elizabeth's so substantial reward is more than merely fortuitous? Does it even imply that an ideological conception of wealth and society is being actively defended? In the past, such questions did not seem troublesome, and, if one could not simply invoke 'luck', then one simply saw an instance of Austen unwittingly or uncritically endorsing the values of her class. Austen's was famously the example of an artist with a strictly limited range, confining herself to the more individual and personal events within a tightly defined single area of society. Arnold Kettle's much noted objection to *Emma*, balanced by the warm assent he gives to the novel's strengths, might seem to be a fair statement of the case against all six novels: the 'inadequacy', he says, 'is not Jane Austen's failure to suggest a *solution* to the problem of class divisions but her apparent failure to notice the *existence* of the problem' (1951, p. 99).

The last thirty years have, however, seen a steady exploring of the connections between the novels and their times, and Kettle's view is now largely untenable. Julia Brown (1979, pp. 4–24, 113–17) offers a closely argued rejection of Kettle's claim, and asserts that Austen took domesticity and its limitations, for women in the ranks of the gentry, *as* her subject, rather than the wider 'masculine' themes to which she could have had only limited access. Others have argued in growing numbers that Austen was actively partisan, in writing a defence of her class in times that were unsettled and threatening. She was never, it has been stated, entirely uncritical of her kind, but was concerned to refurbish their values and so reinforce their position. *Pride and Prejudice* is, like *Emma*, naturally taken to be a more optimistic attempt; *Mansfield Park* and *Persuasion* are seen to be much more pessimistic, in showing the class being defended as most gravely in decline.[8]

But, if it is now impossible to argue that the Austen who, by her own admission, focused on '3 or 4 Families in a Country Village' (*Letters*, p. 401) was blind to the larger national concerns that would have touched these '3 or 4 Families' – one has only to remember Avrom Fleishman's striking observation (1967, p. 7) that the Price family in *Mansfield Park* are war victims – then it is less clear what else has been achieved. For there is an unsatisfactoriness with these arguments – one that, ironically, is also found in the argument they were meant to supersede, represented by Arnold Kettle. One of the necessary arguments against Kettle is that the contrasts and the barriers to be perceived between Longbourn and Rosings in *Pride and Prejudice*, or Mansfield and Portsmouth in *Mansfield Park*, are as telling as anything Austen could have revealed about the lives and crises of the servants, to whom she only infrequently grants the individuality of a name. But, even more than this, the broad class distinctions in which Kettle would have us think, and which he criticises Austen for failing to notice, are themselves inappropriate to the material and the times of the novels, since the form of society he envisages was only just beginning to come into existence. Equally, those who insist that Austen was rushing to the defence of a class that was tottering on the brink of extinction are achieving a strange foreshortening of a process that actually took place in the succeeding hundred years.

J. Steven Watson (1960, pp. 503–4), for instance, notes that, while substantial changes occurred in society in England during the Revolutionary and Napoleonic wars, and they presaged further changes, little enough was obvious or even visible by 1815. The only change, interestingly, that he allows had actually taken place is in literature, in the writings of the Romantic poets. But he also points out that some aspects of society were as they had been in the middle of the previous century, and that 'the hold of the old ruling classes had not been broken'. F. M. L. Thompson (1963 pp. 269–91, 212–37) has argued that the economic crises in the twenty years after the war may actually have been more telling to the history of the gentry, since during the war, 'despite inflation and war taxes, landowners on the whole enjoyed great prosperity and great opportunities either for liquidating old debts or making new savings'. From a very different viewpoint, too, the picture remains substantially the same. Harold Perkin's account (1969, pp. 87–106) of the 'birth of class' – he means the nineteenth-century forms of working and middle class – argues that the 'birth' took place in the five years *after* Waterloo; he also adds that this was merely the birth, and it had 'a great deal of growing up to do before it became the viable class society of mid-Victorian England'. And E. P. Thompson's account (1963; 1968, pp. 111–203) of the formation of the English working class in the period 1780 to 1832 shows it as a growing force, and one that could, on occasion, threaten the established order, but he never claims to be depicting more than the early and often tentative beginnings.[9]

But it is not only history that refuses to support the argument: the novels themselves offer no clear support. In *Northanger Abbey*, General Tilney is the most obvious representative of the landed gentry, and neither he nor the son who is his heir is in any way worthy of our respect. At the other end of the scale there are the Thorpes, aspiring very insecurely to a place in the lowest reaches of the gentry: but what simple moral-social message is to be wrung from the fact that the Morlands are morally much more admirable than either of the other groups, though socially only a little higher than the Thorpes? In *Sense and Sensibility* there is Mrs Jennings, fat, jolly, warm and unrefined, prospering on an 'ample jointure' (p. 36), who has risen, socially, above the origins of that jointure, and who is infinitely preferable to her shallow, cold and correct daughter, Lady Middleton: and Lady Middleton herself demonstrates the possibilities of an even larger social movement. Then, if we consider the good-humoured but quite inane Sir John, if we think of the not-very-honourable hands into which Norland passes, if we remember that Willoughby is in possession of one estate and ruthlessly in pursuit of a second, if we reflect on the typical behaviour of Robert Ferrars, or his mother, then this novel looks more like an attack on the gentry than a defence of what the class stands for. Only Brandon could represent any easy balance between social position and personal merit, but there is no compelling invitation to see this single figure as some kind of prototype for a social class.

Darcy in *Prince and Prejudice* certainly possesses fine qualities, but his defects are fully revealed in his aunt. The only house of unquestioned merit in the novel is that of Mr Gardiner, a man who 'lived by trade, and within view of his own warehouses' (p. 139), and who is the brother of Mrs Bennet and Mrs Phillips. *Mansfield Park* has the Price children, who start so unpromisingly and end, by their own merits, so promisingly, while some of the Bertrams move the other way; but the whole force of the novel works to deny any necessary connection between social and economic status, and intellectual and moral worth. And, if Mansfield is meant to stand for an ideal, then the novel is a failure even as propaganda.

Emma is fuller than ever of amoral social movements: the Woodhouses and the Knightleys may be relatively fixed, but almost everybody else is moving or has recently moved – from the absent Mrs Churchill (an 'upstart' if we are to believe Mr Weston), through the Westons, the Eltons and on, to the newly enriched, never present, but unspeakable Sucklings of Maple Grove, who themselves, as Mrs Elton assures us, find 'upstarts' most 'provoking' (p. 310). Knightley represents Austen's most sympathetic portrayal of one of the landed gentry, yet he exists not as a crude exemplar to the rest of his kind, but as the focus for a vital opposition to Emma, Emma who with her too-easy pleasure in being mistress of Highbury, and her meddlesome ways and little snobberies, is frequently a caricature of what he represents, and a demonstration of how his strengths and advantages can so easily be misapplied. In *Persuasion* it is difficult to find much support for the class in the way that the vain and effete Sir Walter is superseded by Admiral Croft, just as, in his own way, his unadmirable heir is by Captain Wentworth; both naval men having risen to prosperity by their active participation in the just-concluded war.

In none of this is there any consistent, or distinct, concern for the future of the gentry. We may reasonably surmise that Austen would not have relished the complete overthrow of the order that she knew, but there is nothing to suggest that she saw this as imminent, or that in writing her novels she was doing what she could to champion the cause of her class. Rather she seems to be examining, with no particular sense of discomfort or insecurity, the situation of a class, its merits and demerits, its more and less permanent features, the way its composition is susceptible to alternation. Equally, though, only someone already wholly committed to finding the larger social patterns reflected in the novels would see these as the primary meanings in which they deal. Indeed, such assumptions tend to encourage the search for generalisations that Austen habitually does *not* make. Of course she shows an awareness of how the features of a group can be represented in an individual, but she does not, in any sustained way, present us with an individual, and mean to invoke a group at its widest sense: she does not say, 'Here is a baronet', and mean, 'This is the gentry as it can least incisively be defined.' Habitually what she does is to present her readers with particular individuals, each with his own background, status, capacities, tendencies, and then she asks us to consider them in terms of the propositions with which she is working.

This is exactly the point which we found the so-fortunate marriage of Elizabeth Bennet leading to: the novels are not, of course, 'free' from ideology, but any insistent tracing of a defence of an ideology actually thwarts the way the novel works to treat the question in its full complexity, as a social question, and it actually becomes difficult to offer any useful improvement on

Scott's formulation. Worse still, this obscures the dimensions other than of 'class' in which the question is perceived. To assert that the novel is committed, in any serious way, to the defence of the gentry, is to allow for what can never be more than a limited apprehension of the way the novel works so thoroughly to assert its many-faceted nature, and to assert this nature, not as abstractions or ideals, but in terms of the actual and the practical.

It is from the first that the novel works in this way. The much-remembered first sentence actually contains such an assortment of ironies – not least that the 'truth' it asserts will be enacted with literal completeness by the end of the novel – that the only thing we can really know from it is that the narrator is decidedly ironic. Unlike the opening of the earlier two novels, the narrator is strictly curtailed here. The second sentence lodges the idea, in a one-sided version of the narrator's statement, in the minds of Meryton, and after that it exists, still more specifically, in the silly mind of Mrs Bennet.

By the third chapter, when Bingley seems so promisingly to fulfil Mrs Bennet's hopes about rich young men, and Darcy seems equally to frustrate them, Elizabeth (already singled out by her father for 'quickness') begins to command our attention as a witty and intelligent heroine. The Meryton assembly is strikingly like the ball described in *The Watsons*, in its bustle and its schemings, its gossip and its overhearings; and it is not unreasonable to suppose that this is a reworking of some of that material.[10] Emma Watson, though she is never 'insulted' as obviously as Elizabeth is, does overhear some rudely patronising remarks about herself, and the amused irony with which she views the events of the evening must remind us of Elizabeth Bennet, telling the story of Darcy's rudeness 'with great spirit among her friends' – except that, and this is where Elizabeth becomes at once more interesting and more problematic, Emma Watson's is actually the much more secure detachment, and, even as Elizabeth charms us by her witty poise, there are signs that this poise is uncertainly founded. She cheerfully recounts Darcy's snub, 'for she had a lively, playful disposition, which delighted in any thing ridiculous': but nothing is actually 'ridiculous' in the incident; had there been she would probably not have been left with 'no very cordial feelings' towards Darcy. In retelling, though, she can turn the situation, and the man, into the ridiculous, with only slight distortion. We can never tell exactly how much she is actually helping to found, rather than simply lend further support, to a general dislike that is created in the course of the evening.[11]

That also, of course, makes Darcy a figure of some uncertainty. If we accept Elizabeth's view of him unquestioningly, then we have a man who is so abrasively rude as to be, as Mary Lascelles claims, 'quite inconsistent with the Darcy who is described and developed in the rest of the book' (1939, p. 22). Yet if we make the assumption that Darcy does not know he has been overheard – reasonable enough on an occasion when rumour and gossip are circulating freely, and when there are several other interesting overhearings – then his behaviour is neither intolerable nor inconsistent. Do we assume then that he is simply unimpressed by Elizabeth, or is it that he really is, as his remarks later that evening seem to suggest (*Pride and Prejudice*, p. 16), just too easily disdainful? Is it an expression of his subsequently revealed dislike of dancing ('Every savage can dance', p. 25)? Does this dislike combine with the unease in dealing with people that he much later admits to, or is this all – as Elizabeth takes it – no more than another sign of his 'pride' (p. 175)? Once we begin to see the ambiguities, then he is never very easy to place, and too much depends on how the light is seen to fall on his abilities and inclinations. Thus it is possible for two critics to develop two instructive but entirely opposite interpretations, each taking a particular perspective on him and his functioning in the novel. Babb (1962; 1967, pp. 119, 124, 130) shows that there is much more to him than Elizabeth's view suggests, and finds a man who changes only in manner; for Babb, it is Elizabeth who changes significantly, and who becomes more like Darcy. But Moler (1968; 1977, pp. 75, 101, 94) argues that Darcy is actually a parody of the concept of 'patrician hero' to be found in *Sir Charles Grandison*, and the Darcy he discovers is one who undergoes a major change, who 'under Elizabeth's influence, gains in naturalness and learns to respect the innate dignity of the individual', who repents his 'pomposity and pride'.

What is more, because the characters are changing and developing, the instability is perpetuated. The first volume gives readers the advantage over both characters, since we see something of the workings of both minds, but that only means that we are actually made less secure. Darcy, having so decidedly pronounced his opinion of Elizabeth, soon finds her face to be 'rendered uncommonly intelligent by the beautiful expression of her dark eyes', and is struck by the 'easy playfulness' of her 'manners'; while Elizabeth continues to think of him merely as the man 'who had not thought her handsome enough to dance with' (*Pride and Prejudice*, p. 23). As she builds on her version of him, he becomes 'bewitched' by her (p. 52); and when her opinion is strengthened by Wickham's story and she is deliberately offensive to Darcy – more offensive even than she realises – he is most ready to pardon her, because in his 'breast there was a tolerable powerful feeling towards her' (p. 94). Nevertheless, he still has reservations, and apprehends no 'danger', because of the 'inferiority of her connections' (p. 52). Equally, while Elizabeth would scorn such thinking, would find it consolidating her opinion of him, she is still very sensitive to the 'inferiority' of her family, as when for example her mother visits Netherfield (pp. 42–5)

The lesser figures are also seldom easy to place exactly. At first the narrator seems bent on confirming, exactly, Elizabeth's impression of Caroline Bingley, since we are told that she and her sister are 'in every respect entitled to think well of themselves, and meanly of others', and that they have conveniently forgotten their own connection with 'trade' (p. 15). Yet they soon show themselves to be more unpleasant even than this suggests, when they are so maliciously delighted by their 'dear friend' Jane's 'vulgar relations' (p. 37). Caroline's malice is weakened, though, when we discover how silly she is: – with only a little more subtlety than Mrs Bennet could muster, she devotes her flattering attention to Darcy, and betrays her jealousy of Elizabeth. When she insistently echoes Darcy's views she seems simultaneously to be providing support for Elizabeth's view of Darcy, and to be an unwitting parody of Darcy's argument (pp. 37–40).

Her brother is also more than he might seem. At first he appears as the masculine counterpart to Jane, but his deference to Darcy and his sisters (pp. 16–17) makes him seem, as Elizabeth later puts it, 'the slave of his designing friends' (p. 133). Yet when his sisters dwell on Jane's 'vulgar relations' he ebulliently refutes what they say as irrelevant (p. 37) – a gesture that has little to do with slavishness. He can also be surprisingly sharp. When Caroline attempts to flatter Darcy by suggesting that balls are 'unsufferably tedious', and that it would be 'much more rational if conversation instead of dancing made the order of the day', it is he who points, with an acuteness we expect from Elizabeth, to the fatuity: 'Much more rational, my dear Caroline, I dare say but it would not be near so much like a ball' (pp. 55–6). Neither is Jane merely the bland foil to Elizabeth's independence and wit. As Elizabeth herself says, 'to be candid without ostentation or design – to take the good of every body's character and make it still better, and say nothing of the bad – belongs to you alone' (pp. 14–15). Nor is it simply by chance that she is righter, sooner, about Bingley, Darcy, even Wickham (pp. 95–6) and Charlotte Lucas (p. 135), than Elizabeth, since she possesses a useful capacity for doubting her own judgement. Speaking of Bingley's 'desertion', she finds comfort in the fact that 'it has not been more than an error of fancy on my side, and that it has done no harm to any one but myself' (p. 134). Even if, as it happens, this is neither true nor adequate, it does save her from the harsh bitterness which the much-less-involved Elizabeth expresses.

Nor is it only a matter of the complexities of individual characters. The novel employs a variety of contrasting modes, which add to the dislocating effect. The simple humour that such figures as Mrs Bennet or Sir William Lucas generate is connected with but also quite remote from the sophisticated probing of ideas and roles represented by Elizabeth and Darcy. At its most sophisticated, it can function in quite different ways. Sometimes it seems close to the sustained witty exchanges of, for instance, Congreve's *The Way of the World*. Millamant claims to be pleased at having pained Mirabell:

MIRABELL. Ay, Ay, suffer your cruelty to ruin the object of your power, to destroy your lover – and then how vain, how lost a thing you'll be! Nay, 'tis true; you are no longer handsome when you've lost your lover. Your beauty dies upon the instant; for beauty is the lover's gift; 'tis he bestows your charms; your glass is all a cheat. The ugly and the old, whom the looking-glass mortifies, yet after commendation can be flattered by it and discover beauties in it; for that reflects our praises rather than your face.

MILLAMANT. Oh the vanity of these men! Fainall, d'ye hear him? If they did not commend us, we were not handsome! Now you must know they could not commend one, if one was not handsome. Beauty the lover's gift! Lord, what is a lover, that it can give? Why, one makes lovers as fast as one pleases, and they live as long as one pleases, and they die as soon as one pleases; and then, if one pleases, one makes more. (II.i.342–63)

And while they use the debate as a vehicle for their mutual dissatisfaction there is also the sheer pleasure they take in thus vigorously 'out-witting' each other, which suggests the real bond and tension between them that offers an equitable resolution between 'beauty' and 'lover'. It is just the balance that is missing in Fainall's cynical plotting, in Lady Wishfort's lively rages and her blunt comparisons, in Witwoud's insistent 'similitudes', in Petulant's bluster. *Pride and Prejudice* can also provide this balance between wit, feeling and idea, and the dialogue creates its own angles and planes over which the light plays rapidly. Consider the discussion Darcy, Bingley and Elizabeth have of Bingley's character (pp. 48–50). We are already aware of the complicated associations that link and separate all three, but it is dangerous for the reader to seek simple or literal meanings divorced from the play of wit here. Darcy accuses Bingley of being 'proud' (an interesting word, itself, in this context) of doing things quickly:

' . . . you meant it to be a sort of panegyric, of compliment to yourself – and yet what is there so very laudable in a precipitance which must leave very necessary business undone, and can be of no real advantage to yourself or any one else?'

'Nay,' cried Bingley, 'this is too much, to remember at night all the foolish things that were said in the morning. And yet, upon my honour, I believed what I said of myself to be true, and I believe it at this moment. At least therefore, I did not assume the character of needless precipitance merely to shew off before the ladies.'

'I dare say you believed it; but I am by no means convinced

that you would be gone with such celerity. Your conduct would be quite as dependant on chance as that of any man I know; and if, as you were mounting your horse, a friend were to say, "Bingley, you had better stay till next week", you would probably do it, you would probably not go – and, at another word, might stay a month.'

'You have only proved by this,' cried Elizabeth, 'that Mr Bingley did not do justice to his own disposition. You have shewn him off now much more than he did himself.'

'I am exceedingly gratified,' said Bingley, 'by your converting what my friend says into a compliment on the sweetness of my temper. But I am afraid you are giving it a turn which that gentleman did by no means intend; for he would certainly think the better of me, if under such circumstances I were to give a flat denial, and ride off as fast as I could.'

At the same time Austen recognises, like Congreve, that the balance is fragile, so we have also to be alert to those occasions when, as happens later in this same discussion, it is broken. Elizabeth attempts too insistently to use the discussion to 'fix' an aspect of Darcy's character: he replies equally insistently that there must be more particularising, and we are only saved from sterile argument by a vigorous thrust from Bingley, one that turns back, decisively, to the witty mode, and one that should make us wonder how much deference he really pays to his friend. One of the particulars, he insists, must be 'comparative height and size':

' . . . I assure you that if Darcy were not such a great tall fellow, in comparison with myself, I should not pay him half so much deference. I declare I do not know a more aweful object than Darcy, on particular occasions, and in particular places; at his own house especially, and of a Sunday evening when he has nothing to do.'

At other times, we see characters deliberately rather than accidentally resisting the impulse to be witty, and embarking rather more seriously on an explanation of themselves and their world. Here the mode is reminiscent of *The Rambler*: in the discussions between Elizabeth and Charlotte Lucas – Charlotte's views on happiness in marriage could almost have come from *The*

Rambler,[12] in Elizabeth's conversations with Jane and with her
aunt, at least when they can persuade her to be 'serious'; and in
some of Elizabeth's private reflections. But most of all it is Darcy
who displays this tendency. Often the point of these expositions,
for Austen as for Johnson, is that, whatever completeness they
may pretend to, however illuminating they may be, they remain
partial rather than total. Thus, when Darcy is caught between
the rich fulsomeness of Caroline Bingley's compliments, and
Elizabeth's resolution to laugh at him, he chooses to be honestly
self-revealing rather than witty. Elizabeth suggests, with pointed
irony, that he 'has no defect' (*Pride and Prejudice*, pp. 57–8), and
in replying he works towards his proposition, Johnsonian even in
its phrasing, that there is 'in every disposition a tendency to
some particular evil, a natural defect, which not even the best
education can overcome'.

> 'No' – said Darcy, 'I have made no such pretension. I have
> faults enough, but they are not, I hope, of understanding. My
> temper I dare not vouch for. – It is I believe too little yielding
> – certainly too little for the convenience of the world. I cannot
> forget the follies and vices of others so soon as I ought, nor
> their offences against myself. My feelings are not puffed about
> with every attempt to move them. My temper would perhaps
> be called resentful. – My good opinion once lost is lost for
> ever.'

Elizabeth of course labels this an 'implacable resentment': but
the reader is allowed the opportunity of reaching some more
moderate conclusions, of seeing that Darcy is being both honest
and accurate, but also of noting the hint of complacency as a
likely source of error. One passage in *The Rambler* is of particular
interest here: it too demonstrates this capacity for thorough and
competent analysis, but one that is also made with more confidence than is really warrantable. But more striking is the way
that Johnson seems almost to be anticipating the view that
Darcy must have of Meryton and its doings; indeed it is not
improbable that Austen actually had this passage in mind.
Johnson offers us the situation of a rich and frugal young man
who seeks a wife and finds that no other 'virtue' or 'testament' is
required of him.

I saw not without indignation, the eagerness with which the daughters, wherever I came, were set out to show; nor could I consider them in a state much different from prostitution, when I found them ordered to play their airs before me, and to exhibit, by some seeming chance, specimens of their musick, their work, or their housewifery. No sooner was I placed at table, than the young lady was called upon to pay me some civility or other; nor could I find means of escaping, from either father or mother, some account of their daughter's excellencies, with a declaration, that they were now leaving the world, and had no business on this side the grave, but to see their children happily disposed of; that she whom I had been pleased to compliment at table, was indeed the chief pleasure of their age, so good, so dutiful, so great a relief to her mama in the care of the house, and so much her papa's favourite for her chearfulness and wit . . . . [13]

There are only two points at which Johnson's account does not fit the Bennets: the Bennet fortune is decidedly a small one, and it is Mrs Bennet's boast that her daughters are *not* involved in 'the care of the house' (*Pride and Prejudice*, p. 44). But, if this informs and to a degree vindicates Darcy's motives and attitudes, then it should also be a warning to us: not all such 'expositions' in Austen's novel are necessarily made explicit; some can exist in no more certain or clear condition than as implications, in the background.

If there are continuous variations in mode, though, then we have also to attend to the shifts and changes in theme. There are, for example, points at which the whole seems to fit within the framework suggested by the ancient opposition between 'town' and 'country'; subsuming, as that does, the questions of rank, understanding and ethics that predominate in the novel. It is a theme that comes into sharpest focus in the contrast between Caroline Bingley and Elizabeth. It is Caroline who is the most consistent defender of London values and standards, and it is by these that she consistently criticises Elizabeth, that she implies her own merit. The several variants of the debate then current would of course have been familiar to Austen's contemporaries. Fanny Burney's heroines are imbued with simple rural virtues, in *Evelina* (1778) or *Cecilia* (1782), and they battle not unsuccessfully with London sophistications, London fashions, London vices. Robert Bage's *Hermsprong* (1796) takes an aggressively Rousseauistic line, and his hero, having spent his youth in the company of North American Indians, professes that in every essential theirs is superior to anything he has found in the fashionable life of France, Germany or England. Maria Edgeworth is less radical, though following a no less significant line, in *The Absentee* (1812), where she shows the plight of an Irish family, attempting to gain acceptance in London society, and to ape London manners, but succeeding only in acquiring expensive London habits. They have to learn to 'leave all the nonsense of high life – scorn the impertinence of these dictators of fashion' and return to rural life. And Edgeworth's example was to encourage Scott to attempt his own version of the provincial novel with *Waverley* (1814). It was of course also a question which Wordsworth and Coleridge made the subject of a notable disagreement.[14]

Pride and Prejudice is an intriguing variation. Caroline is the not-always-adept defender of 'town' conventions and values in the country; Elizabeth provides an entertaining challenge to these conventions, and suggests vitalised alternatives. Together they embody the conflicts that Darcy has to resolve. But, though Elizabeth's is an important challenge, it is not wholly successful. The 'unconventional' conditions that allow Elizabeth to be what she is are also the conditions which are quite unable to curb or harness Lydia's 'high animal spirits' (p. 45); and, though Elizabeth defends country life by claiming that 'people themselves alter so much' (p. 43), that is not so in such typical inhabitants of Meryton as Mrs Phillips or Sir William Lucas: what is more, the existence of the Gardiners mars the argument, whichever way we put it.

The disconcerting effects of these variations in mode and theme are most intense and concentrated in the first half of the novel. It is appropriate that the effects should be most striking during the gradual progress by which two systems as elaborate and as opposed as Darcy's and Elizabeth's are developed: once they are, and while the opposition lasts, they will themselves help to perpetuate the dislocation. This means that the latter part of the novel is not less interesting or less subtle than the early chapters.[15] Once Elizabeth and Darcy discover doubts where there had been certainties, once they begin the slow and tentative movement towards new attempts at understanding and communication, they are confronting the dislocations, the possibilities for conflict and confusion that, for the reader, have been amplified and sustained from the start of the novel. Now there are new ways in which we can share their experiences.

Darcy's proposal, at the centre of the novel, is the obvious marker. Elizabeth's dislike of him has just been intensified by the certain knowledge of his part in separating Bingley from her sister, and is made stronger still by his confession of having struggled in vain against his love for her. The invigorating quarrel, his letter and her meditations on it, make for a thorough and repeated examination of the differences between them, at first hectically declaimed, then reconsidered, then reflected on. But the moment of illumination is brief indeed, and, even before all has been revealed, the participants are adjusting and redefining their positions. Darcy's letter begins 'in bitterness' but ends in 'charity itself' (p. 368), and when she comes to reread that letter (p. 205) Elizabeth has already moved away from angry and confident opposition, is far into new uncertainties. Then, because we no longer have privileged access to Darcy's thoughts, we have, exactly as Elizabeth does, to attempt an imaginative reconstruction, to guess and predict his meaning. Since Elizabeth proves – for very natural reasons – to be less than reliable, we have also to attempt a measure of that unreliability: for the Darcy she attempts to comprehend is already the Darcy of the past tense.

Elizabeth reconsiders her family and is 'depressed beyond any thing she had ever known before' (p. 209); she also reflects on her own 'blind, partial, prejudiced, absurd' behaviour (p. 208). She can now think of Darcy with 'gratitude', 'compassion' and 'respect', but also finds that she 'could not approve him' (p. 212). Once home, she tries to persuade her father to prevent Lydia's expeditions to Brighton: 'Our importance, our respectability in the world, must be affected by the wild volatility, the assurance and disdain of all restraint which mark Lydia's character' (p. 231). Likewise she reflects on what her father might have done: 'she had never felt so strongly as now, the disadvantages which must attend the children of so unsuitable a marriage' (p. 236). But, though Mr Bennet later acknowledges her 'greatness of mind' on this point (p. 299), he now pertinently asks whether Lydia has already 'frightened away' some of

Elizabeth's lovers, and suggests that 'such squeamish youths as cannot bear to be connected with a little absurdity, are not worth a regret' (p. 231): that, after all, is the view which Darcy himself comes sensibly to adopt. Of course we can recognise his culpability, in merely observing the situation, but it is also as easy to condemn him as it is difficult to suggest practical alternatives, and there is no little truth in his observation that 'Lydia will never be easy till she has exposed herself in some public place or other' (p. 230). In any event, though the Bennets are for some weeks spoken of as being 'marked out for misfortune', they are soon pronounced to be 'the luckiest family in the world' (p. 350).[16]

On the journey to Derbyshire Elizabeth is struck by Pemberley, and more struck by the housekeeper's report of a Darcy who is 'most opposite to her ideas' (p. 248). Then the man himself, his evident desire to renew the acquaintance, to meet her aunt and uncle, to introduce his sister, all speak of a man who is, to Elizabeth, wonderfully changed, and to us rationally softened. As she tries to understand the 'new' Darcy, she finds that her own feelings for him now include 'respect and esteem', and a much-strengthened 'gratitude' (p. 265): she attributes the change she perceives in him to 'ardent love' on his part (p. 266), without quite recognising the effect of her own shifting attitude. But, if it appears that resolution is at hand, then Lydia's elopement seems, as Elizabeth assumes, to crush the possibility decisively. At the same moment Elizabeth learns to 'understand her own wishes; and never had she so honestly felt that she could have loved him, as now, when all love must be in vain' (p. 278).

The return to Longbourn initiates an elaborate process of guessing about Lydia and Wickham, and the possible effects of their actions. Elizabeth feels that only Jane 'could flatter herself with such an expectation' as that Lydia is married (p. 279), and then her uncle provides very cogent reasons for supposing that Jane is right (pp. 282–3). Very gradually the real facts emerge. Wickham and Lydia are found in London, and a suspiciously small settlement is required to expedite the marriage. Mr Bennet is left wondering how he will repay the unstated debt to Mr Gardiner: 'Wickham's a fool, if he takes her with a farthing less than ten thousand pounds' (p. 340) – this was exactly the sum which had earlier rendered Miss King so attractive to Wickham. Later still it is revealed that it was Lydia rather than Wickham who precipitated the elopement, and that it was Darcy, 'exactly among people, where he had apparently least to do, and least temptation to go' (pp. 318–23) who had arranged the marriage and the settlement, at a cost less than a third of the amount Mr Bennet anticipated, and in terms which ensure that Wickham can only benefit indirectly. As a scheming and seducing villain, Wickham has become not only paltry but also incompetent.[17]

When it is known that Lydia is to marry, Elizabeth is 'most heartily sorry that she had, from the distress of the moment, been led to make Mr Darcy acquainted with their fears for her sister'. And yet, with Wickham about to become her brother, she still sees what she calls a 'gulf impassible' between herself and Darcy. Even when she knows of Darcy's part in arranging Lydia's marriage, she concludes, despite her own wishes and her aunt's encouragement, that it is easier to believe his own ostensible motive – the 'endeavour to remedy an evil, which has been brought on by himself' (p. 322). Again (and her choice of words is interesting) she feels 'humbled; but she was proud of him' (p. 327). It is in this mood that she encounters Wickham; and, when he attempts, on the strength of their new relationship, to renew their talk of Darcy, she goes as far as propriety will allow in showing that she knows his real past, and she succeeds to the extent that Wickham never again 'provoked his dear sister Elizabeth, by introducing the subject' (p. 330). But she is now also able to acknowledge, formally, her new relationship to Wickham (p. 329).[18]

The return of Bingley and Darcy to Netherfield renews other speculations. Attention is focused on Jane and Bingley, but it is Elizabeth and Darcy that are the most perplexing. She waits to 'see how he behaves' (p. 335), and, even as she endures an intense 'misery of shame' at her mother's general vulgarity, and her particular ungraciousness to Darcy, she can only see that he is 'silent, grave, and indifferent' (p. 339). Later attempts to communicate are no more successful (pp. 340–2): and the spirited meeting with Lady Catherine, though it subsequently proves to be as useful as Lydia's elopment in giving each a better understanding of the other, actually leaves her fearing his aunt's influence, and anticipating that he will not reappear (pp. 360–1).

He does, and as they move towards a resolution, each in humility and doubt and embarrassment, they also do so with as anxious an expediency as even Charlotte Lucas would have approved, and they are both equally determined to find or make a pretext (pp. 365–6, 381). That too is a salutary instance, because they are trying to fix and stabilise at least some part of a meaning that has hitherto been fleeting and changing for reader and character alike.

5 *Mansfield Park*: Compromises

> *She was, she felt she was, in the greatest danger of being exquisitely happy, while so many were miserable. The evil which brought such good to her!* (Fanny, on being summoned back to Mansfield)

This is the Austen novel about which readers are least able to agree: it therefore appears to be the one that most readily invites an approach concerned with narrative methods and reading-strategies. That at least prevents us from immediately taking sides in the noisy debate. Chapman (1948, p. 194) has succinctly put the problem in terms of the difficulty of being 'sure of the writer's general intention', and of the 'almost blatantly didactic' tone in the novel. That contradiction is central. Critic after critic remarks with relish or fortitude or outrage that this novel is unlike the other five in combining the explication of a theme with a harsh statement of an unpalatable and, for many, unconvincing message. From this it is but a short step to the conclusion that the novel is aesthetically a failure, or to the opposing view that its merits have to be specially and, as they have sometimes been, ingeniously argued.

One line, followed especially by the depreciators, argues that Austen was temporarily persuaded to reject some element in herself and her art. This argument has a suspicious circularity about it, even in the best of hands, since 'defects' in the novel are held to demonstrate some crisis in the life of its author, a crisis which at once cosily explains and is explained by the existence of the novel. Often this becomes no more than an easy means of explaining away parts of the novel which one does not happen to like.[1]

A broader approach looks at the obvious preoccupation in the novel with more and less appropriate modes of behaviour and of education, and with contrasting ideas about society, nature, religion: these have been connected again and again, detail for detail, with the views of Hannah More or Thomas Gisborne or William Wilberforce and other Evangelical writers.[2] But almost all of these concerns were with Austen from the first, and if we remember *Sense and Sensibility* then we can hardly find the seriousness here to be untypical. Some have seen the novel primarily as a means for Austen to refurbish the principles of her class, and very much has been said about the significance of Mansfield Park as a place. Yet others have sought elucidation of the process of refurbishing in the thinking of such figures as Johnson, Burke and Cowper, even of Humphry Repton and Uvedale Price. But the general effect of all these attempts is to make the novel peculiarly a novel of its time and not of ours.[3]

And at the centre of the dilemma presented by the novel there is Fanny Price, the heroine for whom 'good' comes out of 'evil', and happiness out of the misery of others. For many readers she is meant to be flawless, and for them she is either a species of 'insufferable prig' or a kind of saint. In the same way, Mary Crawford becomes either the character whose vitality and wit are too much put upon by the moralising inclination of the author, or the representation of a wicked and sly charm. These are divisions of opinion which do not admit of any useful debate, and the gap has not been much bridged, as yet, by those who have begun to notice that Fanny is not untouched by authorial irony: acknowledging that the heroine has natural flaws does not necessarily make her any more interesting, and in any event such concessions have hitherto been small; a preference for Fanny or for Mary, even if it is shaded a little with uneasiness, still forces a rejection of the other.[4]

But, for all its difficulties, and its supposed remoteness, *Mansfield Park* continues to attract eager attention. The visit to Sotherton is much exclaimed over, though accounts of it are most to be noted for the ways in which they disagree. And more has probably been written about the theatricals than about any other episode in Austen's fiction, but here too opinions diverge. Henry Crawford's proposal, and Fanny's return to Portsmouth, have also not suffered from critical neglect, but once again there have been few signs of a consensus.

In short, it would seem that any attempt to provide an account of *Mansfield Park* requires an unusual degree of circumspection. For the novel appears to do, pre-eminently, what all art does in some measure: to turn the reader back on himself, to baffle him, to leave him revealing more about himself than the thing he would explain.

Forewarned, though, we can proceed with due care. To start with, it is worth noting some of the similarities to, rather than the differences from, the earlier novels. Like Elinor Dashwood, Fanny Price is not so much in need of education herself as she is the observer of the attempted learnings of others. Interestingly, Fanny also has something of Marianne Dashwood's 'enthusiasm' (though not quite her 'passion') for Cowper in particular and nature in general. And, like Catherine Morland, Fanny's reading has given her a taste for Gothic architecture, as she shows in the chapel at Sotherton. Fanny's expectations are not quite as excited as Catherine's, but they are almost as misplaced. It would not be unreasonable to claim that part of the conception of Fanny consists of an attempt to contain some of these qualities and differences in a subtle combination.[5]

But *Pride and Prejudice* separates *Mansfield Park* from the earlier novels. The contrast between these two novels is so striking that one can understand why many critics have been tempted to look for a biographical explanation for the change. Unfortunately, there is no clear evidence. Austen's letters have been ransacked for clues, and too often their characteristics, as letters, have been ignored. They are almost always personal, even intimate; they are typically – and sometimes bafflingly – allusive and elliptical; and they have a persistent tendency to switch lightly from topic to topic. They are also far from complete, and none at all survives from the period, crucial to the present question, of early June 1811 to late November 1812.[6] In the surviving letters that coincide with the writing of *Mansfield Park* there is nothing to suggest convincingly the doubts and perplexities that we might have anticipated. What is more, if the existence of the earlier novel invites a 'biographical' explanation of the later, then it also stands as something of an embarrassment to that explanation. If it is correct to assume with Chapman (1948, p. 79) that the revisions of *Pride and Prejudice* were both late and substantial, then there must have been a considerable period when Austen was at work on both novels, and it is difficult to see how one novel should be so deeply marked by a crisis which left the other so unscathed. *Pride and Prejudice* was published only in January 1813, by which time Austen had been working on *Mansfield Park* for two years, had written at least half of it (Chapman, 1948, p. 82) and was within six months of completing it.

Nor is there anything in her response to the publication of the earlier novel to suggest the weighty moral preoccupations that are supposed to have determined the shape and contents of the latter: rather, the opposite. Two days after receiving a copy of the published novel, her 'own darling child', she writes to Cassandra in a mood, natural enough, of high elation: Elizabeth Bennet is 'as delightful a creature as ever appeared in print, and how I shall be able to tolerate those who do not like *her* at least I do not know'. She goes on to remark on some minor faults in the text, vigorously dismisses them as unimportant, and then makes the troublesome reference to ordination, which is often taken as referring to the subject of *Mansfield Park*: 'Now I will try to write of something else, & it shall be a complete change of subject – ordination – I am glad to find your enquiries have ended so well. If you could discover whether Northamptonshire is a country of Hedgerows I should be glad again' (*Letters*, p. 298). But surely Hugh Brogan (1968, p. 1440) is right in arguing that this is a change of subject within the letter, rather than a statement about the subject of her next novel. There can have been no point in telling Cassandra the subject of *Mansfield Park*, since the letters show that she was intimately familiar with the half that had already been written. The mention of ordination then, like that of hedgerows, probably relates to certain details in the novel which she is checking for accuracy.[7]

Six days later the elation was followed, equally naturally, by doubts.

> Upon the whole, however, I am quite vain enough and well satisfied enough. The work is rather too light, and bright, and sparkling; it wants shade; it wants to be stretched out here and there with a long chapter of sense, if it could be had; if not, of solemn specious nonsense, about something unconnected with the story; an essay on writing, a critique on Walter Scott, or the history of Buonaparté, or anything that would form a contrast, and bring the reader with increased delight to the playfulness and epigrammatism of the general style.   (*Letters*, pp. 299–300)

And despite attempts to see this as a rejection of wit in favour of the pursuit of wisdom, or principle, it surely means little more than it says. She now feels more aware than she was of the novel's limitations. 'Upon the whole', however, these limitations are not thought to be serious. But, even if her doubts are more than temporary, her discussion of the remedies is clearly in part a lively joke, so we cannot in reason go much beyond the simple conclusion that at this point she felt the style of the book wanted a little in contrast and variety. And it is difficult to see in this an Austen who was suffering the agonies of some personal crisis; who was crushed under the graver concerns of the Evangelicals; or who, with profound sorrow, was contemplating the decline of the gentry. Further, if there was sorrow, then its short duration is problematic: *Emma* was begun a year after the publication of *Pride and Prejudice*.[8]

What is more, the differences between *Mansfield Park* and *Pride and Prejudice* can actually often be seen to be no more than different ways of treating the same questions. Though it is less substantially a part of its argument, *Pride and Prejudice* also has important things to say about education, and Darcy's admission, 'I was given good principles, but left to follow them in pride and conceit' (p. 369), reveals a scheme that is less limited in degree but not in kind than that of the Bertrams. *Mansfield Park* has its own proposal scene, also almost exactly in the middle of the novel; it too is unexpected, and Crawford is as much Fanny's social superior as Darcy is Elizabeth's. Both novels reach their conclusions by way of an elopement, and the similarity here is more than can be explained because elopement is a common fictional subject – consider its different and altogether more conventional treatment in *Sense and Sensibility*. Mr Bennet has to be persuaded from his resolve that Lydia will not be allowed to visit Longbourn, while his neighbours happily anticipate that she will be 'secluded from the world, in some distant farm house' (p. 309): in *not* being so persuaded, Sir Thomas is merely the predictably stern enforcer of conventional morality. Mary Crawford sometimes demonstrates how irresponsible wit and sparkle can be, and this is a kind of comment on the mode and substance of *Pride and Prejudice*. But the link is surely not so straightforwardly between Mary and Elizabeth Bennet as to suggest that what is generally recommended in the earlier novel is largely rejected in its successor. Elizabeth's wit is, after all, rather different from Mary's, and, though she certainly laughs at the follies of Mr Collins, the conclusions she is likely to come to are conclusions about fools in general, not clergymen. Equally, there is Mary's complex association with other characters in the earlier novel: with Caroline Bingley, and her defence of town values and manners; with Charlotte Lucas, and her materialistic view of marriage.

If *Mansfield Park* urges the necessity of morality, if it lays out particular sets of principles, then it examines the defects as well as the merits of these principles. It becomes, in fact, a means for considering the limitations of morality in individual lives and in their mutual dealings, as scrupulously as the limitations of wit were considered in its predecessor. If *Mansfield Park* was written under the strong influence of the Evangelicals – the question remains doubtful – then it is about the limitations of those doctrines, about the points they cannot touch.

In summing up the achievements of *Mansfield Park*, Mary Lascelles (1939, p. 35) has suggested that it 'excelled *Pride and Prejudice* in its subtler conception of human relations – by as much as *Pride and Prejudice* had excelled *Sense and Sensibility* in its more subtly planned construction'. It would perhaps be fairer to say that the two later novels both represent a simultaneous advance in psychological and technical subtlety. *Sense and Sensibility* is concerned with ideas as ideas, and we see individuals in complicated and rather formal relation to them. *Pride and Prejudice* concentrates on ideas as they function in relationship with people in practice, through continually shifting emphases and changing possibilities. *Mansfield Park* gives up the wholesale undermining of certainty, and substitutes the doubts and ambiguities of a much smaller scale. The picture seems, almost completely, to say one thing, but enough details do not quite fit to make us hesitate a little. The instances of obvious immorality in the novel are so very obvious that they scarcely require a judgement to be pronounced: the real point is that the kinds of judgement which the novel does offer for our consideration are almost, but not entirely, adequate. We can respond, as many readers do, either by sticking with the judgements or by rejecting them; we can, in short, side wholly with or against Fanny and Edmund. But that is an unsatisfactory choice, since neither side can be made to yield sufficiently to the other: a more promising stance would be one in which we observed, with greater detachment, the discrepancies on both sides and the degree to which a compromise is possible.

The discrepancies are hinted at even at moments that seem to invite the most straightforward judgement. Consider the case of Mrs Norris. From the first pages, when we see her angry bustle in promoting the breach between Mansfield and Portsmouth, then her smugly self-righteous talk of charity for Portsmouth, the narrator allows us only a little time to formulate an opinion before briskly supporting us with a sharply uttered judgement.

> Under this infatuating principle, counteracted by no real affection for her sister, it was impossible for her to aim at more than the credit of projecting and arranging so expensive a charity; though perhaps she might so little know herself, as to walk home to the Parsonage after this conversation, in the happy belief of being the most liberal-minded sister and aunt in the world.   (pp. 8–9)

The same device is used, a little later, against the Bertrams. The girls are shown enjoying their superiority over their cousins: they scorn her poverty ('but two sashes'), her ignorance, her lack of ambition to be 'accomplished'. Their aunt encourages them, while also claiming that the charity to Fanny is her own doing. Then the narrator actually states the strictures we are beginning to formulate, and even extends them to Sir Thomas.

> Such were the counsels by which Mrs Norris assisted to form her nieces' minds; and it is not very wonderful that with all their promising talents and early information, they should be entirely deficient in the less common acquirements of self-knowledge, generosity, and humility. In every thing but disposition, they were admirably taught. Sir Thomas did not know what was wanting, because, though a truly anxious father, he was not outwardly affectionate, and the reserve of his manner repressed all the flow of their spirits before him. (p. 19)

After this we glimpse Lady Bertram, comfortably ensconced on her sofa, preoccupied with her needlework and her pug; Tom Bertram is revealed, a page later, to be 'careless and extravagant'; and we can guess that even Edmund, not lacking in merit, is culpable to the extent that he is his father's son. The defects and the limitations of the whole family are thus economically set before us. And of course, at the end of the novel, there is a severe reiteration of these strictures: Sir Thomas finds not only that the combination of repression and indulgence in the education of his daughters has had the reverse effect to the one he intended, but 'principle, active principle, had been wanting'.

> They had been instructed theoretically in their religion, but never required to bring it into daily practice. To be distinguished for elegance and accomplishments – the authorised object of their youth – could have had no useful influence that way, no moral effect on the mind. He had meant them to be good, but his cares had been directed to the understanding and manners, not the disposition; and of the necessity of self-denial and humility, he feared they had never heard from any lips that could profit them.   (p. 463)

That points to an obvious contrast with Fanny, and might begin to suggest that the novel really is comprised of some distinctly flat-footed moralising. But in fact such moments happen quite rarely in the novel, and the narrator only gives utterance to judgements of this scope and firmness on those few occasions when such judgements are safe. It is as if the narrator is leading us into a consensus about those matters so simple that they do not warrant sustained attention, as a means of clearing space for those that do. And even the most austere of the summary judgements is seldom unmixed: there are, for example, enough scattered clues in the opening pages to make it possible for us, as well as judging Mrs Norris, to undertake the rather different task of understanding her. The less-than-obvious fact, contained in the first sentence, that she is the oldest of the three sisters can help to illuminate the striking difference between her and her passive sisters, just as it underscores the irony by which the younger sisters both attain positions which, though strikingly different, are beyond their 'managing' capacities, but well within that of their under-employed sister. The irony expands as the novel opens out: it is Miss Maria who is 'raised to the rank of a baronet's lady' but it is Miss Ward who takes the more active pleasure in enjoying the 'comforts and consequences'. Her preoccupation with the rights of eldest daughters is reflected in her decided preference for Maria Bertram, and it is she who does most to assist her niece into an ambitious and disastrous marriage. Similarly, it is she who chooses the eldest Portsmouth daughter, rather than any of the 'fine boys' Mrs Price is more concerned about, as the child most suitable for Mansfield charity. Once Fanny is in the context of Mansfield, however, it is also naturally Mrs Norris who is most busy to ensure that she is 'lowest and last' (p. 221).

At many other points, the method of summary judgement is itself made to look dubious. Consider the treatment of Sir Thomas: he is a figure of undoubted but uncertain moral authority and principle; usually the narrator is almost silent about him, and offers only the occasional oblique irony; it is difficult for the reader to get an entirely adequate grasp of the man, and we can find ourselves smiling where we are expected to be most solemn. When we see him giving weighty consideration to the suggestion that Fanny be brought to Mansfield, this is not merely the expression of conventional doubts. If he argues that there must be a 'proper' distinction between Fanny and his daughters, then he also acknowledges that it is a point of 'great delicacy' (pp. 10–11), one on which there should be no rigid enforcement. Everyone notices the larger irony in this: it is because Fanny is not like her cousins, and because the distinction is maintained too rigorously, that she eventually becomes more truly his daughter than either of her cousins. But there is also a smaller irony that is almost as telling, since his lofty speculations carry little weight against Mrs Norris's verbosities, or the rigid distinctions between her nieces that the aunt does so much to support.

The question of his eldest son puts Sir Thomas in an even stranger light. Tom's 'extravagance' costs his brother one of the two livings being held for him, and we might expect that, as with the question of his sisters' education, a few pages before, the narrator will take the opportunity to condemn him roundly, and, through him, his family. But instead, it is Sir Thomas who passes judgement; and, though on this occasion at least he has right on his side, he is also pompous and a little ridiculous.

'I blush for you, Tom', said he, in his most dignified manner; 'I blush for the expedient which I am driven on, and I trust I may pity your feelings as a brother on the occasion. You have robbed Edmund for ten, twenty, thirty years, perhaps for life, of more than half the income which ought to be his. It may hereafter be in my power, or in your's (I hope it will), to procure him better preferment; but it must not be forgotten,

that no benefit of that sort would have been beyond his
natural claims on us, and that nothing can, in fact, be an
equivalent for the certain advantage which he is now obliged
to forego through the urgency of your debts.' (pp. 23–4)

The effect is compounded by Tom's response. He is genuinely
touched, but then he also tries to shrug aside the feelings of guilt
as quickly as possible, so that we can see both the necessity for,
and the unworkability of, his father's 'most dignified manner'.
Indeed, he actually begins to generate a surprising and rough
comedy when, with 'cheerful selfishness', he rationalises himself
away from the little understanding he possesses of what he has
done, and focuses in three easy steps on the death of Dr Grant as
a means of making good to Edmund what he himself has lost his
brother. When Dr Grant's appearance ('a hearty man of forty-
five') seems likely to upset Tom's calculations, he is unper-
turbed: 'no, he was a short-neck'd, apoplectic sort of fellow, and,
plied well with good things, would soon pop off' (p. 24). The
vigorous colloquialisms are entertaining enough; but the question of Dr Grant's health actually becomes a sustained macabre
joke, since the doctor proves to be not only irascible, but also
very eager to be 'plied well with good things'. Thus he provides
telling support for Mary Crawford's views on marriage and on
clergymen; and at the end of the novel he brings on 'apoplexy
and death, by three great institutionary dinners in one week'
(p. 469), thus allowing Edmund to acquire the Mansfield living
conveniently at a point when he has been 'married long enough
to begin to want an increase of income' (p. 473). We have had to
question the efficacy of Sir Thomas's principles, and we have
also been tempted to smile at them.

Equally, though, when Sir Thomas appears to represent a
principle that is most vitiated, when he seems most obviously
open to censure, we should hesitate before condemning him. It
seems at first easy to measure his culpability when, for instance,
we see his attitude to Maria's marriage. He discovers, very soon
after his return from Antigua, that Rushworth is a fool, and he
also begins to understand his daughter's view of the man: 'She
could not, did not like him' (p. 200). Yet, blinded, apparently,
by the worldly advantages of the match, he seems to make no
very strenuous efforts to prevent it. But such a view does not
account for the complicated pressures and circumstances that

exist. He does not begin to understand the mixture of passion and wilfulness that is his daughter, or the way that she is too little governed by 'active principle', and that must be a measure of his inadequacy as a father. But he can know nothing of the part Henry Crawford has played in her feelings, and he cannot know that it is because she has been waiting agitatedly for Crawford to declare his love that it is easy for her father to detect her dislike of Rushworth. He cannot know what the narrator makes plain to us: that the effect of his talk with his daughter is crucially dependent on its timing. Had he spoken to her a few days earlier (that is, 'within the first three or four days after Henry Crawford's leaving Mansfield') then 'her answer might have been different'. By the time that he does speak, she has become 'cool enough to seek all the comfort that pride and self-revenge could give' (pp. 201–2).

And, if we suspend judgement briefly, we shall begin to appreciate that both father and daughter are not just 'wrong' in their different ways, but also radically confused. The narrator speaks, as so often in this novel, only in conditionals and possibilities.[9] Sir Thomas is 'too glad to be satisfied perhaps to urge the matter quite so far as his judgement might have dictated to others' (p. 201). On that uncertain note he is abandoned to his lofty and muddled thoughts: thoughts in which the desirability of the match and the awkwardness of breaking it off, the hope that Rushworth will improve, the belief in Maria's self-confidence, the notion – Edmund makes the same mistake about his sister (p. 116) – that her feelings are not strong anyway, and the idea that she will be happy at Sotherton because it is close to Mansfield, all jostle uneasily together. Maria's thinking, totally opposite to everything he imagines, has its own muddle. She feels that she should not be seen, at least by Crawford, to be rejecting 'independence and splendour for *his* sake', and that she 'must escape' from her father and from Mansfield 'as soon as possible, and find consolation in fortune and consequence, bustle and the world, for a wounded spirit' (p. 202).

The moral points, such as they are, are obvious enough. The novel does not seem to require of us a mere endorsement of these points: rather it invites us to evaluate some states of mental and emotional confusion that can exist in relation to these points, and to examine some of the problems of application. Most telling, perhaps, is the discrepancy between Sir Thomas's intentions, however mixed or muddled they may be, and his actions. He sets out 'with solemn kindness' to speak to Maria, and that is at once a measure of his sincerity in feeling that 'her happiness must not be sacrificed' (p. 200) and an indication that he will fail to communicate with her, just as he failed earlier with Tom.

So the presentation of morality in *Mansfield Park* is neither uncomplicated nor uncritical: but what *is* that morality? The insistence on 'active principle' makes it temptingly easy to see the novel as a sophisticated advocacy of the Evangelicals' cause, but there is almost no real evidence to support this. A couple of years before writing *Mansfield Park*, Austen was decidedly against the Evangelicals: her response to Hannah More's *Coelebs in Search of a Wife* (1808), even before she had read it, is the blank 'I do not like the Evangelicals' (*Letters*, p. 256). And she went back to her own juvenilia, to insert More's title in 'Catherine' (*Minor Works*, p. 232), in a context that heartily satirised its didacticism. Later, shortly after completing *Mansfield Park*, she wrote in a distinctly un-Evangelical way to complain of a Mr Cooper's 'new Sermons; – they are fuller of Regeneration & Conversion than ever – with the addition of his zeal in the cause of the Bible Society' (*Letters*, p. 467, 8 Sep 1816). The one favourable reference to the Evangelicals comes in a letter of 18 November 1814, and that itself is awkwardly late for *Mansfield Park*, being six months after it was published, and only four before *Emma* was finished. It also does little to suggest a fervent personal commitment to their principles, and even less to suggest that her last-published novel was founded on them. Austen writes to a niece who is uncertainly in love; the young man's 'goodness', even his tendency towards Evangelicalism, should not, she argues, be disparaged: 'And as to there being any objection from his *Goodness*, from the danger of his becoming even Evangelical, I cannot admit *that*. I am by no means convinced that we ought not all to be Evangelicals, & am at least persuaded that they who are so from Reason and Feeling, must be happiest & safest' (*Letters*, p. 410). In the circumstances, this calm recommendation of a moderate and rational Evangelicalism cannot be taken as meaning much more than that the aunt would be happier if her niece married a man of firm religious principle. Even if

Austen were briefly, wholeheartedly Evangelical at this time, then it is strange that only two months before she should express a decisive preference for the sermons, not, for example, of the recent and Evangelically inclined Bishop of London, Beilby Porteus, but of one of his predecessors, Thomas Sherlock (*Letters*, p. 406), whose death in 1761 makes him entirely pre-Evangelical – many of whose sermons, indeed, were preached in the first years of that century.[10]

Of course, to test their principles Austen need not herself have been an Evangelical. The matter of 'active principle' is at the heart of William Wilberforce's *A Practical View of the Prevailing Religious System* (1797), and of his distinction, fundamental to Evangelical thinking, between 'professed Christians' and 'real Christianity'.[11] Professed Christians are not only the merely nominal, but also those who mean well yet are insufficiently instructed.

> If we listen to their conversation, virtue is praised, and vice is censured; piety is perhaps applauded, and prophaneness condemned. So far all is well. But let any one, who would not be deceived by these 'barren generalities' examine a little more closely, and he will find, that not to Christianity in particular, but at best to Religion in general, perhaps to mere Morality, their homage is intended to be paid.[12]

But this is really to suggest differences from, rather than similarities to, Austen. Certainly, she argues that principle must be properly inculcated, but where is that special sense of the Christian religion which, for Wilberforce and the other Evangelicals, demanded articulation? The Evangelicals could only have regarded Austen as a professed Christian; a little enlightened, perhaps, but still with a dangerous tendency even on the too-few occasions when Christianity is being explicitly discussed – as when Edmund Bertram defends the role of clergymen (*Mansfield Park*, pp. 92–3 for example) – to confuse Christianity with 'mere Morality'.

But it can still be argued that there are links between Austen and the Evangelicals, in terms of specific applications of principle. Thomas Gisborne, for example, in his *Enquiry into the Duties of the Female Sex* (1797), notes how when a woman is insufficiently instructed in religious principles she can very easily lose the little grasp she has of them. And he warns, emphatically, against encouraging 'emulation' when educating the young. Mrs Norris encourages emulation in *Mansfield Park*, and it is one of the things in which she finds Fanny to be deficient (p. 19). Gisborne also expresses a characteristically Evangelical disapproval of 'ornamental accomplishments', and a vigorous disapproval of private theatricals which it could be argued is reflected in *Mansfield Park*. Then, his view of marriage is very close to Fanny Price's, just as it encompasses almost everything which Maria Bertram leaves out of her thinking. 'Unless the dispositions, the temper, the habits, the genuine character, and inmost principles were mutually known; what rational hope, what tolerable chance of happiness could subsist?'[13]

Almost all these points are expanded upon by Hannah More, in her *Strictures on the Modern System of Female Education* (1799). There is, for example, her argument that the system of education then current tended to encourage 'vanity, selfishness, and inconsideration' – just the vices it ought to be attacking. Equally interesting are the habits which, she asserts, education should be helping to form: 'humility', 'sobriety', 'attention', 'industry'. There is her scorn for the business of 'coming out' – a subject dwelt on by Mary Crawford (*Mansfield Park*, pp. 49–51); and for the practice of learning by rote, at which the Bertram sisters are so adept (p. 18). And one critic has noted how More's notions on 'the religious and moral use of history and geography' are strikingly close to Fanny Price's effusion on the stars, and her praise of evergreens (Moler, 1968; 1977, pp. 114–15, 123–7).[14]

There is one area, though, in which Austen and the Evangelicals must part company decisively. The Evangelicals are united in their disapproval of novels, and it is quite likely that their objections were among those Austen had in mind when she wrote her 'Defence of the novel' in *Northanger Abbey*. For the Evangelicals, even the 'best' novels, those which most accurately depict the world, depict a world which is notably un-Evangelical, and do not adequately acknowledge that defect. When one of their number chose to write a novel – Hannah More – she embodied much of her own *Strictures*, thinly disguised as fiction. *Coelebs in Search of a Wife* (1808), immediately and enormously popular,[15] shows Coelebs surveying the world, and finding it to be notably without 'real Christianity'. An encounter with a family in which the daughters exercise their 'accomplishments' –

just of a kind to be found at Mansfield Park – moves Coelebs to this heartfelt denunciation:

> The piano-forte, when they were weary of the harp, copying some indifferent drawings, gilding a set of flower-pots, and netting white gloves and veils, seemed to fill up the whole business of these immortal beings, of these Christians, for whom it had been solemnly engaged that they should manfully fight under Christ's banner.[16]

But such a dogmatic assertion of principle and practice is remote from anything in *Mansfield Park*, however similar may be the areas of interest. Equally, it would be absurd to argue that the Evangelicals were the sole discoverers of these interests. William Law's *A Serious Call to a Devout and Holy Life* (1728) includes an account of the education of daughters, the necessity for sound principles, and the dire consequences if they are insufficiently instilled. Like the Evangelicals, he saw these results as coming from a plan of education that was well intentioned but misconceived.[17] Similar concerns are to be found repeatedly in the pages of *The Rambler*, for example, or in the lengthy discussions about principled and unprincipled behaviour in *Sir Charles Grandison*.

Nor would it be right to assume that by the end of the century these concerns had become wholly the property of the Evangelicals.[18] Even someone so utterly un-Evangelical as Mary Wollstonecraft matched the Evangelicals to a quite surprising degree, in the details she examined and the remedies she proposed in her *Vindication of the Rights of Woman* (1792) – an agreement noted with amusement by at least one contemporary (Jones, 1952, p. 115). For her central argument, entirely at odds with Evangelical thinking, is that in being treated as inferiors women suffered great wrong, and that it was because they were treated as inferiors that they became so. To change the situation she sought 'a REVOLUTION in female manners'; and she looked forward to the abolition of the distinctions of rank in society as a whole. The Evangelicals, conservative in all that she was revolutionary, accepted unquestionably that women *were* inferior; the question of rank interested them, but merely because they felt that education should provide an adequate preparation for the responsibilities as well as the privileges that rank entailed.[19]

Yet it is precisely when we consider the particular grievances she lists, and the specific ways in which she would achieve her revolution, that we can find Mary Wollstonecraft to have some common ground with the Evangelicals. Her condemnation of the business of 'acquiring a smattering of accomplishments' is as forthright as anything the Evangelicals could muster:

> meanwhile strength of body and mind are sacrificed to liber-
> tine notions of beauty, to the desire of establishing themselves
> – the only way women can rise in the world – by marriage.
> And this desire making mere animals of them, when they
> marry they act as such children may be expected to act – they
> dress, they paint, and nickname God's creatures. Surely these
> weak beings are only fit for a seraglio!

She warns that parents who simply 'extort a show of respect' from their daughters are likely to be bringing up daughters who will become 'adulteresses'. She offers a heavily ironic defence of the practice of making girls learn by rote: 'If they be not allowed to have reason sufficient to govern their own conduct – why, all they learn must be learned by rote!' She scorns the practices associated with 'coming out'. Like the Evangelicals, she contrasts the function of the clergy, as it ought to be, with what it all too often is. Like them also, she is deeply suspicious of the influence of novels.[20]

It is hardly surprising, therefore, that recent feminist accounts of Austen's work have actually tried to make Austen into an ally of Wollstonecraft, using exactly the same evidence as others have used to make her an Evangelical.[21] But, whatever the case one wants to make either for Austen as an Evangelical or for Austen as a feminist, this kind of evidence is inadmissible. The fact that two minds as opposed as those of More and Wollstonecraft, under such different inspirations, and striving for such contra-dictory ends, could nevertheless share this much common ground suggests only one thing. Both were drawing from the same stock of ideas and topics, the subjects of a widespread current debate. It is hardly necessary to add that other contemporaries, Austen among them, had access to the same stock. Byron, for example, made his own particular use of it in his repeated attacks on 'Blue Stockings' in *Don Juan*: in Donna Inez's mock-weighty conversations, for instance, her bogus learning, her theories about education (I. x–xviii, xxxviii–lii). Hannah More was of course among the original Blue Stockings; and she wrote a poem in celebration of the delights of conversation entitled 'The Bas Bleu' (1786). Consider also Byron's mischievous suggestion that an interest in religion was but one of a list of 'accomplishments':

> fits or wits or harpsichords,
> Theology, fine arts, or finer stays
> May be the baits for gentlemen or lords . . . .
> (*Don Juan*, XII.liii)

And, once we perceive that Austen is doing more than merely purveying an already established doctrine, we can properly appreciate the originality of her contribution. Where More or Wollstonecraft lay the greatest weight on the consequences of an insufficient instruction, in order to enforce the proposition that instruction should be more sufficient, Austen does no more than offer a concise instance of insufficient instruction: she takes the conclusion of More or Wollstonecraft as her starting-point and, rather than belabouring the point to make the lesson clear, she indicates that, while the grosser implications are obvious, it would still be useful to examine and test some of the finer possibilities. This at once has her making points that would not have been endorsed either by those who sought to justify the rights of women, or by those who aimed to reform 'professed Christians'. The necessity of sound principles is but half Austen's argument: the other, more difficult and more important half concerns the problems and dangers to be faced in almost any attempt at a practical application of principles, and she looks for the occasions when principle, however sound and however completely digested, may not entirely suffice.

This has a significance for the novel that is beyond the question of the influence of the Evangelicals. It is not merely that the principles Austen would teach and the ideals she would defend are not especially Evangelical; it is that she is not inclined, in any especial way, to teach or to defend principles and ideals. One of the critical commonplaces about the novel is that Mansfield Park, as a place, is the physical embodiment of some kind of ideal. Yet it is almost impossible to see anything beautiful or ideal, even in the most shadowy of implications, in the place as it exists in the novel, since its limitations and faults are held under such tight scrutiny. To argue, as some have tried, that the rightful inhabitants are defective but the place still represents an ideal, is to try to reconcile the irreconcilable.[22] Fanny Price, of course, is usually supposed to be the preserver of the ideal, the redeemer of its virtue, but her own merits are not unambivalent: and she has actually very little to do, either by way of action or inspiration, with making the place what it becomes. Nor do the novel's closing chapters support the notion that the place is meant to be a now established ideal. It is a place where there are patches of light, but where there are also distinct shadows: where memories of guilt and misery linger on in the minds of the characters, however much the author may wish to 'quit such odious subjects' (*Mansfield Park*, p. 461). The one allusion, in these pages, to something like an ideal is to those products of Portsmouth squalor, the Price children: not merely to Fanny, or even to Fanny, William and Susan, but also to 'the general well-doing and success of the other members of the family, all assisting to advance each other' (p. 473).

In the novel, the most cogent and persuasive statement about Mansfield as an ideal comes from Fanny herself one week after her return to Portsmouth.

> At Mansfield, no sounds of contention, no raised voice, no abrupt bursts, no tread of violence was ever heard; all proceeded in a regular course of cheerful orderliness; every body had their due importance; every body's feelings were consulted. If tenderness could be ever supposed wanting, good sense and good breeding supplied its place; and as to the little irritations, sometimes introduced by aunt Norris, they were short, they were trifling, they were as a drop of water to the ocean, compared with the ceaseless tumult of her present abode. (pp. 391–2)

It is easy to see why, given the shock of Portsmouth, Fanny should take this view of Mansfield: but it is a version of the place that exists nowhere, in the novel, outside Fanny's dreams here. Not only is there the obvious and substantial underestimation of the daily pain inflicted on her by Mrs Norris. Few, if any, of the virtues she ascribes to it are to be found there either in the joyless repression occasioned by Sir Thomas's presence or in the boisterous self-indulgence which occurs in his absence. And, if the virtues of Mansfield are to be doubted before, then how much more so when we see what becomes of Tom, Maria or Julia, and how Sir Thomas and Edmund respond. On the rare occasions when Fanny does experience a kind of tranquillity, this is usually undercut by irony. When her uncle returns from Antigua, and the house becomes a scene of a 'sombre family-party' (p. 196), Fanny, alone among the young people, is pleased with the change. Doubtless she welcomes the calm, after the agitation of the theatricals: but then she will also approve of the fact that Henry has fewer opportunities to flirt with Maria; and she must realise that Edmund will see less of Mary.

Fanny's vision of Portsmouth is equally understandable, but here too we must note the biases and the exaggerations: 'Here, every body was noisy, every voice was loud, (excepting, perhaps, her mother's, which resembled the soft monotony of Lady Bertram's, only worn into fretfulness.) – Whatever was wanted, was halloo'd for, and the servants halloo'd out their excuses from the kitchen' (p. 392). It is this shock and this disappointment at coming 'home' that blots out so successfully the unhappinesses of Mansfield, even that of her recent confrontation with her uncle. And that is natural enough, given that the 'home' into which she is given no very warm welcome, and in which she can see little opportunity of being 'useful', is a place of such noisy and often unnecessary confusion. But there is also a real sense in which, at least for the first part of her stay in Portsmouth, she wants the Prices to be what they are not, and will not see them as they are. Sir Thomas intended Fanny to learn from the contrast of the two homes, and he intended the lesson to be, explicitly, an economic one (p. 369). We do not have to adopt his standpoint to see that, while she *is* struck by the contrast, she fails to understand the economics of that contrast. She is very quick to see that her mother is incompetent, but she sees very little beyond that. She does not recognise, consciously, that Mansfield has elegance, and the spaces for privacy and retreat, and that Lady Bertram's voice has no occasion to be 'worn into' the fretful tones of her sister, because Mansfield is wealth, while Portsmouth is poverty. Certainly it takes her some time to begin to understand that the problem of an incompetent servant is more, merely, than a question of bad housekeeping (p. 385). The subject is a serious one, handled seriously; but, since the proposition exists so palpably, and Fanny grasps so little of it, we could also say that Austen is enjoying a gentle joke at the expense of her heroine.

If that suggests that Mansfield has little ideal about it, outside Fanny's rather confused imagination, then it also suggests a Fanny who is rather ill matched to some of the popular critical assumptions about her, as an exemplary heroine. Fanny's moral sense is important, but only because in relative terms it is more pronounced and more comprehensive than that of anyone else in the novel. What we should do as readers, surely, is to observe the difficulties she encounters, the way she attempts to match the moral sense with private wishes and needs, with public require-ments. Consider the complications and confusions that almost any situation generates. The news that Sir Thomas is to go to Antigua brings Fanny a feeling of 'relief' as it does her cousins. Unlike them, she also thinks that 'her feelings were ungrateful, and she really grieved because she could not grieve' (p. 33). But it is her uncle's hard parting words that actually reduce her to tears, plainly showing also why she has difficulty in grieving at his going; and then 'her cousins, on seeing her with red eyes, set her down as a hypocrite'.

The single most important influence on Fanny is of course her cousin Edmund, and here too things are not as clear or as straightforward as they might seem. Edmund is blind to the real nature of her feelings for him; while she soon loves him 'better than any body in the world except William'. In the circum-stances, it is only to be expected that he should be the teacher who 'encouraged her taste, and corrected her judgement' (p. 22), or that she should also acquire a good deal of his youthful solemnity, and something even of his occasional priggishness. The cousins' rather ponderous discussions about Mary Craw-ford, for example, show Edmund still directing and shaping Fanny's opinions, though by now his services as a teacher are required only for a minor 'adjustment'. Equally, while a notable irony attaches to the large area of agreement between them, Fanny is now preparing to disagree. But that is to present us with a dilemma: the opinion of neither character can be wholly relied upon, once Edmund begins to see Mary through the eyes of a lover, and Fanny to use her principles in the service of her feelings and wishes, as she considers and judges her rival.

We must move carefully here: Fanny can be unreliable, and she can reveal a surprising degree of hidden aggression, but those critics who descry a Fanny Price turning her principles into weapons, to be used aggressively against her situation, are usually confusing a part of the picture with, the picture as a whole.[23] Take the matter of the riding-lessons for Mary Crawford: we can see Fanny as fretful, self-pitying and hypercritical; we can concentrate, rather, on the way the situation points to Fanny's lonely, dependent and unhappy condition. But these are only two of a number of threads tangled together, which we have to pick out. There are the complexities created by Fanny's established but secret love for Edmund: it was Edmund who reasoned Fanny out of her own fears when she began to ride; it was Edmund who later acquired a horse, himself, for her use (pp. 35–7). Now she has to watch Mary learning to ride on the same horse, and inevitably her judgement is coloured.

It is as easy to judge Mary's part in the affair, and as easy to be wrong about her. We could, like Fanny, take her actions and her frank admission of selfishness as proof of her blighted and wilful nature, but this is a view which the circumstances do not actually support. For Mary (as it is, surely, 'objectively') the half-hour delay is no more than a minor piece of discourtesy – certainly she cannot, at this stage, understand Fanny's situation, as Edmund does. Equally, when the horse is handed over to Fanny, she does not, like Edmund, make gratuitous excuses, thought up after the event, about 'time' and 'shade' (p. 68). Instead, she apologises simply and directly: then, and this too is characteristic, she turns the matter into a joke against herself. Indeed, the narrator makes it clear that Mary's actions are understandable, and hardly more than venial: 'and to the pure genuine pleasure of the exercise, something was probably added in Edmund's attendance and instructions, and something more in the conviction of very much surpassing her sex in general by her early progress, to make her unwilling to dismount' (pp. 66–7).

The two sentences that follow this, though, take us forcibly back to Fanny's plight, and the consequence for her of Mary's 'genuine pleasure': 'Fanny was ready and waiting, and Mrs Norris was beginning to scold her for not being gone, and still no horse was announced, no Edmund appeared. To avoid her aunt, and look for him, she went out.' Yet, while that is a powerful appeal for us to ally our sympathies entirely with Fanny, there is

something in her stance that makes this a little difficult, and can
actually make us smile. When she goes out, she sees Edmund
and Mary in the distance, both on horseback, with Henry and
the Grants standing by. Fanny feels the inevitable 'pang' at
being excluded, and at the thought that 'Edmund should forget
her', but it is also interesting that she honestly appraises Mary's
quick competence on horseback: the cross jealousy will be felt
later (p. 69), when she listens to the coachman's lengthy praise
of Mary, and his pointed comparisons with her own nervous first
attempts at riding. Now it is something else that swiftly focuses
her attention.

> After a few minutes, they stopt entirely, Edmund was close to
> her, he was speaking to her, he was evidently directing her
> management of the bridle, he had hold of her hand; she saw it,
> or the imagination supplied what the eye could not reach. She
> must not wonder at all this; what could be more natural than
> that Edmund should be making himself useful, and proving
> his good-nature by any one? She could not but think indeed
> that Mr Crawford might as well have saved him the trouble;
> that it would have been particularly proper and becoming in a
> brother to have done it himself; but Mr Crawford, with all his
> boasted good-nature, and all his coachmanship, probably
> knew nothing of the matter, and had no active kindness in
> comparison of Edmund. She began to think it rather hard
> upon the mare to have such double duty; if she were forgotten
> the poor mare should be remembered.   (pp. 67–8)

It is the contact of hands, seen or imagined. She cannot, of
course, bring herself to blame Edmund for what happens, and so
she obliges herself to see that he is 'making himself useful, and
proving his good-nature' – a convenient explanation that does
not commit him to any particular interest in the object of his
usefulness. Yet the emotion generated in her by the touching of
the hands can only momentarily be contained. Deflected from
the principals, it is concentrated in an ill-tempered attack on
Henry; and, whatever defects he may elsewhere reveal, Henry is
innocent enough here. Then there is a brief flash of self-pity,
quickly turned into the more respectable, if also rather ludicrous,
concern for the 'poor mare'.[24]
Now, the point is not that Fanny's 'active principle' is in

abeyance, but that she gets relatively little help from its functioning presence, and it is her emotions which play a large part
in shaping her interpretations and her responses. Nor is this a
momentary aberration. Everyone notices that Fanny is 'the only
heroine to get a headache cutting roses', and while conventional
explanations either point to this frailty as a weakness which is
meant to make Fanny endearing, or remark that she is part of a
long tradition of frail heroines, it is perhaps more important to
understand the degree to which this frailty has an emotional,
rather than a merely physical basis.[25] Typically, Fanny's situation, and her feelings, are obscured, in the four succeeding days,
when she gives up her claim to the horse, by the rather more
importunate Bertram demands. On the fourth evening Maria,
out of temper because she was excluded from an invitation to the
parsonage, succeeds in putting her aunt even more than usually
out of temper; and so Mrs Norris shrilly scolds Fanny for 'idling
away all the evening upon a sofa' (p. 71). Julia, just back from
the parsonage, good-humouredly defends Fanny; Edmund notices that she is ill. Then the story of the roses comes out, and of
the walks to and from Mrs Norris's house, and, as cause and
blame are debated, it would seem that Fanny has more than
enough reasons for her headache. It is only at the end of the
chapter, when every other explanation has been fully canvassed,
that we are introduced to the 'possibilities' that relate to Fanny's
emotions: 'As she leant on the sofa, to which she had retreated
that she might not be seen, the pain of her mind had been much
beyond that in her head; and the sudden change which Edmund's kindness had then occasioned, made her hardly know
how to support herself' (p. 74). Similarly at Sotherton, it is when
Edmund appears to be completely engrossed with Mary, and
Mary to be at her most worldly, that Fanny becomes aware of
how 'tired' she feels (p. 94). So, too, her arrival in Portsmouth,
after a long journey, and to a very noisy household, are circumstances that more than sufficiently explain her 'aching head' (p.
382). Yet it is the effect of the unfriendly welcome that is most
significant: Susan's kind words and considerate actions soon
dispel much of the pain in 'head and heart' (p. 384).

It is interesting that this account of 'psychosomatic illness' to
some extent prefigures the psychological theorists, but the pre-
figuring is less important than our seeing what else Austen is
doing here. It is within *Mansfield Park*'s deliberately constructed

moral framework that feelings are given this large scope. It is emotions that so often give shape to the meaning of events and situations. 'Active principle' is doubtless essential, but it is not always fully active, and it is feelings, half understood and muddled as they are, which are often more fully in control. Nor is it that this happens only at moments of high crisis. Almost any attempt at understanding has the potential for skirmishings between feeling and principle.

That is one kind of answer to Charlotte Brontë's famous claim that, to Austen, 'the passions are perfectly unknown'. Indeed, it goes to show that, despite the obvious differences between the two novelists, there are also interesting similarities. It would clearly be absurd to suggest that Brontë conceives of a world that has no noticeable use for 'active principle', or one that is conceived wholly in emotional terms: but emotional terms are predominant, and they give first meanings to ideas and to actions. It is also a world of strong contrasts in primary colours, rather than one of more minute variations and shadings: even more, perhaps, it represents an attempt to render these *poetically*. It was just on this point that Brontë considered herself to be fundamentally different from Austen. When G. H. Lewes suggested to her that Austen was 'one of the greatest artists', without being poetic, her pointed reply was not, of course, a claim to greatness herself; but it was an emphatic denial of the title to the earlier novelist. 'Can there be a great artist without poetry?'[26] But, whether or not Austen is a great artist, whether or not she is 'without poetry', there is one important sense in which her scope is larger than that of her successor. It is Austen who makes the detached *novelistic* survey, who locates emotions within the context of a total picture: of head and of heart, of feeling and of principle. Likewise, while she sees the possibilities for a harmonious and unified whole, she also recognises the more powerful potential for conflict and confusion. Most of all perhaps, because she is fully aware of the context, she is fully able to allow for the shaping influence and the sometimes chaotic effects of emotions.

And, as it is with Fanny, so it is, in different ways, with everyone at Mansfield: Lady Bertram's emotional range is like her ethical reach in only occasionally stretching beyond her sofa and her pug; Sir Thomas is principled but also worldly, loving but also austere; Mrs Norris has her active and ill-tempered

bustling; Tom, his unthinking and self-centered pursuit of pleasure; Julia forms a self-centered conception of the future as soon
as she meets Henry, while her sister's thinking is 'more confused
and indistinct' (p. 44), both about Henry and about Rushworth;
the solemn yet sympathetic Edmund becomes almost a parody of
the young man conventionally in love, doing it 'without studying
the business . . . or knowing what he was about' (p. 65). And the
Crawfords are particularly interesting, in this regard, once we
learn not to see them simply, in Fanny's terms, as the spreaders
of corruption, or else, and equally simply, as the bringers of
vitality and fun to a staid Mansfield. They enter the novel
declaring their 'wickednesses' more openly than any other Austen characters: Henry is named, is criticised by the narrator, as a
'flirt' (p. 45), while his sister as quickly states her hard-headed
ambition to achieve a mercenary marriage. But no other 'vil-
lains' also leave us so unsure of what they will do and what they
will become. With Henry, for instance, we find that, just at the
point when we expect to be able to label an active vice, there is
mere thoughtless selfishness; and he can even appear, engag-
ingly if not unambivalently, as the reformed trifler, so that his
attempts to make Fanny a little in love with him leave him in
love with her and – ironically – with the most complete sense in
the novel of her merits, and the difficulties of her life at the Park.
Even as he confuses us, Henry is himself caught in the confusion
between principle and feeling.

In a more complicated way, so is Mary, and, though she is
continually set in contrast to Fanny, the distinction (as became
clear in the matter of the horse) is almost never absolute or clear.
If we are told that Mary, unlike Fanny, is unresponsive to
nature, has 'none of Fanny's delicacy of taste, of mind, of
feeling', then we have also to remember that 'her attention was
all for men and women, her talents for the light and lively' (p.
81). And her liveliness is valuable, even if it is sometimes
misplaced, just as Fanny's admirable seriousness can turn all too
easily into solemn moralising. If Mary confidently and compla-
cently attaches a saying from 'the court of Lewis XIV' to her
finding herself in the shrubbery of a country parsonage, then
that is not necessarily better or worse than Fanny's prolix and
second-hand response to that same shrubbery (pp. 208–9).[27] If,
in the much-noted matter of the necklace and the chain (pp.
257–71), we condemn Mary for the trick she plays on Fanny,

then we must also acknowledge that, cynically knowing though she is, she also makes the mistake of assuming that Fanny is almost equally so ('You were as conscious as heart could desire' – p. 362). We may be inclined to praise Fanny for only dimly guessing at (and then after a pointed hint) what Mary takes to be obvious; but what of Fanny's crudely sentimental response to the gift of a chain from Edmund? It is, as the narrator suggests, understandable, but then it is also uncomfortably amusing: and, for all Fanny's 'heroism of principle' and sense of 'duty', it is suggestive of the behaviour of Harriet Smith, in *Emma*.

We can be shocked by Mary's repeatedly expressed intention to marry ambitiously, until we realise that she is merely stating explicitly the principles that are elsewhere implicit, and further that she wants to be provocative in exaggerating, and contrasting them with those of Edmund (*Mansfield Park*, pp. 212–14, for example). When she states her belief in the 'true London maxim, that every thing is to be got with money' (p. 58) we can take this, as many critics do, to be the ultimate proof of her corrupted and mercenary nature: until, that is, we see that all she is doing is acknowledge she does not understand country customs. The 'London maxim' is nothing but the statement of an elementary fact of economic life in a large city: money can do 'every thing', because, in a real sense, only money can do anything. Her mercenary principles are, in general, the same as those advocated by Sir Thomas Bertram until the closing pages of the novel, just as they accord exactly with 'almost the only rule of conduct' which Lady Bertram offers her niece (p. 333). And, if she is more sophisticated than the younger Bertrams, then the contrast between them nevertheless usually works in her favour. It is clear that Mary regards Maria's 'captivation' of Rushworth as natural and appropriate, but it is also clear that she would never herself be tempted by a Rushworth, however rich. Mary finds that Edmund is 'agreeable to her', despite the fact that he is a younger son, and, in addition, 'not pleasant by any common rule'. She can 'hardly understand it', but then she does 'not think very much about it' (p. 65). She, too, is caught up in the emotional confusion, and in her case, the confusion is actually a sign, albeit uncertainly, of grace.

What, though, of the Crawfords' context, their background? Neither the passing direct reflections of London life supplied by

the Crawfords, nor the more substantial account of the place and
its delights offered by Mary in her conversations with Fanny and
her letters to Portsmouth (pp. 359–62, 393–4), are more than
decidedly second-hand renderings, conveying only a little more
than a sense of meretricious glitter, shallowness, selfishness. It
could be argued that the delicate balance elsewhere held between Fanny and Mary is lost: Mary appears to be a fool to trust
to such dubious pleasures, while no great virtue can be ascribed
to Fanny for not being tempted by them. But that is to exag-
gerate, and the picture in fact has unexpected complexities. The
most likely models for Austen's London are those of Fanny
Burney and Maria Edgeworth, but there is actually only a fairly
remote connection with *Mansfield Park* and the perspectives are
rather different. In a Burney or an Edgeworth novel, fashionable
London society is presented as the outsider's view, seen and
rendered as a life of profligacy and dissipation, actively to be
countered by a Cecilia or a Belinda. Fanny Price remains quite
remote from urban sophistication, and to the extent that she
opposes its influence she does so passively for the most part, and
by being what she imperfectly is. What is more, the view of
London society is almost entirely that of the insider: complacent
and assured, not blind to defects but too ready to condone them.
It is a picture which is surprisingly like the London in which
Byron places his hero in *Don Juan*.

> In the great world – which being interpreted
>   Meaneth the West or worst end of a city
> And about twice two thousand people bred
>   By no means to be very wise or witty,
> But to sit up while others lie in bed,
>   And to look down on the world with pity –
> Juan, as an inveterate patrician,
> Was well received by persons of condition.
>
> (XI.xlv)

It is a world where

> Daughters admired his dress, and pious mothers
> Inquired his income, and if he had brothers.
>
> (XI.xlviii)

There is Byron's vivid rendering of the interminable bustle, and
real boredom, of a grand ball (XI.lxvii-lxx). There is his advice
to the man who

> hath higher views
> Upon an heiress or his neighbour's bride,
> Let him take care that that which he pursues
> Is not at once too palpably descried.
>
> (XI.lxxi)

At times, he seems almost to have had Mary Crawford's career
in mind:

Some who once set their caps at cautious dukes
  Have taken up at length with younger brothers.
Some heiresses have bit at sharper's hooks;
  Some maids have been made wives, some merely mothers. . . .

(XI.lxxxi)

There is a similar aptness, given the ending of *Mansfield Park*, in
his view of newspapers, and the 'evidences which regale all
readers'.

> For 'tis a low, newspaper, humdrum, lawsuit
>   Country, where a young couple of the same ages
> Can't form a friendship but the world o'erawes it.
>
> (XII.lxv)

Interestingly, his opinion is the opposite of Sir Thomas Bertram's, when he suggests that, while Society usually banishes the
fallen, this does

> But aggravate the crime you have not prevented,
> By rendering desperate those who had else repented.
>
> (XII.lxxx)

Byron speaks as an 'insider', though one who is more percipient that those he describes; one whose acumen is perhaps
sharpened by his sense of exile from that community, and
enriched by some of the livelier autobiographical details he includes in his argument. And he is constantly shifting his relation-

ship to his material: sometimes the matter is personal and even intimate, at others it is public and general; at points he is convivial and partisan in his attitudes to those he is describing, then he can also be remote and austere. The overall effect is to create a picture that is three-dimensional, and to allow the reader to see things both from the inside, and (more detachedly) from the outside. Austen was never an 'insider' herself, but this should not obscure from us the extent to which she herself achieved a three-dimensional picture, by recording the ambivalences of Mary Crawford's connection with London, in the balance between Fanny's rigid strictures on London life, and Mary's view as the not uncritical, but still indulgent, 'insider'.

The conflict between more and less adequate principle and feeling is perhaps most clear with the question of religion. It is appropriately in the disused chapel at Sotherton that Mary expresses her doubts about the value of family chapel services, and her suspicions about the attitudes of those who attended them (*Mansfield Park*, pp. 86–7). Some critics find this shocking; yet there is nothing very outrageous, or even very new, in what she says. A hundred years before *Mansfield Park* was published, *The Rape of the Lock* offered an amusing picture of the kind of confused irreligiousness Mary Crawford has in mind, and one of the effects of the 'Cave of *Spleen*' is to 'send the Godly in a Pett, to pray' (IV. 64). The question of inappropriate behaviour, often decidedly flirtatious, in churches, was a recurrent theme, not always handled with due seriousness, in the pages of *The Spectator*. It was a topic which Richardson took up in his single, ponderous, contribution to *The Rambler*.[28]

One kind of response to Mary's views on family devotions represented in the novel is that of Fanny: she feels 'too angry for speech'. Edmund's response is much less extreme; is indeed the most appropriate, even if it is a compromise between his sense of Mary's attractions and his dislike of her opinion. 'Your lively mind can hardly be serious even on serious subjects' (*Mansfield Park*, p. 87). And Mary does have an acute sense of the world *as it is*: her account of the 'Mrs Eleanors and Mrs Bridgets' in the chapel at Sotherton and 'starched up with seeming piety' is apt enough, as Edmund himself admits. Equally, it is not clear what value Edmund or Fanny place in the chapel, beyond its literary–Gothic significance; or what importance they attach to family devotions that is more than a respect for a useful social custom.

When Edmund is drawn to defending the function of the clergyman (pp. 92–3), he is most concerned to stress the general significance of the clergyman's role. In his view, the clergyman 'has the charge of all that is of the first importance to mankind, individually or collectively considered, temporally and eternally – which has the guardianship of religion and morals, and consequently of the manners which result from their influence'. And, when challenged by Mary, he elaborates on the question of 'manners': 'The *manners* I speak of, might rather be called *conduct*, perhaps, the result of good principles; the effect, in short, of those doctrines which it is their duty to teach and recommend. . . . ' It is little wonder that Mary's view of fashionable life in Regency London should so clash with Edmund's thinking, when we see that he is invoking the authority of *The Book of Common Prayer*. The stress laid on the 'great importance' of the clergyman's function in the Service of Ordination exactly matches Edmund's argument. For example:

> and see that you never cease your labour, your care and diligence, until you have done all that lieth in you, according to your bounden duty, to bring all such as are or shall be committed to your charge, unto that agreement in the faith and knowledge of God, and to that ripeness and perfectness of age in Christ. . . .

There is also, quite precisely, Edmund's sense of 'manners': 'consider how studious ye ought to be in reading and learning the Scriptures, and in framing the manners both of yourselves, and of them that specially pertain unto you, according to the rule of the same Scriptures'.

At the same time, the words in Edmund's mouth are rather sententious. Edmund is speaking with the naïve and idealistic enthusiasm that is typical of any young man who is willingly entering a profession: it may indeed be a part of the narrator's irony that his enthusiasm is of a kind more usually excited by the professions that Mary would have him enter. Certainly, we can share at least something of Mary's impatient joke, when she later wonders at his delay in coming to London: 'There may be some old woman at Thornton Lacey to be converted' (*Mansfield Park*, p. 394). There are also the emotional connections and complications. When Mary provocatively declares on the nothingness of clergymen, she does so not only because this is her opinion, but also because her more than ordinary interest in Edmund makes it natural that she should wish him to be something she can more easily esteem. So, too, Edmund, shocked though he sometimes is by her, is still securely caught by her attraction; while Fanny disapproves of Mary so strongly, of course, partly because she fears that Edmund does not do so sufficiently.

The episode of the theatricals allows the reader a further opportunity of exploring the connections and differences between emotional and moral energies. When Maria hopes for, and obtains, the role opposite to Henry's, she is committing herself to playing the part of a 'fallen woman', and that is of course a significant foreshadowing.[29] Even more important is the way in which Henry and Maria deliberately exploit their roles. They play the parts of mother and of long-lost son. Their much-rehearsed embraces accomplish, in the context of the play, what they could never so easily do outside it, and the mere attempt later in London bundles them impetuously into an elopement. Ironically, they would not have been permitted this degree of freedom of physical expression had they been playing the parts of lovers in the play. It is by yet another irony that the lovers of the play are enacted by Mary and a rather reluctant Edmund; and they offer a brisk caricature of their own roles and debates in the novel. It is Edmund who plays Anhalt, the clergyman, who has to talk to Mary's Amelia of marriages happy and unhappy, compatible and incompatible; Mary who must talk of love with a frankness that even she finds a little embarrassing (p. 168).

The 'morality' of the theatricals is an especially interesting question. Here we see 'active principle' at work, at least in those who oppose the theatricals, and it is significant that this is not wholly convincing. It is easy enough to find objectionable elements in what actually happens; in the quarrels and the flirting, the scheming and the extravagance: but then this is no more than an intensification of what the novel has already demonstrated as typical. Nothing in the stated opposition is wholly coherent or convincing. Partly, it is the result of an ambivalence in the arguers themselves: Edmund's lengthy arguments against the project, against the play chosen, lose much of their conviction when he realises that Mary takes a different view (p. 129). Even his absolute refusal himself to act is turned about out of consideration for her (p. 154). Fanny too is strongly opposed to the enterprise, and yet her refusal to act probably has more to do with a feeling of embarrassed shyness than it has with any real moral conviction. It cannot be said that she regards the business of acting as in itself dangerously corrupting, else why should she take such pains to help Rushworth master his part – indeed, master it for him (pp. 224–5)? Why should she take such a thorough general interest in the proceedings? 'For her own gratification she could have wished that something might be acted, for she had never seen even half a play, but every thing of higher consequence was against it' (p. 131). That nicely catches the ambivalence in Fanny's attitude; just as the characteristic slight self-pity makes the 'higher consequence' a little doubtful.

And, while of course she and Edmund are right in claiming that Sir Thomas would disapprove, they are, all three, on very uncertain ground when seeking the basis of this disapproval: instead of there being a single compelling principle to invoke, there is a dubiously large and mixed collection of quite good reasons, advanced by Edmund. There is the objection to ama- teur acting *as* amateur; there is the question of a 'want of feeling' for Sir Thomas, at a time when he is 'in some degree of constant danger'; there is Maria's 'very delicate' situation; there is the suggestion that it would be 'taking liberties' with the house, in its master's absence; there is the point that it would be 'wrong as an expense' (pp. 124–7). Sir Thomas does indeed echo most of these arguments: but what seems to be foremost in his mind is a dislike of Mr Yates, the man who brought the idea of theatricals to Mansfield, and, by implication, of aristocratic habits and pleasures (Chapman, 1948, pp. 198–9). And nothing more secure or absolute as a moral structure is to be founded on the sadness which predominates in his feelings, a sadness at the way his family seem so easily to have forgotten him and his dangers. What is more, the reader who is inclined to take matters only and wholly seriously will be thwarted by the narrator's sense of the comic potential to be found, even in moments that are very painful to the participants, as they argue, manipulate, justify. It is a potential which increases as the tensions rise, and the performance approaches; and it takes on a sharp actuality with the sudden return of Sir Thomas, and his unwittingly dramatic appearance, with rather bemused dignity, on the stage (pp. 182–3).

After the theatricals, after Maria's wedding, when Fanny

comes to be at the centre of life at the Park, there are further
opportunities for the reader to observe the interplay between
feelings and principles. When Henry plans 'to make Fanny Price
in love' with him, the narrator devotes an unusually long and
detailed comment to the matter, noting the degree to which
Henry is blamable (pp. 231–2). Equally though, Fanny's position is not untouched by irony, and, while her moral objections
to Henry are strong, they make her by no means impervious to
his charms. It is her love for Edmund which secures her from
their effects, and, even then, not entirely. At the end of the novel,
the narrator's retrospective view allows considerable force to the
possibilities – albeit now unattainable – of this relationship:
'Would he have persevered, and uprightly, Fanny must have
been his reward – and a reward very voluntarily bestowed –
within a reasonable period from Edmund's marrying Mary' (p.
467).

What is more, as that last quotation might begin to suggest,
while there are many sombre and oppressive moments associated with Henry's attempts to court Fanny, they can be not a
little lightened by the comedy. When Henry first begins to notice
Fanny, when he first tries to draw her into a conversation, he
lights, unluckily for him, on the subject of the theatricals, and of
his great happiness during the time of the rehearsals. Fanny's
first response is unspoken, and it perfectly comprehends the
differences between them. 'With silent indignation, Fanny repeated to herself, "Never happier! – never happier than when
doing what you must know was not justifiable! – never happier
than when behaving so dishonourably and unfeelingly! – Oh!
what a corrupted mind!" ' (p. 225). And the comic effect tells
equally against both, keeping us once again from taking sides or
making easy judgements. He is shown, confident of his charms,
ignorant of how ill they are succeeding; she, over-reacting, and
being a little too self-righteous. Then, as we watch him attempting to awaken her interest, finding this an unusual challenge,
becoming engrossed, and then himself in love, so we can see how
he appears to be rapidly acquiring 'active principle': equally, we
can never be sure of the measure of his sincerity, of the extent to
which he is responding to emotional pressure or moral conviction.

The confrontation between Sir Thomas and his niece on the
question of Henry's proposal (pp. 312–25) has rightly been

stressed by critics. In standing by her preference for love, rather than money, Fanny has to challenge the authority of her uncle, and to imply that his principles are insufficient to the degree that they are merely materialistic. Yet it is all too easy to over-emphasise the significance of Fanny's challenge, to be overly struck by the fact that she is capable of making it.[30] Of course it takes courage on her part; of course the narrator makes it clear how close she is to being crushed (p. 321). But it would surely be rather surprising, if, in fact, she did not resist the elsewhere-compelling authority of Sir Thomas on this occasion, given that everything else she is – morally and emotionally – makes her completely antithetical to his advice. Once again, too, it is the covert factors in the situation, as much as the overt, that the reader has to weigh. Fanny's reasons for refusing Crawford are sounder than her uncle can know, but she cannot vindicate her decision in his eyes, because to do so would also be to blacken her cousins. At the same time, we do not have to share Sir Thomas's values to see that, from his point of view, Fanny's explanation must appear thin, her decision wilful. The apparently amiable relations that exist between Park and parsonage, between Henry and his niece, are quite contrary to the spirit in which she makes the curt and resolute rejection of the proposal.

This acquired capacity on Fanny's part to hold back, to give so little away, plays a significant part in determining the way the novel ends. It means, as Henry discovers, that wooing her is a very unrewarding task for any man who is not Edmund. Even when Henry is most careful, most assiduous, most delicate in the exercise of his charms, as when he reads Shakespeare, as when he talks of sermons (pp. 336–44), she reveals only minimal interest, however much her attention is caught. And, on an 'uncommonly lovely' day in Portsmouth (pp. 409–12), when she is unusually happy, and happy in his company, when even the comparison she inevitably draws between Henry and Edmund tells less weightily against Henry, she is able to conceal so much of this that, when they part, her formal, reserved and cold manner jars against his enthusiastic warmth, and is indeed a distinct rejection of what he offers. It is not necessary to repeat Mary's error (p. 437), and blame Fanny for what follows: but it is surely entirely understandable that Henry should return to London frustrated and disappointed; and, being Henry, should be too easily tempted by the diverting prospect of Maria's company.

Indeed, while Portsmouth offers new occasions for the reader to sympathise with Fanny's plight, it also excites more doubts about the way her feelings and her morality combine. Thus her response to Tom's illness is a decided mixture: there is her lack of 'any particular affection' for her cousin, but there is also her 'tenderness of heart'; yet there is also the uncompromisingly severe, if primly qualified, review of his life, in which the 'purity of her principles' directs her to notice 'how little useful, how little self-denying his life had (apparently) been', and in which she happens to find him wanting in the two virtues she can most easily claim for herself (p. 428). We must notice her response to Mary's letter about Tom (pp. 433–6), in which she is so quickly and surely outraged by what is little more than Mary's habitual lightness.[31] She has also to perform some dubious distortions in order to justify her refusal of the Crawfords' offer of the means of returning to Mansfield, while not quite acknowledging the extent to which she is under the impulse *not* to receive a favour from Henry, and the even more distinct wish not to bring Mary and Edmund together. Then the news of the elopement leaves her on the verge of a shrieking hysteria,[32] offering a moral condemnation that is grossly inappropriate, and is comically offset by her father's laconic comment on Maria: 'by G – if she belonged to me, I'd give her the rope's end as long as I could stand over her' (p. 440): ' . . . it was too horrible a confusion of guilt, too gross a complication of evil, for human nature, not in a state of utter barbarism, to be capable of! – yet her judgement told her it was so' (p. 441). And this very quickly and easily dissolves into a guilty, but scarcely suppressed, happiness when she discovers that the elopement is also the means of getting her, and Susan, to Mansfield. Thus the elopement becomes the 'evil', with *all* its attendant confusion of emotion and principle, 'which brought such good to her!': this is what makes her 'exquisitely happy, while so many were miserable' (p. 443).

By the same token, we can find that Edmund and his father respond to the elopement with an excess of 'active principle', so that we are left with a residual doubt about the value of that principle. Sir Thomas is too preoccupied merely with the matter of not offering 'an insult to the neighbourhood' (p. 465), and his son is rather too apt to emphasise the 'dreadful crime' (p. 457), as his last encounter with Mary shows. If Mary is wrong to see only 'folly' where there is 'guilt' (and it must be said in her defence that one of her motives is, doubtless, to keep open the

possibility of a relationship between herself and Edmund), then
he is wrong to see 'guilt' only and always. It is understandable
that he should feel, at this point, that the differences between
them are greater than anything that is in their mutual attraction,
that he must separate himself from her. We can even begin to
anticipate that he will soon be in his cousin's arms. But we can
also wonder about the kind of sermon he might preach on the
woman taken in adultery.

That *Mansfield Park* finds such a resolution, less than perfect
and less than perfectly happy as it is; that the novel also allows
us to conceive of other resolutions, perhaps more satisfactory as
real possibilities; that it is preoccupied less with recommending a
particular set of principles to its readers, more with considering
the nature and function of principle in general, and the dangerous difficulties of practical application: to the extent, and it is
substantial, that *Mansfield Park* achieves these ends, it is not a
novel that is obstinately and defensively a novel of its time. It is
also provocatively and even disturbingly a novel of our time.

6 *Emma*: Mystery and Imagination

'What an air of probability sometimes runs through a dream! And at others, what a heap of absurdities it is!' (Mr Weston, when his son 'blunders' and forgets which story he is telling to whom)

It has become commonplace to observe that *Emma* resembles a detective story. In reading it we try to solve a set of connected mysteries: there are plenty of clues but we will very likely go wrong, we can only be certain that we shall not be wholly right. It has also become commonplace to treat the novel as an account of the functioning of the imagination, Emma's in particular.

But if both commonplaces are valid – and each modifies the other, to an extent – then both are in need of qualification. *Emma* presents us with a 'conclusion', but this does not constitute a 'solution' in any sense that is appropriate to the label 'detective story'. And, if its subject is the imagination, then it cannot be (despite widespread critical assumptions on this subject) that it approaches its subject in a narrowly critical spirit, or at best that it finds a safe, restrained and chastened expression for the imagination. Whatever faults one may find with Emma's imagination, hers is only one of many varied imaginative conceptions of the world of Highbury offered by the novel. With everyone in the novel busily imagining their conceptions of its world, it could be said that *Emma* offers an examination of more and less adequate uses of the imagination, but not that it considers the faculty to be necessarily dangerous.[1]

The world of Highbury exists, self-defining, and yet not quite coherent. Some of the accounts of that world supplied by its inhabitants are by their very simplicity compelling (even if they do not quite convince). Mr Woodhouse, 'having been a valetudinarian all his life' (p. 7), with his 'habits of gentle selfishness', and his complete inability to 'suppose that other people could

117

feel differently from himself' (p. 8), provides a version of this
world that makes it consist almost entirely of threats to his own
health and happiness. It is a confined and rather airless world, in
which appetites are too easily satisfied by basins of 'nice smooth
gruel, thin, but not too thin' (p. 105). It has almost nothing in
common with other versions of this world, but it is a version that
is tolerated, and those who are too sharply critical of it are apt to
sound merely churlish.[2] By contrast, his daughter Emma's rich
and varied creations appear to be almost as large as the novel
itself, and to be often formidably persuasive – consider for
example how many critics who allow themselves a first-name
familiarity with the principal characters in other Austen novels
feel obliged to refer to *Mr* Knightley in deference to Emma's
views. Yet Emma's power is largely illusionary, as becomes clear
when we perceive that her creations are often manifestly incomplete, and that they exist in competition with the conceptions of
other characters.

In its preoccupation with mystery and imagination, and with
ways of understanding the world, *Emma* has particular affinities
with *Northanger Abbey*. *Sense and Sensibility*, *Pride and Prejudice* and
Mansfield Park are, of course, all concerned with ways of understanding and imagining the world, but with ways that relate to a
specific aspect of the world, a set of questions, a defined vocabulary. Sensibility and sense for instance, or prejudice and pride, or
morality and emotion: these are the terms that most economically illustrate the point. *Emma*, like *Northanger Abbey* (though in
rather different ways), is more preoccupied with the antecedent
question of what actually constitutes understanding and imagination.

For all this, the novel's subject and its form are likely to
appear, at least to a casual glance, to be strikingly lucid and
coherent. Emma has a large pre-eminence in the novel, unique
in Austen's novels, and reflected uniquely in the title. Jane
Fairfax, Mrs Elton and even Harriet Smith can challenge
Emma's position in Highbury in some way, but none can touch
her position in *Emma*: each invites nice and significant contrasts
with her, reflecting different aspects of her self and situation,
reinforcing her position in the novel. It is something that the
structure of the novel emphasises, as it subtly yet unmistakably
marks out the stages of Emma's experience, etched in the pattern
of the successive details, and marked by the effective use of

balance and repetition. For all these reasons it is clear what *Emma* is about, and there is a degree of consensus among the critics that is obviously lacking in regard to *Mansfield Park*. *Emma* is usually said to be about the educating of Emma Woodhouse: the process by which she blunders, and the means by which she comes to adjust the basis for her perceptions and her understanding.

Beyond that very general formulation, though, there is very little easy agreement. Emma's education has been seen as a matter of intellectual or moral or social or emotional or sexual development: for some readers there is actually a strain of half-hidden lesbianism in her. Some have insisted that Emma learns significantly, and becomes fully adult; others that she learns and changes little. For some her affectionate concern for her father shows a saving grace; for others it is a sign that to the end she is unwilling to give up childish ways. Her schemes and devices for ordering the lives of her friends are of course 'wrong', but have been regarded as the merely misguided attempts to apply an impressive creative vitality, or as the wilful faults and follies of an over-indulged young woman. In the same way Knightley is the wise and mature force of correction, or he is flawed, but only enough to make him seem the more convincing, or he is notably flawed. So too, we could continue with the other characters.[3]

One consequence is that the argument has tended to become rather self-preoccupied, another is that it has become less than fully responsive to the novel's potential as a brilliantly enlightening and enlivening comedy about understanding and misunderstanding, imagination and confusion. Nor, as readers, do we buy our laughs too cheaply. We too must set about the business of 'conjecturing', we too must venture our own explanations, and match them to the often contradictory explanations offered by the characters. Highbury, the imaginative construction of its author, comes to exist as a series of imaginative constructions of its imagined inhabitants: and, in responding to this series, the reader has in part to reconstruct it, in part to attempt his own ordering. Emma herself shows us what we have to do, just as she can show us how not to do it. She declares herself to be 'an imaginist . . . on fire with speculation and foresight' (p. 335): she is also one who 'sets up', however mistakenly on occasion, 'for Understanding' (p. 427). To read

Emma is to chart a course between imagination and judgement, to attempt the very necessary business of accommodating to both.

Wayne Booth's much cited account of *Emma* (1961, pp. 243–66) offers the most sustained attempt, to date, to explain Austen's handling of her material, and our response to it. Booth points to the need for a balance between 'sympathy' and 'judgement' in the reader. Austen achieves this, he notes, by ensuring that we see a great deal of the novel through Emma's eyes, but that other characters, chiefly Knightley, provide a corrective to her views. When we move beyond the generalities, though, then Booth's conception proves to be too simple and too stylised. Booth is unhappy about the process by which the reader is 'mystified', especially about the secret engagement of Jane and Frank, and he observes that this 'inevitably' (p. 255) reduces the dramatic irony. But Booth's formula for connecting mystery and irony has nothing to do with the actual experience of reading *Emma*, since there is never a crudely mechanical trading between the two. If, like Emma, we are mystified by Frank and Jane, that does not directly limit our ironic understanding of the heroine, since we do not have to establish the precise measure of her error to guess at a good deal of its substance. We have the history of her blunders and surmises, we know the methods she habitually employs, and we have the contrary opinions of other characters.

The most useful answers to Booth's case have come from W. J. Harvey (1967, pp. 48–63). For him, the novel is 'binary': 'Around the visible star, Emma herself, circles an invisible planet whose presence and orbit we can gauge only by measuring the perturbations in the world we can see. . . . The written novel contains its unwritten twin whose shape is known only by the shadow it casts' (p. 55). The 'unwritten twin' is of course the story of Frank and Jane: but the novel is very rich in fictions and possibilities; this 'unwritten twin' is only one of them. Nevertheless, on the problems of actually reading the novel, Harvey comes much closer to the experience, as it must strike most readers, than Booth:

we, too, share the frailty of the characters, not merely by being human, but also, in a special sense, by being readers. In other words, *Emma* is a novel which constantly tempts us into surmise, speculation, judgement; the process of reading runs parallel to the life read about. Hence the need for mystification and hence the delayed revelation which shows how we, too, are liable to mistake appearances for realities and to arrive at premature conclusions. The novel betrays us to ourselves. (p. 57)

Even this, though, is limited. It takes no adequate account of the actual functioning of the imagination in reader or character, and for Harvey the whole experience occurs between the doubts of the first reading and the certainty of the second. The special pleasure of subsequent readings he can only explain by the meagrely argued possibility that 'our attention is so diversified and diverted by the thick web of linguistic nuance that we do not concentrate single-mindedly on the ironic results of the mystification' (p. 63).

The most striking limitation of both accounts is that, while they describe mechanisms for reading *Emma* that are actually quite elaborate, this does not match their sense of what is *in* the novel, which is deemed, by both, to be very straightforward. Harvey sees it as the portrayal of a heroine whose faults are snobbery and pride; faults which result from her 'failure to control an over-active and perverted imagination' (pp. 49–50), while Booth (1961, p. 244) comments on Emma in these terms:

> charming as she is, she can neither see her own excessive pride honestly nor resist imposing herself on the lives of others. She is deficient both in generosity and in self-knowledge. She discovers and corrects her faults only after she has almost ruined herself and her closest friends.

Both versions, it must be said, are also a little too insistently grim.

And we discover why Booth is so pressingly opposed to the mystification when he reveals his conception of Austen's narrator as a 'friend and guide' to the reader, one who also has 'learned nothing at the end of the novel that she did not know at the beginning' (p. 265). This is surely an illusion which, from the first pages of *Northanger Abbey* onwards, Austen creates *in order to destroy*. Reading her novels is not actually an easy, comfortable and soothing experience, through which we are carefully guided by the friendly, genteel, aunt-like and all-knowing figure of the narrator.[4] Booth's preoccupation with what the narrator 'knows', and what the narrator reveals, leads him to conclude that, but for the mystery of Frank and Jane, all would be easy and obvious. Harvey offers an apt corrective on this point, when he suggests (1967, pp. 53–4) that Booth 'assumes a rather too sophisticated first reading to be the norm'. But then none of the six novels yields up its significances quite as easily as Booth envisages *Emma* doing, to a first-time reader. *Pride and Prejudice* is the most obvious point of comparison, with the deliberately maintained mystery of the real nature of Darcy and Wickham. If we were better informed on these points then we should, obviously, be much more able fully to savour the ironies of Elizabeth's mistakes about both men.

But then if we are invited to consider both *Emma* and *Pride and Prejudice* as vitiated by Austen's desire to maintain mysteries, we might well want to consider whether these mysteries are perhaps actually performing some important function other than that of beguiling the reader. Booth (1961, pp. 254–5) rather casually concedes that 'every author withholds until later what he "might as well" relate now', but the emptiness of this gesture can be seen if the proposition is turned around. It is impossible for a novel to reveal everything at once; it is a bald axiom that the author must choose what will be told, how and when. The reader who would avoid mystification should avoid fiction altogether, and should confine his reading to something like the *Dictionary of National Biography*. Even that reveals sequentially, but it does not deliberately mystify.

There is of course a kind of novel in which the part played by mystery is deliberately confined, and every character is introduced by a tidy biographical summary, with a neat underlining of significant details. It is exemplified in Scott's *Waverley*, where the very process of orderly explanation to the reader actually works by way of a mystification of the hero, a mystification which the reader will at once penetrate unless he is historically illiterate or else incapable of performing a simple arithmetical subtraction. Scott subtitles his novel *'Tis Sixty Years Since*, he pointedly takes his retrospective from the year 1805, he gives the novel a romantic–military flavour, and he sets it principally in Scotland. It is not possible for any reader to take as long as

Edward Waverley does to discover that 1745 is the year of the coming of Charles Edward Stuart. But even Scott mystifies his reader on some points. Exact details of the process by which Waverley is persuaded and deceived into exchanging Hanoverian for Stuart loyalties are only partially revealed, and then only at the end of the novel. But this means that we see as and what Edward Waverley sees: because we too are mystified we have had an uninterrupted view of his capacities. A fuller understanding of his situation than he himself has would make that assessment more difficult.

This sheds an interesting light on the much more substantial mystification in *Emma*, and especially on Booth's proposed 'remedy'. Even a first reading, he says, could have been full and complete, had Austen 'been willing to sacrifice her mystery' (1961, p. 255). True, but at what cost? One important consequence, already pointed to by Harvey, is that the reader would not have to risk his own guesses and interpretations, and the novel would be a safer and duller experience for him. But, equally, the more precisely we can note each wrong judgement of Emma's, the less we shall be able to perceive as Emma perceives: the less we shall be able to sense the degree to which Emma's views are reasonable, and her mistakes natural. The very balance which Booth himself insists upon, between sympathy and judgement, would be destroyed.

But what of second readings of the novel? This should allow us to seek a balance between achieving a new experience, given that we now know of the mystification in advance, and of remembering that we now have the advantages of hindsight.[5] At the same time, there are special uncertainties that remain, even at a second reading of *Emma*. This is the kind of difficulty we find, for instance, in *The Portrait of a Lady* (1880–1). In James's novel, the mystification of the reader is a slighter matter than in *Emma*, but it is no less necessary. James allows us some significant glimpses beyond the reach of Isabel Archer's consciousness: even on a first reading we can, for example, make more than Isabel very tentatively does of the 'anomaly' of one day finding her husband together with Madame Merle, she standing and he sitting. But it is merely that we are a little ahead of the heroine, not that we are completely informed of a level of ironic meaning. We know, long before Isabel does, that he and Madame Merle are in collusion but we know insufficient about the nature of the collusion, and we can never do more than guess at the actual history of their relationship. Whether for first or subsequent readings, we are always caught between the possibilities of knowing *more than* Isabel does, and of knowing *as* she does.[6] And the experience of a second reading includes the recognition of those elements that are still unresolved.

In *Emma*, this measure of the unfixed is much larger, and the compacted fragments of actual and possible meaning can never be completely resolved into a single and articulate totality. For second and subsequent readings, we shall of course have the advantage of hindsight: but it is only a reading that is mechanical and mindless that will be wholly determined by that foresight.

Reginald Farrer (1971, pp. 23–4) was probably the first to record something of this quality in the novel when he claimed that twelve readings of *Emma* 'give you . . . pleasure, not repeated only, but squared and squared again with each perusal, till at every fresh reading you feel anew that you never understood anything like the widening sum of its delights'. His point was taken up by Lionel Trilling (1957; 1967, pp. 45–6), who commented also on the 'difficulty' of *Emma* – a difficulty which, he argued, was different from and greater than the 'literal' difficulty of Proust or Joyce or Kafka, since with them it diminished with 'each sympathetic reading'. With *Emma*, he suggested, there can be no such progressive resolution, and we can never fully understand it. Virginia Woolf (1925, p. 174), writing in general about Austen's novels, has noted something that especially applies to *Emma*, and to this characteristic of the novel. Austen is, she says,

> a mistress of much deeper emotion than appears upon the surface. She stimulates us to supply what is not there. What she offers is, apparently, a trifle, yet is composed of something that expands in the reader's mind and endows with the most enduring form of life scenes which are outwardly trivial.

In his attempt to provide a phenomenological account of the reading process, Wolfgang Iser (1972; 1974, p. 276) cites Woolf's comment on Austen, adding that, as the reader's imagination supplies or completes the unwritten details, so what he contributes will 'influence the effect of the written part of the text'.

Thus begins a whole dynamic process: the written text imposes certain limits on its unwritten implications in order to prevent these from becoming too blurred and hazy, but at the same time these implications, worked out by the reader's imagination, set the given situation against a background which endows it with far greater significance than it might have seemed to possess on its own. In this way, trivial scenes suddenly take on the shape of an 'enduring form of life'.

Iser is, of course, moving from the case of Austen to a much more general account of the process of reading. But it is worth noting how *Emma* is specially illuminating, specially appropriate for his argument, as an example from the ranks of 'traditional' (Iser, 1972; 1974, p. 280) texts. Indeed, to the extent that Iser has identified something that is specific to *Emma*, *Emma* is not a useful example of what can, in general, be applied to 'traditional' texts.

Emma is also an interesting example – though not one he actually cites – in connection with Iser's views on second readings of the same text. A second reading, he notes (1972; 1974, p. 280),

often produces a different impression from the first. The reasons for this may lie in the reader's own change of circumstances, still, the text must be such as to allow this variation. On a second reading familiar occurrences now tend to appear in a new light and seem to be at times corrected, at times enriched.

He also observes that a second reading is not necessarily 'truer', but simply different: 'even on repeated viewings a text allows and, indeed, induces innovative reading' (p. 281). Once again, though, *Emma* is not merely a typical, but a specially appropriate, instance of Iser's argument, in that it makes an unusually large allowance for variations from reading to reading.

That is not meant as a claim that the uncertainty in *Emma* is wildly and chaotically unlimited. As Iser suggests in general, so with this novel the felt pull lies between what the text specifies and what the reader imagines. And indeed the substantial uncertainty of *Emma* exists in a paradoxical relationship with a measure of certainty that is unusually high even for Austen. The settings in time, in place, in social class are all precisely and strictly limited; and the events and circumstances of the novel are rendered with a degree of particularity that seems to allow for only the minutest variations in possibility. Nevertheless, it is within this apparently rigid and clear structure that so much flexibility, so much conjecture, so much doubt is allowed to exist.[7] It could even be said that this is a new and special application of the traditional defence of Austen's limited scope – that we have depth instead of width – since within the defined there is so much undefined. It is with this novel that Austen turns the 'limitation', triumphantly, into a crucial part of what she achieves. She can say and do so much about 'understanding' and 'imagination' because so many possibilities are seen to exist within the seemingly determined: because she has managed to combine the maximum of certainty with the maximum of doubt.

This play between certainty and doubt is declared from the novel's opening words, and it is something that has been strangely undernoticed. Many readers see only the certainties, and are content to echo Booth's assertion (1961, p. 257) that nothing in the opening paragraph 'could have been said by Emma'. Even those who disagree have been rather tentative: Mansell (1973, p. 148), for example, suggests that the opening sentence 'seems slightly coloured already by Emma's own vanity'. And he takes the point no further. In fact, while all Austen's novels start by introducing the reader to a kind of uncertainty, this is usually less radical than in *Emma*. Only *Northanger Abbey* goes as far, and rather different effects are being sought there. We can best appreciate what Austen's narrator achieves in *Emma* if we contrast the novel with the practice of some of her successors. In *Middlemarch* (1871–2) George Eliot shows us, fully and fairly, both the inner life of a character, and the way that character connects with, and is perceived by, other characters, but these distinctions are always much more clearly marked than in *Emma*. The much-noted instance at the start of chapter 29 takes us, through a series of steps, from the mind of Dorothea, her hopes, ideas, beliefs and her growing awareness that her marriage is not at all what she had anticipated, to the views of Casaubon himself, by way of comments of the narrator about the shift, and the necessity for the shift:

One morning, some weeks after her arrival at Lowick, Dorothea – but why always Dorothea? Was her point of view the only possible one with regard to this marriage? I protest against all our interest, all our effort at understanding being given to the young skins that look blooming in spite of trouble . . . .[8]

All the time, as we move from one mind to another, or as we explore the ground between them, we know where we are in relation to them and to the narrator.

With Austen and especially with *Emma*, the shifts in narrative perspective are almost never as clearly defined. We become aware of the complexity of the material, and of its ambivalence, just because we are made uncertain of exactly how we are examining it.

Emma Woodhouse, handsome, clever, and rich, with a comfortable home and happy disposition, seemed to unite some of the best blessings of existence; and had lived nearly twenty-one years in the world with very little to distress or vex her.

She was the youngest of the two daughters of a most affectionate, indulgent father, and had, in consequence of her sister's marriage, been mistress of his house from a very early period. Her mother had died too long ago for her to have more than an indistinct remembrance of her caresses, and her place had been supplied by an excellent woman as governess, who had fallen little short of a mother in affection.

Sixteen years had Miss Taylor been in Mr Woodhouse's family, less as a governess than a friend, very fond of both daughters, but particularly of Emma. Between *them* it was more the intimacy of sisters. Even before Miss Taylor had ceased to hold the nominal office of governess, the mildness of her temper had hardly allowed her to impose any restraint; and the shadow of authority being now long passed away, they had been living together as friend and friend very mutually attached, and Emma doing just what she liked; highly esteeming Miss Taylor's judgement, but directed chiefly by her own.

The real evils indeed of Emma's situation were the power of having rather too much her own way, and a disposition to think a little too well of herself; these were the disadvantages which threatened alloy to her many enjoyments. The danger, however, was at present so unperceived, that they did not by any means rank as misfortunes with her.   (pp. 5–6)

The process of development represented by these paragraphs seems at first to be simply linear, and the portrait of Emma becomes more and more complete, with the gradual accretion of detail. But in fact considerable ambivalence is being generated from the way in which the narrator unobtrusively offers several points of view.

The first paragraph should begin to alert our suspicions, with its slightly complacent string of adjectives and qualifying phrases, its air of having been a little too carefully and consciously chosen. Clearly, it is a point of view that is close to Emma's, but how close exactly? Then, of course, the word 'seemed' is ambiguous: it could either be that the terms do not quite apply to Emma, or that the terms are a not-quite-appropriate formula for the 'best blessings of existence'. The second paragraph requires a change in thinking from us. We must retain a sense of these doubts, but they must be consigned, momentarily at least, to the back of our minds. The narrator, in this paragraph, is a significant distance from Emma and has, very much, the appearance of a conventional narrator composedly setting out the biographical details of the heroine. Here too, though, the description begins to edge into implied comment, as the sense of comfort is stated and reiterated: here too, the comment has its own ambivalence, and we can either welcome the placid and secure context for the heroine, or we can find it to be too easy, too undemanding, too unchallenging.

In the third paragraph the narrator is again very close to Emma, but not quite in the position of the narrator of the first paragraph, since the line of vision is differently angled. This narrator is connected with and responsive to the relationship between Emma and Miss Taylor, and can give us a sense of how each views the relationship, can begin to search out the range and the limitation of each perspective, can reflect on the ironies of the interaction. But the general attitude remains quite friendly, quite indulgent to the principal subject, like almost everything else in Emma's world. There follows, at the start of the next paragraph, an almost violent jolt away from Emma, the more striking since it follows so closely the line of argument at the end of the previous paragraph, but from such a decidedly different standpoint. The narrator has acquired a liking for crisply decisive judgements; and, if not actively hostile to Emma, is certainly determined not to be too easily charmed and delighted by her. The narrator now seeks to achieve a not-uncritical detachment in relation to Emma, and will err, if at all, on the side of severity. The effect of these shifts is very complex: it goes a long way in helping to create the sense of a fully three-dimensional picture; it makes for a subtle and comprehensive exploration of that picture, so that the seeming order and tidiness of the picture *is* only seeming; it ensures that the progressive movement forward is also a shifting retrospective view of what has already been established; and it persuades us to an active concern for the way that even a slight change in perspective or distance can make for a significant change in what is perceived.

It is never again, after the first four paragraphs, that the narrator is quite so sustainedly busy, moving back and forth over the ground between characters, exploring the possibilities of differing perspectives that are within and also beyond their capacities. But it is also a movement that never ceases for very long. The visit to Box Hill, for instance, is memorable partly because it is a period of increased movement for the narrator, exploring the individual perspectives and the way they combine, the different levels and possibilities of meaning within and between the characters. It is thus that we measure not only the workings of the simpler links, as between the Eltons, Miss Bates and Mr Weston, but also those more complicated connections, actual and possible, between Emma, Knightley, Harriet, Frank Churchill, Jane Fairfax; it is thus that we acquire a sense of the whole. Emma's snubbing of Miss Bates is at once witty and apt, and a piece of gratuitous cruelty to one who has no defences; we can smile at it, but we must recognise that it entirely deserves Knightley's rebuke. Yet the sequence of events forms another pattern, one that, perhaps, we can never wholly comprehend. Knightley's words gain a particularly cutting edge because it is Emma to whom he is speaking; because it is *she* who has been cruel, but also because it is *she* who has just been flirting so 'excessively' with Frank (p. 368). Likewise, though the shame Emma feels is certainly penitential, it is also in part a response to an only slightly apprehended bond between herself and Knightley, and to a sudden sense that the relationship is in some way at risk. It is the striking of this very complicated chord that has Emma leaving Box Hill with 'tears running down her cheeks', tears that are 'extraordinary' (p. 376).

But *Emma* also contains a more substantial mystery, the one presented by Frank Churchill and Jane Fairfax. Jane is often considered to be something of a failure on Austen's part, but it would be more appropriate to say that she is interesting just because her existence poses so many large questions. It is even tempting to seek outside the novel for 'facts' about Jane that might allow us to understand what is so elusive in the novel. Austen told her family that Jane Fairfax lived only 'nine or ten years' after her marriage [9] and Chapman (1948, p. 186n.) has argued that this shows that 'Jane Fairfax was too good for Frank Churchill'. If Austen intended so decided a moral judgement though, then it is odd that she should have left the matter unclear in the novel, and should have offered the judgement casually, and far from its pages: one must also doubt the wisdom of going to the lengths of killing Jane off in order to make the point. In any event, Jane's early death is much more easily ascribable to the ill health she suffers in the novel.

But even that measure of sureness quickly dwindles away if we reflect on its basis: almost all the discussion of Jane's health comes from the doting Miss Bates and the officious Mrs Elton, while the narrator offers only the briefest and least alarming account, telling us that she 'had never been quite well' since the time of the Dixon's marriage (p. 165). Once we know of it, we can recognise that the period of her illness also coincides, almost exactly, with the period of the secret engagement (pp. 161, 395): but we still have no means of measuring that significance exactly. We learn, eventually, that she loves Frank deeply, but we also know that she fears the prospect of being a governess: and we know, equally, that this prospect is never far from her mind, as long as the secret engagement offers her so uncertain a future. We discover that the secret itself generates a powerful sense of guilt in her; we find also that she feels that Frank is too cavalier and too frivolous about the secret. Yet on occasion she shares the joke (pp. 242–3), while on Box Hill she is touched by jealousy, when she feels that Frank goes too far in his 'flirting' with

Emma. At times her frailty is little more than an interesting symptom of a wider problem; at times it appears as an exact counterpoint, as when she terminates the engagement and Mr Perry finds that her 'health seemed for the moment completely deranged' (p. 389); but even at such times it is fiction as much as truth, a fiction which Jane herself can manipulate. When she is emphatically determined to reject favours from Emma, and claims to be too ill to ride in a carriage, she is also seen on the same day, 'wandering about the meadows, at a distance from Highbury' (pp. 390–1). Indeed this confusion of physical and mental states is such as to place her in the company of Mr Woodhouse, and, by an even more interesting irony, of Mrs Churchill. And, because Jane's situation is so complexly but so incompletely rendered, there is no single coherent explanation for her behaviour. Too much depends on how we decide to see things; and we understand, we judge and we imagine what, very largely, we *choose* to understand and judge and imagine.

Frank offers us a repetition and an enlargement of these difficulties, and we have to try to balance his naturally high spirits with his careless wilfulness. We do not have to be blind adherents to the manners of Regency England to see why secret engagements are regarded as wrong and foolish: but if we consider *this* engagement, then we encounter a never-resolved ambivalence. Frank's love is genuine enough, but how much can actually be built on it? Is the engagement a secret because he is pusillanimous or irresponsible, or is it justifiable in the face of unresolvable circumstances? Is the delight he takes in duping Highbury the result of occasionally excessive high spirits, or does it reveal a deep and sinister tendency to deceive? When he appears in the very worst light, on Box Hill, there are still too many hidden possibilities, too many visible complications, for us to be sure what to make of him. When Emma and Frank try to enliven the untoward dullness of the company, Emma herself recognises that the phrase 'flirted together excessively' (p. 368) will be used by some of their observers to describe what she and Frank are doing: but there is also a sense in which they are both 'innocent' because, imperfectly though they understand each other, they both know that neither is seriously attached to the other. At the same time, of course, Frank and Jane are covertly continuing a quarrel begun the previous day. But even here, when he is behaving petulantly and selfishly, we can never be quite sure of the measure in which this is so. Too much about him, as about Jane, and the history of their relationship, has to be guessed at. In the same way, when Jane translates her words into actions the next day by terminating the engagement, we can never know, exactly, the degree to which she is complying with what she takes to be his wishes, and the degree to which she is expressing her own.

And, symbolising the fact that we can never achieve certainty, there is the daunting figure of Mrs Churchill, who plays an important part in Frank's story, and about whom we actually know very little. She exists for much of the time remotely from Highbury, in Yorkshire, and the closest she comes is to Richmond, still a crucial nine miles away. Apart from Frank, the only person in the novel who actually knows her is Mr Weston, and he, of course, is naturally prejudiced in favour of his son, just as he has a strong prejudice against Mrs Churchill. We can view Mrs Churchill in a number of different ways: her illness is genuine, and it naturally makes her fretful and demanding; her illness is largely a thing of her imagination, and a device for her to get her own way. Likewise we can combine, variously and with varying results, Mrs Churchill's ill temper and her tendency to dote on Frank. None of these different possibilities is, after all, very much more than the conjecture of Mrs Weston, or Emma, or Knightley (pp. 121, 145–51). And what we make of her depends, absolutely, on what we make of Frank himself: whether we judge that his difficulties are real, even insoluble, or whether we think him careless and cowardly.

There is, though, a point at which the mystery of Mrs Churchill, and so of Frank, seems to be decisively resolved, and the question of whether she is a genuine Yorkshire ogress, or whether the ogress is merely the *ad hoc* creation of her nephew's imagination, is apparently settled unexpectedly by her sudden death.

> Goldsmith tells us, that when lovely woman stoops to folly, she has nothing to do but to die; and when she stoops to be disagreeable, it is equally to be recommended as a clearer of ill-fame. Mrs Churchill, after being disliked at least twenty-five years, was now spoken of with compassionate allowances. In one point she was fully justified. She had never been admitted before to be seriously ill. The event acquitted her of all the fancifulness, and all the selfishness of imaginary complaints.   (p. 387)

The startling flippancy of the narrator's comment should put us on our guard. The medical evidence does nothing actively to support Highbury's new interpretation, and points rather to the persisting ambiguity. It is a 'sudden seizure of a different nature from any thing foreboded by her general state' (p. 387) that kills her. She may, or she may not, have been really ill before: her mind and her temper may, or may not, have been affected.

And the taking-off of Mrs Churchill is supremely to Frank's advantage, giving a grimly ironic particularity to the label of 'child of good fortune' (p. 443) that Emma gives him. His aunt's death removes the chief obstacle to Frank's marriage, exactly at the point where its removal is most useful to him: she is dead a convenient two or three hours before he receives the letter from Jane that terminates the engagement. For his response to the letter we have only his version to rely on, in his letter to Mrs Weston, and that is an entirely characteristic piece, elegantly told, plausible, incomplete (p. 442). Yet, even the details that are revealed show other ways in which he is a 'child of good fortune'. It is because Jane is compelled to write a second, bleaker letter, one that so commandingly requires an immediate reply, that he is forced to broach the matter with his uncle: it would have been all but unthinkable for him to do so within hours of his aunt's death; it is entirely conceivable that he should do so three days later, when the second letter arrives.[10]

Other important consequences follow from this death. Emma is made to understand Harriet, and therefore herself: and Knightley is moved to propose to her, just at the point when she is most anxious that he should, least sure that he will. Even Harriet is directly touched by this death, since one of its consequences is that she is allowed to rediscover her love for Robert Martin. Most importantly it is a signal that Frank is *never* going to be an unambivalent figure to us: his aunt's death relieves him of the responsibility of ever facing the choice between submitting to her will and insisting on his right to marry Jane: such a useful method of fixing and settling the matter of Frank Churchill is not going to be used.

It is not even that we can settle matters to the extent of placing Frank as a cunning manipulator of facts. He does of course enjoy spinning out versions of his world, but he also holds to a version of the world, the one which he actually understands to be *the* world: he is therefore himself subject to muddle and misconception. Here some elements reflect to his credit, ironically, just because they show him to be less than all-knowing. Preoccupied as he is with plots and schemes, it is almost inevitable that he should anticipate, much too quickly, that Emma guessingly comprehends the existence of the secret engagement, and is prepared to join in the game of flirting, as a means of helping to keep the secret (p. 324, for example).

Then, we must notice the way in which others in the novel, quite independent of Frank's efforts, are quick to offer their own interpretations of his reality. Before ever he appears in High-bury, he is 'one of the boasts' of the place, and the letter he writes to Mrs Weston excites considerable – if repetitious – discussion (pp. 17–18). The Westons have early but substantial dreams of connections between Frank's future, and Emma's (p. 41). Emma herself has her own dreams about Frank, long before he sets foot in Highbury, and 'the name and the idea of Mr Frank Churchill . . . always interested her'; she frequently thinks that 'if she *were* to marry, he was the very person to suit her in age, character and condition'; she even has 'a sort of pleasure in the idea of their being coupled in their friends' imaginations' (pp. 118–19). Then, though she never doubts that she will refuse him, she busies herself 'forming a thousand amusing schemes for the progress and close of their attachment, fancying interesting dialogues, and inventing elegant letters' (p. 264). When she learns of the secret engagement, her vigorous strictures seem to have the force of objective comment: 'It has sunk him, I cannot say how it has sunk him in my opinion. So unlike what a man should be! – None of that upright integrity, that strict adher-ance to truth and principle, that disdain of trick and littleness . . . .' (p. 397). But her words actually have as much to do with what have been her own dreams and speculations about herself, about Jane, about Frank, about Harriet, even her uncon-scious thoughts about Knightley, as they do with Frank's ac-tions. 'She was extremely angry with herself. If she could not have been angry with Frank Churchill too, it would have been dreadful' (pp. 402–3).

Frank is the subject of a spirited disagreement between Emma and Knightley, a clash between different versions of his past and his future (pp. 145–51). Knightley is predisposed to dislike Frank, almost to the same extent as Emma is to like him, before either has seen him. His dislike is soon fixed (p. 206), and it is the existence of this prejudice, of course, that alerts him to his feelings for Emma (p. 432). By the end, his understanding of Frank is governed entirely by his understanding of his relationship with Emma. He has just joined Emma, after returning from London:

> He had found her agitated and low – Frank Churchill was a villain. – He heard her declare that she had never loved him. Frank Churchill's character was not desperate. – She was his own Emma, by hand and word, when they returned into the house; and if he could have thought of Frank Churchill then, he might have deemed him a very good sort of fellow. (p. 433)

But, then, it is not just Frank and Jane who excite speculation of one sort or another. It is rather that they help to focus our attention on a process that happens continuously and everywhere in the novel. It is carried out, sometimes with propriety, sometimes entirely without: its results can be startlingly apt, or they can be embarrassingly wrong. Emma's first act in the novel is to congratulate herself on what she imagines to be her part in forming the Westons' marriage; soon her powers are concentrated on the prospect of making something of her friendship with Harriet, and we glimpse, also, what others make of her makings. When she paints Harriet's portrait, she paints an idealised version (p. 48). Emma and Knightley have their fiercest argument over their differing senses of Harriet and Robert Martin (pp. 60–6). Emma fashions a match between Harriet and Mr Elton, and she persuades Harriet into a fanciful contemplation of the man, while Elton is cultivating his own ambitious dreams that are entirely at odds with Emma's. Later, it is one of the most obviously ludicrous elements in the Box Hill visit that Emma should contemplate the prospect of educating Harriet to be Frank's wife (p. 373) while what Harriet has actually learnt is to imagine that Knightley is in love with her (p. 407).

Nor is this process confined to the principals. Emma makes the mortifying discovery that the collective speculations of Highbury have neatly circumscribed the possibilities of her relationship with Elton, possibilities that she had liked to think of as secret. And Miss Bates, who inadvertently allows Emma to make this discovery, acts as the very capable spokesman for Highbury conjecture, even as she denies that she is 'quick at those sort of discoveries' (p. 176). Mrs Elton's arrival generates almost as much conjectural interest as does Frank Churchill (p. 267). In pointed caricature of Emma herself, she brings an active sense of the world and of her place in it, one she will rudely assert, as she does in an early encounter with Emma (pp. 272–9), an encounter that leaves Emma veering between rage at her impertinence and delight that Mr Elton should have sunk so low.

Knightley appears with significant frequency in Emma's speculations, even though she does not notice the significance: so, for example, his arrival at the Cole's party is especially noticed by her, and she observes that he comes as he 'should', in his carriage, 'like a gentleman'; later she discovers that he comes in his carriage in order that Jane and her aunt may be fetched in it. This is the occasion when Mrs Weston gives breath to her idea that he is in love with Jane, an idea that so disturbs Emma, and one that we later find Mr Cole has independently formed (pp. 213, 224, 228). Knightley himself is imaginatively active: he shows, in the opening pages, how he can master and even exceed Emma's range. (pp. 12–13); and, alone of those in Highbury, he suspects – and it is a measure of the man that he doubts his suspicions as he entertains them – a hidden connection between Frank and Jane (p. 344). Of course his apprehension is not perfect, nor is it only with Frank that his limitations are revealed. When he tries to explain Jane's tolerance of Mrs Elton in a way that will put an end to Emma's rather unkind probings on this question, he arrives at an interpretation which, while a sensible account of the way things ought to be, has little to do with the way they are, as is soon revealed (pp. 286–7, 295–6, 299–302). But he is the most competent apprehender in the novel.

And what of Emma, sorrowfully contemplating a marriage between Knightley and Harriet, and reflecting on likely changes in her own circumstances, in the course of an evening that is 'very long, and melancholy'? The sense of the physical aspect of the day allows us to glimpse imaginatively the workings of her imagination: 'The weather added what it could of gloom. A cold stormy rain set in, and nothing of July appeared but in the trees and shrubs, which the wind was despoiling, and the length of the day, which only made such cruel sights the longer visible' (p. 421).

Again and again, then, the novel offers us a collection of ways of viewing the world and the self; each self presenting a different perspective, different biases and prejudices, different acuities of vision, different blind spots. And yet each attempt to order the world is also necessarily in some measure an imaginative reaching out, an attempt to complete a pattern that would otherwise remain partial, an attempt to establish the obscure or missing details: and all attempts exist in a noisy simultaneity. In the circumstances, all we can expect, all we get, are rash or brave skirmishings for the truth, some more well-armed than others. And for the reader, too, to understand is also to imagine; in considering the different versions of the world, we too must reach out, must reconstruct what is merely implied, and we must venture to choose between them.

This is an experience that is of course common, to some degree, to the reading of any novel, but *Emma* renders it pervasively and intensively. In this regard, reading *Emma* can be compared with reading *The Ring and the Book*. Browning's poem, indeed, offers us a greater measure of certainty than *Emma* does, and the central 'fact' is never disputed: Count Guido killed his wife and her parents. It is as we consider motive and justification, and as we come to weigh circumstantial details, that we move, more and more, into uncertainty. Guido is a brutal murderer or a wronged husband or something in between. Pompilia, his wife, is more or less a saint, more or less an adulteress. Caponsacchi is exercising his priestly function appropriately, if unconventionally, in rescuing Pompilia from the tyrannical Guido; he is seduced by her; he seduces her. Thus Caponsacchi for instance has one whole book in which to persuade us to the view of the circumstances he wants to take, but he nevertheless appears, from the first and even as Browning outlines the subject at the start of the poem, to be a richly ambivalent figure, one who does not imply a single composite and actual truth so much as several possible ones.

Also hear Caponsacchi who comes next,
Man and priest – could you comprehend the coil! –
In days when that was rife which now is rare.
How, mingling each its multifarious wires,
Now heaven, now earth, now heaven and earth at once,

Had plucked at and perplexed their puppet here,
Played off the young frank personable priest;
Sworn fast and tonsured plain heaven's celibate,
And yet earth's clear-accepted servitor,
A courtly spiritual Cupid, squire of dames
By law of love and mandate of the mode.
                    (*The Ring and the Book*, I.1016–26)

It is precisely this sense of a contained and yet restless uncertainty, one which we must attempt to resolve, and can never wholly resolve, that is so close to the problem of *Emma*: To make any attempt at coherence, it is necessary that we commit ourselves and that we choose, and thus inevitably risk being wrong. Browning goes so far as to declare that his point is to make us discover the size of the risk: his 'lesson', he says at the end of the poem, is

       that our human speech is naught,
   Our human testimony false, our fame
   And human estimation words and wind.
                    (XII. 834–6)

In one sense *The Ring and the Book* is actually the more 'open'. It exists as a succession of more or less completely imagined possibilities and explanations, each having essentially the same status. In *Emma*, the heroine is centrally important, and however significant the other characters are, or other versions of reality, they remain secondary to those in which she is a part, and to those she generates. In another way, it is the novel that is the more open. Browning is recovering the past, is attempting to give life back to a complicated mess of truth and rumour. But it is dead and past and forgotten: we can join the argument over how to interpret what has happened, but it has all happened; it is, in a sense, finished and fixed. Austen's novel exists, by contrast, in the present tense, where things are still happening. To understand is to explain the past and predict the future as well as to comprehend the present: and the attempts within the novel to explain its meaning are so completely enmeshed that they can, whether accurate or not, influence or even determine what the reality becomes. In that sense, the reader is more implicated in Austen's novel than in Browning's poem, and with the novel we must rather more actively establish the differing possibilities. Sometimes we are offered too many possibilities, but sometimes we are offered almost nothing. Jane Fairfax, for example, gives us only a few clues: an occasional and almost hidden smile, a habitual and rigid self-suppression, a plaintive acknowledgement on one occasion that she is 'wearied in spirit' (p. 363), on one occasion an angry rejection of a belated offer of friendship (pp. 389–91). Yet even these fragments can tell us a good deal about the possible ways in which life appears to her, once we are alert to the significance of their existence.

So, *Emma* demonstrates that 'understanding' and 'imagining' are, both of them, continual and essential activities, that their work is never finished. But what exactly are these activities? From what, if anything, do they derive? Usually, with *Emma* the questions are perceived, quite straightforwardly, to be a matter of literary sources. Lascelles (1939, pp. 68–9) suggests that Emma is

> more elaborately deceived than Marianne Dashwood, betrayed further into active folly than Catherine Morland . . . by the false notions current in the world of illusion. . . . Such a young woman as Emma, so constituted and so circumstanced, could have become acquainted with legitimacy as an interesting situation, infidelity as a comic incident, only in her reading.

Lionel Trilling (1957; 1967, p. 53) has observed that, 'like Don Quixote and Emma Bovary, her mind is shaped and deceived by fiction'. Walton Litz (1965, p. 134) makes Emma's position in the tradition a pivotal one, by suggesting that Emma is 'deceived as to the outside world (Don Quixote) and deceived as to her own emotions (Emma Bovary), and . . . the two kinds of deception are related'. And Kenneth Moler (1968; 1977, pp. 155–81) elaborates on the tradition.

Yet, every attempt to be specific on this point has brought the inevitable acknowledgement that there is actually no particular source that will support these claims; there is no equivalent to the functioning of *The Mysteries of Udolpho* in *Northanger Abbey*. The most favoured explanation has been Lascelles's: 'Jane Austen had no particular novel or comedy of intrigue in mind', and, in order to exist, the 'bookish origin of such follies does not need to be stated explicitly' (1939, pp. 68–9). But, by itself, that is a weak assertion; and the idea, crucial to Lascelles and to those who follow her, that it is only through novels that Emma would find illegitimacy and infidelity entertaining, will not stand very much scrutiny. Emma is young, and she knows little enough of the world outside Highbury. But she also has an unusually large scope (for a young woman of her time and class) for action and independence, and has had from an unusually early age.

The first two decades of the nineteenth century could hardly be described as a period noted for the practice of high and austere virtues, or even of a merely polite discretion. The remarkably sordid doings of the Prince of Wales, later the Prince Regent, and of Princess Caroline, his estranged wife – indeed of most members of the royal family – were frequently regaling the nation at large.[11] Nor of course would it be at all accurate to say that such scandals were only connected with the royal family. The newspapers were capable of greatly shocking Fanny Price – and of annoying Lord Byron – by publishing the details of breaking marriages. It is easy enough to conceive of a sensibility, a little more robust than Fanny's, that would sometimes find such revelations amusing rather than shocking. Austen was herself only about four years older than her Emma when she congratulated herself for having 'a very good eye at an Adultress', one she exercised in the Upper Rooms at Bath (*Letters*, p. 127). All of which suggests that a young woman need not have been entirely dependent on novels for a full and lively understanding of the possibilities of life. Highbury is certainly no Bath, but there is no reason to suppose that its inhabitants are especially imbued with decorum and virtue. As for Emma's curiosity about Harriet Smith's origins, the question all but asks itself: it is the only interesting thing about her. Nobody in Highbury is shocked by her illegitimacy, except for Mr Elton, and then only when he is forced to think of her as a possible wife. Emma's fanciful speculations about her high birth could derive something from her reading, but have a great deal more to do with the honour that Emma deems her friendship to bestow on Harriet (p. 62).

And, if we consider dispassionately the tradition from which *Emma* has been supposed to derive, then it should be obvious that *Emma* depends, even less than *Northanger Abbey*, on the inspiration of Charlotte Lennox or Eaton Stannard Barrett. The tradition of more sophisticated borrowing from Cervantes to which *Northanger Abbey* does belong, the tradition we find developing through Fielding and Smollett and Scott, also has little to do with *Emma*. Trilling's attempt to connect *Madame Bovary* with the tradition by way of *Emma* would have been more convincing had he used Scott as a link. It is Scott who distinguishes his own efforts from the simple imitators of Cervantes, and is also the teller of high heroic stories that come *themselves* to be the source of delusions for the characters of other people's novels. One of the authors that the young Emma of Flaubert's novel avidly reads is Scott: part of her later experience is to reflect on the difference between words in literature and words in life.[12] In *Emma* there is no named source for Emma's more fanciful notions, and it is Harriet Smith who is known to delight in the novels of Ann Radcliffe and Regina Maria Roche (p. 29). Austen's subject is the workings of the understanding and the imagination, but it is not in any special sense in this novel that there is a study of the way literature can shape or deceive the understanding and the imagination.

And, without actually stating the point explicitly, Austen goes a long way towards emphasising it. Knightley, for example, supplies an early warning that Emma is to be noted more for her general than for her particular knowledge of literature; for knowing what ought to be read, but not for having read it. Typically, of course, what he says reveals a tendency in him to be rigorous, perhaps unduly so, where Emma is concerned; this must qualify the significance we attach to his words, but we can still recognise their appropriateness.

> 'Emma has been meaning to read more ever since she was twelve years old. I have seen a great many lists of her drawing up at various times of books that she meant to read regularly through – and very good lists they were – very well chosen, and very neatly arranged – sometimes alphabetically, and sometimes by some other rule. The list she drew up when only fourteen – I remember thinking it did her judgement so much credit, that I preserved it some time; and I dare say she may have made out a very good list now. But I have done with expecting any course of steady reading from Emma.' (p.37)

Knightley's assertions are given a substantial confirmation a little later, when we see more of Emma and Harriet.

> Her views of improving her little friend's mind, by a great deal
> of useful reading and conversation, had never yet led to more
> than a few first chapters, and the intention of going on
> tomorrow. It was much easier to chat than to study; much
> pleasanter to let her imagination range and work at Harriet's
> fortune, than to be labouring to enlarge her comprehension or
> exercise it on sober facts; and the only literary pursuit which
> engaged Harriet at present, the only mental provision she was
> making for the evening of life, was the collecting and tran-
> scribing all the riddles of every sort that she could meet with,
> into a thin quarto of hot-pressed paper, made up by her friend,
> and ornamented with cyphers and trophies.   (p. 69)

Once again, this contradicts the notion of a strong and sustained
literary influence on Emma, and it directs us rather to the people
and events of the novel, the difficulties they pose in the matter of
imagining and understanding.

For an Austen heroine, Emma also makes remarkably few
literary allusions. Apart from a reference to *Elegant Extracts*, as
the source for a riddle (*Emma*, p. 79), there are only three made
by her. What is more, two of them tend to confirm her habit of
not getting beyond first chapters. One takes her no more than
134 lines into the first act of *A Midsummer Night's Dream* (*Emma*, p.
75); another, to Madame de Genlis's *Adelaide and Theodore*, gets
her no further than pages 11 and 12 of the first volume, before
preliminary introductions have been completed (*Emma*, p. 461).
Of course, it does not have to be the case that *all* Emma's
reading is of opening pages for the argument to stand, and in fact
the third allusion she makes is to the fifth act of *Romeo and Juliet*,
to the scene in which Romeo buys poison from the apothecary
(*Emma*, p. 400). But it is also, interestingly, the case that Emma
is not making an excessively literal application of literature to
life. She does not make a simple analogy between Romeo's
situation, or the apothecary's, and that of Jane Fairfax – she has
just been told of the secret engagement. Rather, her use of the
quotation is a measure of the quite surprising degree to which
she is able, sympathetically and imaginatively, to understand
Jane's situation: even her anger with Frank does not blind her.

It should be noted, though, that both passages from Shakespeare are included in *Elegant Extracts*. Now, we must be careful
not to make too little or too much of the links between *Emma* and

Elegant Extracts. For one thing, though Emma gives it as the source of 'Kitty, a fair but frozen maid', the riddle is not to be found there, as Chapman points out (*Emma*, p. 79n). For another, even if we assume that Emma reads all her poetry in *Elegant Extracts*, then that does not mean that she turns the pages of a slight, pocket-sized collection of puzzles and quotations: there is a selection of riddles and epigrams, but the collection as a whole deserves the status of an extremely long and comprehensive anthology of poetry, in which riddles and epigrams occupy a very small place.[13]

And there are other things to be said about *Emma* and *Elegant Extracts*. One irony that links Emma with Robert Martin is that he too is a reader of *Elegant Extracts* (*Emma*, p. 29). Then, since everyone points to the parallels between Emma and Mrs Elton, it is interesting to note that she too is a likely (not, in her case, a certain) reader of *Elegant Extracts*, which includes both 'L'Allegro' and Gray's 'Elegy' (*Emma*, pp. 308, 282). But even more telling is the one other literary allusion Mrs Elton makes; and that is also to be found in *Elegant Extracts*. When she seeks to refer, in a pointedly covert manner, to Jane's engagement, she acknowledges that she has forgotten the source, but nevertheless proceeds to quote (*Emma*, p. 454):

> For when a lady's in the case,
> You know all other things give place.

Chapman gives the source and quotes the context in the footnote, but it is perhaps worth spelling out the significance of that context. The poem, one of Gay's *Fables* (1727, 1738), is 'The Hare and Many Friends' (the poem Catherine Morland learned with such ease); Mrs Elton's borrowing puts Jane's marriage, inadvertently, into a rudely agricultural context. The Hare has just asked for help from the Bull, who excuses himself thus:

> Love calls me hence; a fav'rite cow
> Expects me near yon barley mow:
> And when a lady's in the case,
> You know, all other things give place.[14]

When quotations are being used to such precise and telling effect, then the very scant evidence that Emma herself presents of a knowledge of literature must be taken as evidence that she is not widely read. Austen is making the point that, though Emma's imagination and her mind are the subject of the novel, it is not a mind and an imagination that has been too richly fed on literature.

But, if the imagination, as Austen conceives of it, is not merely that ability to indulge in fanciful speculations, and if it is not merely that part of the mind that can become easily infected by an indiscriminate reading, if indeed it can perform some necessary part in the process of understanding, then how, exactly, does she conceive of its functioning, and from what does she derive her idea? The concept of imagination is a crucially important landmark in the intellectual and ideological battlefields of the eighteenth and nineteenth centuries, and it is a notoriously problematical one. The word has one cluster of meanings, largely pejorative, largely to do with the wrong or the false: it has another set of meanings, usually favourable, to do with useful and pleasing acts of creation, or creative interpretation, of coherent selection and ordering. Traditionally, Austen has been regarded as being distinctly on the side of an Augustan 'sense', rather than a Romantic 'imagination': certainly, late in her life she expressed the decided opinion that an excess of 'imagination' could easily be inimical to good judgement (*Letters*, p. 486).

Of course the matter is not as simple as this implies. Austen is on the side of 'sense', she tends to question the excess of 'feeling', she can reflect on some of the dangers of an unrestrained 'imagination'. But she is not all and always for 'sense', all and always against 'feeling' and 'imagination'. She is indeed inclined to make a dispassionate examination of all three, to consider the strengths and the limitations of each, and to reflect on some of the more and less appropriate ways of combining them.[15] Can there be any doubt, by the time we reach the end of the first chapter, that Emma is playing a game that has its dangers? That, rather than trying to understand her world, she is merely making of it what she pleases? Yet, if the novel is preoccupied with the errors of the imagination, then it is strange, as several critics point out, that the imagination is never wholly routed. Emma is chastened, certainly, and she acquires a sense of the ways in which her imagination can play her false, but there is, equally, nothing to suggest that she is going to stop making errors of the imagination. Part of the comedy of the concluding chapters comes from her successive attempts to dream up a solution to the problem of Harriet, attempts which are always thwarted, attempts which are made even as Emma claims to be forswearing the arts of the imaginist. And the novel shows imagination, whatever its limitations, to be a universal activity.

It is of course true that in the century before Austen there were some immensely influential attacks on the imagination. John Locke's *An Essay Concerning Human Understanding* (1690) declared, famously, that it is in '*Experience*' that 'all our Knowledge is founded; and from that it ultimately derives it self': experience that is either, directly, from '*Sensation*', or indirectly, when 'the Mind comes to reflect on its own *Operations*, about the *Ideas* got by *Sensation*'.[16] But equally that does not mean that as a concept imagination was more or less in abeyance, until the coming of the Romantic poets. In *Imagination* (1976, pp.13–130), for example, Mary Warnock starts her account of the subject with a consideration of the degree to which Hume thought of the faculty as creative in his *A Treatise of Human Nature* (1739–40). From him, she traces a line of development through Kant and Schelling, to Coleridge and Wordsworth.

Unfortunately, this can tell us almost nothing about Austen. We have no indication that she read the philosophical writings of Hume, though she would doubtless have encountered some of the ideas, at least at second hand. But she can have known little, if anything, of Kant and his German contemporaries; and *Biographia Literaria*, which might have informed her, was published in the month of her death. She knew of Wordsworth, but there is no way of telling what she knew of him.[17]

Nevertheless, while Coleridge's distinctions between fancy and imagination are the most influential of such attempts in English thought, they are by no means the first, and, independent of anything he borrowed more immediately from Kant, have been shown to be part of a developing line of thought that goes back at least as far as Dryden. Shaftesbury, Addison and Steele are notable early instances: they see the limitations of the imagination but they also praise its products, can see literature as something that will actively educate individuals and nations. Addison makes surprisingly large, surprisingly unempirical claims for poetical creativity: 'It shews a greater Genius in

Shakespeare to have drawn his Calyban, that his Hotspur or Julius Caesar. The one was to be supplied out of his own Imagination, whereas the other might have been formed upon Tradition, History and Observation.'[18]

In the middle of the century Johnson is even more assiduous in warning that the imagination can deceive, and in insisting that it should be trained and curbed. But then merely to read Johnson, to see what he says on one side of an argument, usually to misread Johnson; and we can also find him forcefully observing that 'men of study and imagination' are not troubled by 'that weariness which hangs always flagging upon the vacant mind'. He also asserts that 'All joy or sorrow for the happiness or calamities of others is produced by an act of the imagination.' Likewise, he asserts that the artistic imagination is not to be rigidly proscribed; indeed, for him it is a vital, growing force, the despair of those who would categorise, or define, or explain, always seeking the new and the unknown.[19] In *Rasselas* (1759), there is Imlac, the wise and informed guide to Rasselas and his sister, who discourses on the 'dangerous prevalence of imagination' but who, nevertheless, when moved by the 'enthusiastick fit', makes such extraordinarily large claims for the poet: the claims are striking because they are not wild and impossible assertions, but are part of a serious argument that has been taken a little too far.

> He must divest himself of the prejudices of his age or country; he must consider right and wrong in their abstracted and invariable state; he must disregard present laws and opinions, and rise to general and transcendental truths, which will always be the same. . . . He must write as the interpreter of nature, and the legislator of mankind, and consider himself as presiding over the thoughts and manners of future generations; as a being superior to time and place.[20]

And what is perhaps the most remarkable thing about this remarkable passage is its similarity to some of the ideas advanced by Shelley in his *A Defence of Poetry*. The language of poets, Shelley says, is 'vitally metaphorical; that is, it marks the before unapprehended relations of things and perpetuates their apprehension'. Poets 'imagine and express' what is an 'indestructible order'; they are the institutors of laws and the founders of civil society and the inventors of the arts of life and the teachers, who draw into a certain propinquity with the beautiful and the true that partial apprehension of the agencies of the invisible world which is called religion . . . .[21]

That is not to suggest that Imlac is possessed of the inclination to write *Prometheus Unbound*. Shelley argues the matter more fully, and he goes a good deal further. Johnson sees the poet as having a greater reach for the permanent truths: Shelley sees in the creative imagination a capacity actually to reform the perceptions of truth. And the differences between them are accentuated by the fact that Shelley is making a serious declaration of his position, while Johnson's Imlac is asserting something that is justly founded, but seen to be grown to excess. Even so, it is clear that, while Johnson was, as it were, with one arm reaching back to the last decades of the seventeenth century, he was, with the other, stretching forward to the first decades of the nineteenth.

And after Johnson it became easier to resolve tension, widely felt, between an imagination that is in some sense artistic, and is to be encouraged, and that of ordinary people, in whom it is to be restrained. Cowper, for instance, can function as the poet who shows his readers how to exercise their own imaginations. Thus in book IV of *The Task* he describes the delight he feels when he sits comfortably at home, by the fire, ranging widely in his imagination. In this, he is an interesting precursor of the Coleridge of 'Frost at Midnight', where in addition to the common theme of the imagination's journeyings there is the similarly deployed imagery of a winter's evening.[22] Cowper starts with the sound of 'the twangling horn', which brings into his mind the vivid and particularised picture of a bridge over the river, the moon, and a man bringing the post,

> the herald of a noisy world,
> With spatter'd boots, strapp'd waist, and frozen locks;
> News from all nations lumb'ring at his back.
> (*The Task*, IV.5–7)

He deliberately contrasts this active imagining with the passive slighter dreams induced by a low-burning fire. Again, the link with Coleridge is interesting, and both poets connect the slight

flames with the superstition that they foretell the coming of
strangers. Cowper dreams of

> houses, tow'rs,
> Trees, churches, and strange visages, express'd
> In the red cinders, while with poring eye
> I gaz'd, myself creating what I saw.
>
> (IV.287–90)

And he goes on to observe:

> 'Tis thus the understanding takes repose
> In indolent vacuity of thought,
> And sleeps and is refresh'd.
>
> (IV.296–8)

Of course Cowper was a favourite of Austen's; and we can
assume that Knightley liked Cowper, since he quotes the words
'myself creating what I saw' (*Emma*, p. 344). Indeed, he is the
only poetry-reader in the novel who – we can be sure – does not
read his poetry in *Elegant Extracts*.[23] He applies the quotation to
his suspicions of a secret connection between Frank and Jane,
because he doubts his suspicions. He does not, therefore, quote
from Cowper's accounts of the imagination actively going out to
interpret the world, but his description of the slighter, much
more trifling activity of mechanically toying with an assortment
of images, 'In indolent vacuity of thought'. Knightley knows that
the imagination can deceive: and he is consciously seeking to
avoid Emma's 'errors of imagination' (*Emma*, p. 343), so for him
it is not an irresponsible game in which one can assume that
something is, just because the possibility of its being so has
entered one's imagination. He also recognises something of the
way his own feelings and prejudices are tangled up in the whole
question. But, though he doubts his suspicions, he is right about
Frank and Jane. He has imaginatively conceived of and imaginatively interpreted their relationship.
  Thus, Austen inherited from her eighteenth-century background not the narrow and restrictive conception of the imagination that popular critical belief allows her, but an altogether
larger conception, and one that she herself steadily enhanced.
Where she differs most notably from the poets who were her

contemporaries is in the kind of question she asks about the imagination, and hers are, properly, novelistic questions. She is not preoccupied with those who have a superabundance of imagination; who are poets and who will, as a matter of course, define themselves and their world. Austen concerns herself with those in whom the imagination is no less crucial, in the business of understanding the world, but who have not climbed Snowdon or Mont Blanc; those who will regard it as a special expedition to spend the day on Box Hill. Her questions are directed to the fundamental paradox that the imagination is, essentially, an expression of the self, a matter of individual colourings and shadings and interpretations: but that it is just this individual choice and perspective that can distort and deceive. At the same time, this necessary combination of understanding and imagination, which determines what we 'make' of the world, can itself help to determine what the world will become.

On all these points there are significant contrasts to be drawn between Knightley and Emma – though the distinctions are to be felt everywhere in the novel, and Knightley could as interestingly be contrasted, for example, with Frank Churchill. Knightley's imaginative understanding is notable in being the most complete in the novel. It is hardly surprising, indeed, that so many critics treat him as if he were meant to represent an ideal; but this, surely, is to go too far, and his faults and limitations, though minor, are obvious, as for example in his jealousy of Frank. Knightley is remarkable, though, for the flexible and full sense he has of the world and his place in it – a point which should strike us forcefully, if we compare him with other characters in the novels, in roughly similar positions: General Tilney for example, Sir Walter Elliot, Sir Thomas Bertram, or Lady Catherine de Bourgh; only Darcy comes to approximate what from the first he stands for. Knightley is continually to be seen actively administering his estates; he is even, it is hinted, subject to the petty tyrannies of his housekeeper and of William Larkin (pp. 238–9). Naturally, he must be judged in terms of his class and his times, and we should not expect to imagine him helping to dig manure into his strawberry-beds; but he is proud to be the friend and adviser of his tenant farmer; he is active, but not too predominantly, and never autocratically, in the affairs of Highbury and Donwell; he is open and amenable, not unaware of social niceties, but not too bound by them, and with a tendency to think, rather, in terms of need, or merit, or ability, or virtue. He is to be found walking everywhere, and mixing rather more freely than Emma likes – she would also have him make much greater use of the ceremony and parade of the carriage (p. 213). He is able to listen to the unsolicited, if well-meant, advice from a rising tradesman about the affairs of his own heart, without seemingly taking offence (p. 288). He can deal amicably with almost all his fellow creatures, without compromising his integrity, even when they are tediously loquacious, or meddlesome and mean-minded.

And the contrast with Emma is so telling just because he is 'better' but not 'perfect'. Though some readers, especially those given to Freudian thinking, try to see theirs as an unhealthy 'father–daughter' relationship, that is to ignore the strong evidence, never more apparent than in their not-infrequent quarrels, that they are vitally connected equals. The important difference between them is not one of ability: it is the difference Knightley himself points to, the sixteen-years difference in their ages; and, as Emma points out, that is of diminishing significance (p. 99). But it does make for other differences: her relative youth expresses itself in her tendency to be a little self-centred and self-indulgent, as we can tell from the first page of the novel. She sees the world, and she draws distinctions in what she sees, too much in terms of her own importance, or else too much on the basis of idle guessing, guessing that she trusts merely because it is *hers*. She does speak, habitually, with a vigour and confidence that can mislead the unwary: and some of her notions, though 'wrong', have a decided currency, so that it is possible to find, even in the second half of the twentieth century, critics who write Emma-like nonsense, in defence of Emma's views, about the inherent kindness of the English 'caste system' because it means that everyone knows his place in society.[24]

But the real problem with Emma's views is not whether or not she is trying to defend the indefensible: it is that her arguments are sometimes so feeble that they are what Knightley aptly if intemperately calls 'Nonsense, errant nonsense, as ever was talked!' (p. 65). Debates about tradition and change, arguments for and against egalitarianism, were not then new, indeed had acquired a vivid topicality with the revolutions in America and France. One has only to consider the vigorous debate about change in general, change in France, between Edmund Burke and Tom Paine two decades before *Emma* was written.[25] It would of course be unreasonable to judge Emma's arguments simply in terms of the range and competence of Burke and Paine – Austen herself never mentions either. The point is that Burke and Paine were the leaders in a debate that spread across the nation, and their terms became part of the general currency of thought. Emma's attempts to espouse some elements of conservative thought are slight indeed, and they put her in the company of Lady Catherine de Bourgh and Sir Walter Elliot in precisely the ways in which Knightley is not.[26] It is 'nonsense' which derives not from the excesses of a deceiving imagination, but from the insufficient and improper use of the imagination, from a toying with fanciful possibilities. Instead of attempting a complete and imaginative interpretation of her world and her place in it, she is sometimes so self-preoccupied that her thinking breaks up into confused and contradictory fragments of the half-thought-out and the half-imagined. As a measure of her general wrong-headedness, she is wrong even on the question of mercenary marriage, and she applies the right principle to the wrong case. Since she does so merely to support her casually preconceived scheme for Harriet and Mr Elton and Robert Martin, she comes to be a parody of Elizabeth Bennet's spirited assertions, or of Fanny Price's agonised reflections, when she declares that a man 'always imagines a woman to be ready for anybody who asks her' (p. 60).

There are even wider inconsistencies in her thinking. Her objections to the Martins are, we can suppose, allied to her objections to the Coles. They, she feels, are tainted by their connections with trade, and they need to be put in their place – that is, 'down' – because their rising prosperity encourages them to pretensions above their deserts. Yet it turns out that she is notably inconsistent about the Coles. And Mr Weston, who has himself only very recently broken his direct links with trade, is allowed by her, almost unreservedly, to be a gentleman. That, presumably, has something to do, for her, with the fact that he has already completed the upward movement, has purchased a gentleman's residence, and so on – a dubious-enough piece of reasoning. But his status, in her eyes, also has a great deal to do with the fact of his marriage to her own dear governess. Even the (mostly) commendable warmth of mutual feelings between Emma and Mrs Weston leads Emma to see her friend sometimes

as an adjunct of herself rather than as an independent individual, with her own history. So she can make a pointed allusion to
the destined 'situation in life' of Jane Fairfax, as a governess,
with a clear implication of its inferiority, while actually in the
company of Mrs Weston (p. 201). The occasion is one of those
wonderful and recurrent moments in the novel when individuals
bring together, inadvertently, different possibilities of meaning
and misunderstanding: Mrs Weston is concerned that Emma
might be embarrassing her newly acquired stepson by this
reference to governessing, which seems to touch herself; Frank is
embarrassed, but only because he is anxious to avoid being too
closely questioned about Jane, and uncertain how much Emma
knows; and Emma makes her remark because she is intent on
pursuing her Dixon theory.

And it is on those occasions when Emma is contemplating the
great glory of the Woodhouses, exactly as Mrs Elton extols the
grandeur of Maple Grove, that we can appreciate just how
slightly Mrs Elton is an exaggerated version of herself. As when,
for instance, she receives an unexpected and entirely unwelcome
proposal of marriage: in support of her indignation, she insists to
herself that Elton must know

> that the Woodhouses had been settled for several generations
> at Hartfield, the young branch of a very ancient family – and
> that the Eltons were nobody. The landed property of Hartfield
> certainly was inconsiderable, being but a sort of notch in the
> Donwell Abbey estate, to which all the rest of Highbury
> belonged; but their fortune, from other sources, was such as to
> make them scarcely secondary to Donwell Abbey itself, in
> every other kind of consequence . . . .   (p. 136)

These are stolid-enough musings; but there is irony in the
importance attached to Donwell. And, if Emma lacks the completeness of a Knightley, she also lacks the completeness of a
Mrs Elton, and that is the completeness of the irredeemable. For
she goes on, immediately, to attempt fairer assessments of
things: and her imagination, which can only have been soundly
asleep while she sifted uncritically through the hackneyed
phrases of a second rate genealogist, comes by the end of the
paragraph to be alert and probing. Her own behaviour was such,
she realises,

as (supposing her real motive unperceived) might warrant a
man of ordinary observation and delicacy, like Mr Elton, in
fancying himself a very decided favourite. If *she* had so misin-
terpreted his feelings, she had little right to wonder that *he*,
with self-interest to blind him, should have mistaken her's.

She goes on, with due seriousness, to forswear matchmaking. It
is true that, barely half a page later, she is beginning to conjecture again about a husband for Harriet, but then she does stop,
here, to 'blush and laugh' (p. 137) at herself, and that is a
capacity that is considerably enlarged by the end of the novel. Of
course she is not going to stop imagining, or to stop committing
errors of the imagination; of course she will not always make full
and proper use of her imagination. But there are reasonable
grounds for hope.

And that, surely, is the point we should arrive at. It is all too
easy to notice and dwell on Emma's faults: certainly critics have
spent more than enough time annotating them. Such efforts,
even the moderate and sensible ones, inevitably muffle the
comedy and that must be a blunder, since the most striking thing
about the novel is its comedy. It is by amusing us, not by
moralising at us, that Austen explores her material: and we do
not have solemnly to record each error or potential error, if we
can laugh at them and at their consequences. But reading *Emma*
also means that we must commit ourselves to the risk of finding
that we must laugh at ourselves, and at our own lazy or mistaken
imaginings. If we laugh at Emma, then we must also laugh with
her. Thus too, perhaps, the moments that can touch us most
effectively are those few but memorable occasions when Emma
can conceive of a possible set of consequences to her own folly,
can imagine a future that is bleak, contracting, unvaried. At these
moments, the 'fact' of being 'handsome, clever, and rich' (p. 5)
seems to be devoid of consoling meaning; and the opportunity to
'take to carpet work' when she grows older (p. 85) appears to
lack any human significance. We are touched because we have
laughed so much, but also because we have risked ourselves.

7 *Persuasion*: Becoming a Novel, Creating a Heroine

There is a quickness of perception in some, a nicety in the discernment of character, a natural penetration, in short, which no experience in others can equal, and Lady Russell had been less gifted in this part of understanding than her young friend.   (Praise for Anne Elliot)

There are special difficulties in the way of getting a hold on the scope and the substance of *Persuasion*, and they are typified by the late and slow-coming vindication of Anne Elliot's 'quickness of perception'. In the earlier novels there are doubts about the future of the heroine, but there are seldom any doubts about whether that future will be worth recording. This degree of security is Anne's only remarkably late in the novel; for, as long as she is less than central, there are other matters making larger claims for our attention.

One such 'matter' is the novel's lateness. *Persuasion* shares the fate that tends to befall any 'last' work: the word 'valedictory' is rather too easily applied, its pages are searched for any sign of an abjuring of rough magic, and it is assayed for evidence of new and sadly unfulfilled beginnings.[1] But even if these temptations are avoided there still remains one problem to be dealt with before we get to the novel itself: *Persuasion* is unfinished. It is of course no mere fragment like *The Watsons*; it has not been perfunctorily rounded off, as was *Lady Susan*. But, like *Northanger Abbey*, it has not come to us in a form which we can be sure Austen would have been happy to send to her publisher.[2]

It is indeed possible that *Northanger Abbey* suffered less in being 'unfinished'. Austen thought it fit for publication in 1803, and there was the opportunity for substantial revision later: *Persuasion* would have been disadvantaged by the very fact of its lateness. In the letter in which she mentions that *Northanger Abbey* is 'put upon the Shelve for the present', Austen also mentions

Persuasion as 'a something ready for Publication, which may perhaps appear about a twelvemonth hence' (*Letters*, p. 484). A bare five days after writing this, she stopped working on *Sanditon*, and in the remaining four months of her life it seems that she never again attempted any serious literary work. But this letter was written six months after, by her own account, the novel was 'finished', and anyway 'a twelvemonth' is much more than would have been necessary for the process of publication. So 'finished' and 'ready for Publication' must mean 'complete, but not completely revised'. Austen subjected all her other novels to a period of testing in reflection, before publication, though this period shortened significantly for the later work. *Mansfield Park* was published about a year after being 'completed', *Emma* after only nine months.[3]

Internal evidence for the unfinished state of *Persuasion* seems easy to find. Most obviously, there is the treatment of Mrs Smith – the way she is clumsily jerked into the novel, and the apparent muddle about her nature and function. Is she the enduring cheerful sufferer or is that the necessary mask for a sick, angry and helpless woman? What too is the point of the story she so lately tells Anne about Mr Elliot? Anne has always known of his doubtful past, has questioned his reformation, and has discovered a retained preference for Wentworth that makes it impossible for her to marry Mr Elliot (pp. 160–1). The issue, though, is not as simple as it seems, and all six novels assert that the consolations of a neat and comprehensive resolution will not be offered, without an ironic probing of their necessity.

In any event, as we try to separate the deliberately under-formed from the accidentally unfinished, we have to remember that if there are faults then they are nothing more than minor – consider the finely coherent way in which the novel resolves its central preoccupations. And there is another point. If we must concede that we cannot know that the novel is finished, then we must also acknowledge that we cannot know how or what Austen would have revised. We can probably accept, given the almost universally expressed dissatisfaction with Mrs Smith, that something would have been changed here, though what aspect and to what degree can only be guessed at, and the same applies to anything else we might deem 'unfinished'. If we approach the novel with too secure a sense that it is unfinished, it is fatally easy to find faults in everything we do not immediately assimilate. In Andor Gomme's much-noted declaration of his unpersuadability, for example (1966, pp.178,181–3, 175), he acknowledges that the novel has some fine things, but is much too readily taken up with the task of noting all the things that may be unfine, is consequently unbalanced, and is sometimes careless. To find that Lady Russell's attitude to Anne's friendship with Mrs Smith is significantly different from her attitude to Elizabeth's friendship with Mrs Clay is not to find a noteworthy inconsistency in Lady Russell, and in Austen's thinking: even Gomme could not argue that Mrs Smith has it in mind to seduce Sir Walter. To record a persisting doubt about whether Anne was right to take Lady Russell's advice is not to have found evidence that the novel is so badly flawed that we must doubt whether Austen could ever have revised it. It is rather that the novel deals subtly with complex material, in ways that preclude straight answers to simple questions, and that it works to make us notice this.[4]

Those who have attempted to explain away the blemishes have fared no better. Several more or less ingenious attempts to account for the functioning of Mrs Smith as wholly coherent and necessary have been made. Paul N. Zietlow, for instance (1965, pp. 179–95), argues for luck and chance in the novel. He justifies Mrs Smith partly on the obviously fallacious ground that, as Austen chose to revise the adjacent chapter but not the one containing Mrs Smith's revelations, she must have been content with that chapter; but he also concludes that Mrs Smith functions as a *deus ex machina*, brought in 'at a crucial moment to avert catastrophe' (p. 193). However, since Mrs Smith makes her revelation only when she is sure, beyond reasonable doubt (*Persuasion*, p. 199), that Anne does *not* intend to marry Mr Elliot, it is pointless to invoke either chance or the gods. There is no catastrophe to avert and no illusion to dispel, and Mrs Smith exists to bring a so-important message that turns out not to matter.[5]

So the argument about incompleteness is a dangerous one but we cannot do without it. Yet this does not necessarily commit us to endless and pointless doubts. No novel is 'perfect', and the 'completeness' of any novel must in some sense be arbitrary: it can never be at the point at which no revision is possible, it is always at the one beyond which the novelist decides, for whatever reason, that further revision can be left undone. Once that

decision has been taken, readers can enter into their dealings
with that novel, in the surety that, however difficult or obscure or
unsatisfactory it is, the novel is not going to be forever sliding
into the teasing indeterminacy of the 'might have been revised'.
Apparently this decision was not taken for *Persuasion* – or, for
that matter, for *Northanger Abbey* – but there is also no gross
sense in which either is incomplete: we should not forget the
incompleteness but we should also take care to invoke the
argument only when our grounds are surest; and then, perhaps
to temper but never to establish our judgement. We should, in
short, treat *Persuasion* and *Northanger Abbey* as far as we can as if
they were as 'finished' as the four 'finished' novels.

But no sooner do we come to terms with the unfinished nature of
Persuasion than the vexed question of its background begins to
assert itself. This is the only one of the six novels to be fixed in
time, and it is fixed decisively on its first page with the stating of
the heroine's date of birth. Austen began writing the novel some
eight weeks after the battle of Waterloo, and the novel has hero
and heroine renewing their engagement three and a half months
before the battle. The first substantial attempts to develop the
argument about *Persuasion* and its times was made by Joseph
Duffy (1954b, pp. 274–89). The novel, he said, contrasts an
'effete' and 'static' aristocracy – in the person of Sir Walter –
with a 'class' of naval persons in the process of supplanting them.
Since Duffy's piece appeared, the argument has hardened into
an orthodoxy to be reiterated with minimal variation. Yet it is
an argument that creates difficulties rather than resolving them,
and as we saw with *Pride and Prejudice*, this concept of a conflict
between classes squares with neither the novel nor its times. Not
only was Sir Walter's class not under particular threat, but the
difficulties faced by Sir Walter have very little to do with the
future of his class, and a great deal to do – as the novel makes
abundantly clear – with his constitutional inability to live within
his income. Indeed, within six months of Duffy's piece being
published, Chapman offered a brief and sadly unheeded 'Reply'
(1954) in which he pointed out (p. 154) that Sir Walter was not a
member of the aristocracy; that neither the aristocracy nor the
gentry were especially 'effete', or in danger of being superseded
in 1815; that there was no such thing as 'an "energetic naval

class", rising in opposition to the old privilege'; that the naval officers were likely, themselves, to be the sons of gentry or even aristocracy.

Just as we have seen that there is ample support for Chapman's conception of the gentry, so it is equally easy to substantiate his views on the navy. The Austen family itself supplies instances of naval captains who were the sons of gentry: many of her naval details must have come to Austen from her brothers Francis and Charles. Francis has been thought of as a model for Wentworth, while he himself thought that he helped with the formation of Captain Harville (Chapman, 1948, p. 125n.) More general evidence is to be found in something like Michael Lewis's account of the navy during the Napoleonic wars, in which he clearly shows that naval officers could make very large claims for being 'gentlemen', and that many were the sons of titled persons, gentry or professional men (1960, pp. 23–58). Yet more evidence is to be found in *Persuasion* itself, and, if Austen intended the navy to be seen as the symbolical repository of national strength and virtue, then it is difficult to see why she included the account of Dick Musgrove (whatever one makes of his treatment by the narrator) since his is clearly (p. 51) the description of a typically *un*satisfactory midshipman; or why, at the other end of the profession, we should be told of the existence of Admiral Brand and his brother, 'Shabby fellows' who played a 'pitiful trick once' on Admiral Croft, in order to deprive him of some of his best men (p. 170).

All four of the central naval figures in the novel are, in differing degrees, 'gentlemen', at least as Anne uses the term, though not as her father understands it, or in a form to which Lady Russell could give unqualified support (pp. 23, 97, 127). All have been united in testing and vigorous activity, and are linked by a warm fraternal bond: but, rather than representing a naval 'type', they are also four very distinct individuals, as we can see if we but for a moment compare the other three with Wentworth: Harville, the unliterary, the practical contriver who is also sensitive and sympathetic, the one who makes a cheerful best of limited means and confined spaces; Admiral Croft, straight-seeing and plain-speaking, whose every gesture shows his strong good nature and his plain, unsubtle sense; Benwick, gentle and quiet, full of the literary sensibilities of love and grief, and yet also sometimes strangely insensitive. Indeed Benwick is an embarrassment to any attempt at drawing a line between navy and gentry, for, though Admiral Croft says that he is 'a very active, zealous officer', he also speaks of him as being 'rather too piano' (pp. 171–2), and he is a figure who remains more appropriate to a drawing-room than a poop-deck.

But, unmindful of these many objections, those who hold to the orthodoxy continue to declare its terms. Some, such as Malcolm Bradbury (1968, pp. 383–96) or Tony Tanner (1981, pp. 180–94), insist on the primary importance of the conflict between aristocracy and navy; and, though that is to mistake Sir Walter's rank, it does mean that the argument has a certain simple consistency, and it is possible, with Bradbury, to ignore the existence of the Musgroves; or merely, with Tanner, to note them briefly as being something of which Anne is not a part. Once we try to apply the argument using the terms of social distinction more accurately, then it simply will not work. David Monaghan, for example, attempts to restate the orthodoxy more appropriately, in terms of gentry and navy. But then what about the Musgroves? The Musgroves are cheerfully, sufficiently, even thrivingly of the landed gentry (p. 28): they are possessed of none of the Elliot faults, just as the Elliots, with the obvious exception of Anne, have none of their virtues. It is just on this point that Monaghan founders: his account of the novel shows us (1980, pp. 143–6) an Austen trying to 'cobble together a somewhat fantasised version of the future', one in which the Musgroves are, like the naval persons, the representatives of what he labels as an 'idealised bourgeoisie'; yet also not so ideal, since they 'lack any sophisticated knowledge of the language of manners', for which, we are to believe, they are duly criticised in the first half of the novel, and then unduly praised in the second. It is, thus, Austen's fault, rather than that of the orthodoxy, that the orthodoxy does not work, and Monaghan concludes (p. 162) with a damningly easy circularity: the society in which Jane Austen lived was 'finally falling apart', and so too, at least in some degree, was her 'art'.

One of the commonest effects of the orthodoxy is to encourage a reading of the novel that is pessimistic about its society. Yet a 'pessimistic' reading is a half-reading, one that is overly responsive to the first volume, and underestimates the second: a too-easily optimistic reading would be equally destructive of the balance which the novel in fact represents. Alistair Duckworth

(1971, pp. 180, 184) exactly illustrates the problems of such an approach, since he takes the metaphor of the estate and its treatment to be central. For him *Persuasion* is the novel in which responsibility for the estate is 'abandoned', and in which 'society never really recovers from the disintegration evident at the beginning'. But Duckworth can only sustain his solemn prognostications by a very dubious reliance on some of Mary Musgrove's peevish reflections. Mary finds 'powerful consolation' for the fact of her sister's marriage in the view that 'Anne had no Uppercross-hall before her, no landed estate, no headship of a family' (*Persuasion*, p. 250). Is this the condition newly perceived by Austen, in which the world is suddenly made strange and perilous? No. Landed estates and headships of families have never been, in Austen's novels, the inevitable reward for the heroine, or the sign that she has achieved security. True, they are obtained by Elizabeth Bennet and Emma Woodhouse; in a lesser way, too, by Marianne Dashwood. But they do not go to Catherine Morland or Elinor Dashwood or Fanny Price.[6]

Each heroine is placed, at the end, in a group that has at least the potential to become sound and balanced, but one that is also made up of varying strengths and capacities. Anne certainly faces a special risk in the 'tax of quick alarm' demanded of the wife of a sailor, and which we are told of, significantly, in the novel's concluding sentence: but this significance can be overdone, especially if we fail to remember that it is only part of a comprehensive statement of the advantages and disadvantages of Anne's position. And a properly responsive reading of the penultimate chapter should show us that Anne is already placed in what has the makings of a workable and worthwhile group. As the company gathers in the Elliot drawing-rooms – and it is a gathering of almost everyone in the novel – Anne is supremely happy, and the glow of her happiness warms everything that she sees: but her vision is certainly not unrealistic, and what it encompasses is a coherent life in society, one in which some relationships are in decline, and others merely static, but some where there is the hope of fruitful growth. When Anne complains that, in exchange for all his friends and family, she has 'but two friends in the world to add to his list' (p. 251), she is reflecting on the fact and the irony of her seriously impoverished past, and there is the added shading given that one of her 'two' is Lady Russell. But she is also acknowledging that they are already in a community, one in which they have friends and ideas and experiences in common.

It is not just that the gentry-and-navy argument has no secure foundation: it can actually limit our understanding of what the novel is doing. Any attempt to argue that Austen is criticising in order to defend her class, or that she despairs of its future, is apt to blunt the criticisms that she is in fact making. It is no mere pedantry, for example, to insist that as a baronet Sir Walter is not a member of the aristocracy: it is an essential part of the sharp irony under which Anne discovers, when she sees 'her father and sister . . . in contact with nobility', that she wishes 'that they had more pride' (p. 148). As D. W. Harding (1965, p. 18) has said, the story is 'embedded in a study of snobbery':

> Jane Austen created the perfect starting point for her satire by giving Sir Walter Elliot a baronetcy, thus putting the family in a twilight region between the nobility and the gentry – still no more than gentry but distinguished among them by the hereditary title. His scorn for those beneath him and his anxious toadying to 'our cousins, the Dalrymples' who are of the nobility (Irish), provide a good deal of the astringent comedy of the book.

And it is the fact that the Dalrymples are Irish that clinches the matter (p. 158). Situated as the Elliots are, and only too anxious to claim the relationship to nobility, they are precluded by their particular snobbery from participating in the more general snobbery by which the Irish peerage was regarded as greatly inferior to that of England. Maria Edgeworth's *The Absentee* (1812) vividly shows how fashionable London society in general regarded the Irish peerage, and its representative in the person of Lady Clonbrony as inferior to a degree only a little short of clownish.[7]

Of course, to a full-blown reformer, polemically insisting on how things should be, any account of how they are, however critically put, is doubtless apt to sound merely palliative. We might prefer to declare with William Godwin that the principle of inherited rank and authority is such that no other could 'present a deeper insult upon reason and justice'; we could join his approval of the way Tom Paine challenged the notion of hereditary power by pointing out that the concept of 'an hereditary poet-laureate' is 'ridiculous'.[8] But every good satirist knows that a freshly and sharply observed account of things as they are can be as devastating as any prophetic dream or speech from the barricades. In *Gulliver's Travels*, Swift forcefully illustrates the point: Gulliver praises the England of Queen Anne to the king of Brobdingnag, and to the Houyhnhnms, but succeeds only in appalling them.

And in *Persuasion* there is some of the most cutting satire in all Austen on the question of rank – cutting just because it is manifestly and calmly a statement of things as they are. Once we have got the measure of Sir Walter Elliot, then we do not even have to argue that this conceited, mean-spirited, stupid, idle baronet is in any way typical of his rank, in order to say that the concept of inherited rank is indefensible. What the novel presents is an element of its society that is at once endowed with permanence and absurd. It surely is not by chance that Anne Elliot expresses so decided a preference for earned rather than inherited privilege; or that it is she who argues that 'good company . . . is the company of clever, well-informed people, who have a great deal of conversation', while it is her father's heir-presumptive who insists that her standards are too high, who says that good company 'requires only birth, education and manners, and with regard to education is not very nice' (p. 150).

Once the background of the novel is properly in perspective, is its shape revealed a little more clearly? Certainly there is an almost universal consensus about its strengths and beauties. Everyone admires the skill with which the material is shaped to fit the seasonal progression from autumn to spring, and the heroine's movement from a state of 'desolate tranquillity' (p. 36) to one in which she is 'glowing and lovely in sensibility and happiness' (p. 245). Everyone remembers the painful first meetings of Anne and Wentworth, the moment at which he relieves her of the attentions of an over-lively nephew, the walk to Winthrop, the visit to Lyme, the happy resolution. But everybody also agrees over what there is to disagree about: the question of whether the 'lost' years are inevitable, or whether we can blame Wentworth or Anne, or Lady Russell, or the 'Elliot pride' or anything else. Both the consensus and the dispute were marked out by the novel's very first readers.[9]

We can try, as is often done with Austen's novels, to see the matter in terms of a process of education. But who does the learning? Is it Anne or Wentworth or both? And what is learned? The critics have offered an impressive range of possibilities: persuasion and persuadability, advice and evidence, growth and decay, dignity and duty, reason and feeling, perception and feeling, memory and feeling.[10] Yet other issues are also worth noting, and a contrast between this novel and its immediate predecessor is interesting. Anne has no need to learn Emma Woodhouse's lessons, and could in fact be said to have learnt them too well. Anne is almost too ready to conceive of others' point of view, is actually in danger at times of effacing herself. So, too, *Persuasion* is less concerned with an active faculty such as 'imagination' than with the more passive 'taste'. And, in returning to this topic, in conceiving of a heroine who has disadvantages in almost all the areas where Emma Woodhouse has special advantages, Austen makes some striking points about the plight of women in general, in the society of the novel – points which are the more compelling because they are plainly and unsententiously put. Anne is obliged to be stationary, passive, contemplative, in the exercise of her 'elegant' mind: her psychological state is matched in the physical world, where for any journey greater than the distance from Kellynch-Hall to Kellynch-Lodge she is dependent on other people. It is no accident that, at the end of the novel, one symbol of her marriage and the freedom it bestows is that she becomes 'the mistress of a very pretty landaulette' (p. 250).

Wentworth, by contrast, has the opportunity to go abroad in bold and testing action. He has a large and not unjustified self-confidence; he is always in search of sweeping and decisive action, always impatient of mere convention. He will where necessary defy authority, and he has an understanding that is as quick, emotionally, as it is in every other way. When Benwick returns to Portsmouth, for instance, unaware that Fanny Harville has died, it is Wentworth who leaves his own ship, who 'stood his chance for the rest – wrote up for leave of absence, but without waiting the return, travelled night and day till he got to Portsmouth, rowed off to the Grappler that instant, and never left the poor fellow for a week' (p. 108). It is true that, when he leaves it, Wentworth's ship is in 'no danger of . . . being sent to sea again', but then the point is that the risk should be nicely calculated. Yet, and this is a measure of Austen's impartiality, it is also Wentworth who, because of his nature and because he assumes too completely that Anne's nature is different, takes so very long to discover that the engagement is renewable.

A similar impartiality is revealed in the treatment of Anne. It is just when she claims her 'seniority of mind', and tastefully recommends that a taste for Romantic poetry should to some degree be balanced by a taste for the prose of the moralists, that she must also admit that she has been 'eloquent on a point in which her own conduct would ill bear examination' (p. 101). Throughout the novel, where she evinces her characteristically 'aesthetic' response it is always tinged by circumstances, mood, desire, idea. Thus the fundamental movement of the novel has Anne finding the world to be a place of blank sorrow at the beginning, and fulfilling joy at the end. It is nowhere more clearly displayed than on the autumnal walk to Winthrop, when Anne half-overhears the conversation of Wentworth and Louisa Musgrove, and tastes the 'sweets of poetical despondence' (p. 85): it is the narrator, not the melancholic Anne, who perceives that Anne is actually in an unspoken debate with the more hopeful farmer who looks to the return of spring. At times, even the highest and noblest claims for taste seem to be wan and frail: when Anne contrasts herself with the Musgrove sisters, she seems, almost, to be drawing attention to her own taste and elegance *as* a standard.

> Anne had always contemplated them as some of the happiest creatures of her acquaintance; but still, saved as we all are by some comfortable feeling of superiority from wishing for the possibility of exchange, she would not have given up her own more elegant and cultivated mind for all their enjoyments; and envied them nothing but that seemingly perfect good under-standing and agreement together . . . .(p. 41)

Except, of course, that this also sounds like someone who is a little desperately clinging to a shred of dignity and self-regard, and is perhaps making a not-quite balanced assessment of that shred. This in turn points to the implication that, given the state of isolation, of uncommunication, which is Anne's for half the novel, her taste (good though it no doubt is, and except for the very doubtful consolation that it can offer her) is irrelevant.

There is, proverbially, no point in disputing matters of taste. By the beginning of the nineteenth century, this had become at once a well-worn cliché and a proposition about which there was still much to debate. Austen implies that where no disputing is possible then it is also the case that taste – whatever it is – ceases to matter significantly.

That is not to turn the complex diversity that makes up the subject of *Persuasion* into a homily. As R. S. Crane has said (1967, II, 287), the novel is

> pervaded with morality of what seems to me a very fine sort, however, it has no moral and argues no thesis. It is a novel of personal relations. . . . It is a love story, in short, which moves us as all good love stories do, not because its hero and heroine are embodiments of abstract values, ideological or social, larger than themselves, but simply because they are particular human persons who have fallen in love and suffer and are happy in the end.

Equally, though, Crane's account cannot really help us grasp the unresolvable debate in and about the novel. The arguments about Anne and Lady Russell and Wentworth have persisted and will continue because they deal with problems that are never shaped into the form of a balance sheet of 'rights' and 'wrongs'; are much too tentatively and partially put. At the end all we are left with is a significantly qualified defence of her past actions from Anne, and a statement from Wentworth not necessarily convinced that Anne's version is wholly right, but conceding that he is himself blamable for part, though only for part of the past. In the circumstances, all that we can do, perhaps, is agree with Anne that Lady Russell's advice was 'good or bad only as the event decides' (*Persuasion*, p. 246). Any further and more extensive resolution must be reached by our own efforts, and by going beyond what the novel specifies. That means that we must recognise that we are venturing on possibilities, not looking for certainties: else we may find ourselves pushing the novel into what is for this novel the sadly reducing tidiness of a moral.

But if, in one sense, the 'problem' of *Persuasion* is such that it can tempt its readers to find less in it than there actually is in the novel, then, in another sense, the history of the past and present of Anne Elliot and Frederick Wentworth can remain always vividly alive to us, just because it is not all told, and cannot be finished, finalised, parcelled up, but must always be partly guessed at. And this marks a significant change in method for Austen: *Emma* showed how far she had developed her skill in suggesting and using the uncertain and the incomplete, but the structure of that novel makes inevitably for a certain degree of simplication and stylisation. Other conceptions of the world of Highbury exist, but they exist in a world that is Emma's. Frank Churchill is the single dazzling exception, quite unfixable, always hinting at the possibility of other versions of himself, and utterly destroying the illusion of an Emma-centred world. But, given that we work so much through the large and accommodating consciousness of Emma, *Emma* remains an Emma centred novel, one in which, paradoxically, the more we find out about her limitations, the more we reinforce our sense of Emma as heroine. There is, thus, in spite of the stress on alternatives and variations, an inevitable and artificially heightened sense of coherence, pattern, unity. *Persuasion* seeks for conditions in which this structuring and focusing is, if not eliminated, then at least tightly limited; and its context appears to be one in which there is, radically, less order and shape.

Principally it is a matter of heroineship. *Persuasion* is a novel that is very significantly less heroine-oriented, one in which conceptions of the world other than the heroine's loom much more portentously. Similarly, the heroine is much less predominantly the object of the narrator's attention; and from the opening pages this difference is strikingly apparent. The earlier novel starts with the utterance of the name of the heroine, and proceeds to make immediate and large claims for her; before the end of the first paragraph we can begin to sense that shifts to the consciousness of others will be largely in order to make explicit contrasts with the heroine's. In the later novel, we have to read some twenty-three pages before we know much more than the bare facts of Anne's existence – and that as the drily recorded detail on the pages of the *Baronetage* – or before she begins to function properly even as a minor character, one whose story is already history to be summed up as a piece of background information.[11]

As everyone notices, Anne is a telling twenty-seven, and her unhappiness has, at the point when the novel starts, already been of long duration. She has had time to settle into a sad calm neutrality, in which she can watch the events of others' lives and in which her own life can be regarded as a minor detail in those other lives. For half the novel, in a word, it does not seem to be her novel: the paradoxical workings of *Persuasion* are such that this is the way we come to discover that it splendidly *is* her novel.

We find ourselves apprehending the method and the means as they are in the act of becoming *novel*. Consider the problem of first and second readings. As *Emma* shows, all novels make possible an innovative second reading, but some have an unusually large element of the imprecisely and incompletely rendered. In these cases a second reading is essential if we are merely to obtain an adequate measure of the range and diversity that we can set against what is actually specified. And *Persuasion*, in its own special way, presents just such a problem. Or is that to make unnatural claims for the novel? Even those critics who make large claims for it often suggest that there is a straightforward clarity in its workings. Sheldon Sacks, for example (1969, p. 288), is actually contending that Austen's novels are 'crucial and even experimental developments in expanding the bounds of morally serious comic plots in comic novels' in claiming that

> when, at the end of the third chapter, Anne says, 'with a gentle sigh, "a few months more, and *he*, perhaps may be walking here"', only an imperceptive reader would fail to recognise the traitless 'he' as her future husband, though until the subsequent chapter, 'he' is nameless and exists only in Anne's single passionate remark.

And that, of course, is to suggest that, whatever else *Persuasion* achieves, it does offer, even to the first-time reader, an unusually large measure of unambiguous security.[12] Doubtless the perceptive reader will recognise the unnamed Wentworth as a possible husband for Anne, but the perceptive reader who sees Wentworth, at this point, unqualifiedly, as her future husband will be the same perceptive reader who saw Willoughby, as certainly, as the future husband of Marianne Dashwood, or Wickham as the future husband of Elizabeth Bennet. It is dangerous, at least with Austen, to have this uncritical reliance on fictional conventions. Nobody could deny that Austen recognised the inevitability of fictional conventions as a means of connecting novel with reader, but then nobody could deny that Austen knew – had known as a child – that such conventions could be turned into hilarious parody, if mechanically or ineptly invoked.

It is therefore not needlessly complicating, but essential, to ask whose novel *Persuasion* is: it is certainly Anne's, once her future with Wentworth is secure, and it is almost as clearly hers once we begin to approach that point more closely. But it is also a very gradually attained state, the result of a slow movement from the condition in which Anne exists to reflect only on other people's stories, and through a consideration of the varied possibility these stories represent. That is why even a second reading of *Persuasion* need not simply be a processing through a pleasant interim, before the anticipated happy ending is confirmed, but an opportunity, once we know what the resolution is, to re-examine the means of reaching it, to see how far we travel along paths that seem to be alien to it, to consider just how many paths there are.

Certainly, at the start of the novel there is very little to show that it is Anne's novel: Anne who is, whatever her merits, 'of very inferior value', who is 'nobody', who has 'no weight', who is 'only Anne' (p. 5); the 'only' might suggest a potential uniqueness, but the context seems to negate this possibility decisively. It is not merely that she does not matter at Kellynch-Hall, but that she does not seem to matter in *Persuasion*. None of her views on the payment of the debts are made known to her father; none of her wishes for the future are noticed or heeded. We begin to learn that she has had a past that might be 'interesting', but then it seems to be a past that is finished and irretrievable. When Anne feels that 'time had softened down much, perhaps nearly all of peculiar attachment to him' (p. 28), the news that Wentworth might be at Kellynch again brings the 'revival of former pain' (p. 30), but is no particular cause for her to hope or us to expect.

No, for the first five chapters it is the Elliots as a group who are the subject of *Persuasion*, and Anne has the minor role of passive observer in that story. The contrast between Anne and her family works to expose how fine Anne is, potentially, and how appalling are her family. Is that all? Is that enough? We might ask, as some of the critics have done, whether the Elliots are not just simply and crudely drawn abstractions of vanity and folly, at once lifeless and too easily dislikable.[13] If they are, then they are certainly out of place in a novel that contains the complexity and depth of an Anne Elliot, and any comparison between Anne and her family must either be tiresomely obvious, or false. It could be said that Sir Walter and Elizabeth are lifeless machines, existing only to demonstrate, wearisomely and simply, what they are. But perhaps they are not a failure of conception, something that the novelist has been unable to bring adequately to life; perhaps they are a striking success, a disturbing picture of life that is notably less than lived.

Dickens's last completed novel presents a similar problem. It is often said of *Our Mutual Friend* (1865) that the Veneerings and their friends come from a Dickens who was decidedly less than at his best; a Dickens who was tiredly, incompetently, mechanically making mere jottings, mere lists of traits. But it is rather that the Veneerings and the people they assemble round their dinner table are all people who, as people, are deficient in life; who, as they view themselves and each other, have become fractured and distorted, and who cannot make coherent statements about themselves but merely dubious assertions. The truth about 'charming' Lady Tippins, for example, is that she is a painted and animated corpse. The picture – and it comes to us with the frozen stasis of a picture, reflected and framed in the mirror – shows us, not the declining powers of the novelist, but the comprehensive vision he has of the limitations of life in the society he portrays. The mirror, among other things,

> Reflects charming old Lady Tippins on Veneering's right; with an immense obtuse drab oblong face, like the face in a tablespoon, and a dyed Long Walk up the top of her head, as a convenient public approach to the bunch of false hair behind, pleased to patronise Mrs Veneering opposite, who is pleased to be patronised.[14]

Sir Walter and his eldest daughter represent, in their own way, the same kind of unlived life. We have already seen how, being as they are, they make all questions of rank, as rank, absurd. What they stand for as individuals is equally significant in its insignificance: quite consumed by vanity, they are totally preoccupied with the trivial surface detail of dress and cosmetic and social distinction, and beyond this they have almost no existence. They are without the capacity to discriminate, beyond the point of telling whether or not attention is being paid to them, and so they are prey to the grossest flattery, and are pathetically easy dupes. They are quite unable to conceive of any real notion of self-respect, and when, at the end, they are deprived of the soothing attentions of Mrs Clay and Mr Elliot, it is entirely appropriate that they should console themselves by paying yet more craven deference to the broad-backed and slight-minded Viscountess and her dull daughter. 'They had their great cousins, to be sure, to resort to for comfort; but they must long feel that to flatter and follow others, without being flattered and followed in turn, is but a state of half enjoyment' (p. 251). The chief point about the Elliots is that their essential nullity is conveyed just because at the start of the novel, and more briefly on occasion later, they are at the centre of our attention, and it is seemingly their novel. By giving them, even only for a while, a significance in the novel that is equivalent to the significance they claim in the society of the novel, their claims to significance are shown to amount to nothing.

Now, if we think of Anne in relation to what her family represents, then we shall find the opening of *Persuasion* has a sufficiently rich complexity, because, if Anne does not seem to count, then we can get a full measure of the potentially tragic irony if we properly see that *this* is her context, and the reason for her not counting: Anne, whose intelligence and sensibility are vitally evident in the first words she utters, words that are surprisingly forthright, but are also totally without effect; Anne who, however we interpret the difficult events of eight years before, has helped determine her own situation. For Anne to waste the length of her years in the splendour and nothingness that is Kellynch-Hall, with its copy of the *Baronetage*, its too-many mirrors, its bottles of 'Gowland' (p. 146), would, without exaggeration, be tragic. And, for as long as the novel appears to be 'about' the Elliots, that does seem to be her fate. Equally, we have to recognise that Kellynch and the story of the Elliots is not merely the dull, blank, barren point from which we move to more promising scenes. One way of viewing the novel, as Lascelles suggests (1939, p. 181), is as the 'bursting open' for Anne of the 'prison' that is Kellynch. But it is also the case that the threat of reimprisonment remains real, if muted, until comparatively late in the novel. We may often almost forget the existence of Sir Walter and Elizabeth – though Mary is a potent reminder of family characteristics: we may find, as Anne herself does, that the concerns of her father and eldest sister, which seemed so bulky at the start of the first volume, have shrunk decidedly by the start of the second. But the possibility remains that the novel will turn back into the Elliots' story, with Anne having seen brighter and more hopeful futures, but back at the point where there are no grounds for hope. It is, after all, quite late in the novel when she has to listen to her father's obnoxious remarks about her friend Mrs Smith ('a mere Mrs Smith, an every day Mrs Smith, of all people and all names in the world, to be the chosen friend of Miss Anne Elliot' – p. 158). We cannot blame Anne for seeing but not pointing to the way her father is being inane and contemptible; we cannot blame her for leaving it to 'himself to recollect' the obvious comparison with Mrs Clay: but we must also see that this is a wasted charity, and that the measure of her father is that he will not 'recollect'.

But, while the threat that the novel is the Elliots is real enough, it is soon pushed somewhat to one side by other, widening possibilities; and the subject on which Anne first speaks, the debts of her family, becomes the occasion for these possibilities, experienced with the Musgroves, then at Lyme, at Kellynch Lodge, and finally at Bath. Only at the end do we find that *the* story has become the best and happiest of Anne's stories.[15]

Consider, by way of contrast, the example of James's *The Wings of the Dove* (1902). With this novel, even more daringly than in *Persuasion*, there is a holding-back of the heroine: she is of course frail, but in no sense insubstantial, yet two of the novel's ten books elapse before we know anything of her existence. We find her (and it is also typical of the novel that we do not get directly to Milly herself, but are introduced to her through Mrs Stringham's guessing attempts to understand her friend) sitting on the 'dizzy edge' of a mountain path in Switzerland 'in a state of uplifted and unlimited possession. . . . She was looking down on the kingdoms of the earth, and though indeed that of itself might well go to the brain, it wouldn't be with a view of renouncing them. Was she choosing among them or did she want them all?'[16] The first two books are not just a preliminary setting of the scene in which Milly will be placed as a result of her 'choosing': the characters peopling that scene have dreams and visions quite as large as anything vouchsafed to Milly, and seldom in compliant harmony with hers. Kate's conception, at the start of the novel, of the possibilities represented by her future, and of her father, her aunt, her sister, of Merton Densher, are so elaborate, and so enmeshed with the conceptions of others, that we can only dimly glimpse and guess at their entirety. In such circumstances, to talk of differing possible stories is obviously to make a very large simplification; but it is a means of enabling us to perceive that the psychological drama that makes up the novel is a conflict between stories. Given the range and the fullness of versions that each individual holds, given that different individuals will have different versions of the same possible events, specific versions will only survive by fighting or accommodating. That leads, inevitably, to the kind of double and triple thinking so common in the novel, by which Kate or Densher, or Mrs Lowder or Mrs Stringham, or even Milly, will build into their sense of the world and the future an attempt at approximating or circumventing a sense of how others view that prospect.

It is of course obvious that *Persuasion* does not quite have this scope, but it must be said that the earlier novel is not simply making less use of the method, but is actually making the method work to a somewhat different end. *The Wings of the Dove* plunges us directly into the middle of things, with the differing versions already fully in existence, already in conflict. *Persuasion*, on the other hand, introduces us stage by stage to the different aspects of the debate, starting with the smallest, least interesting fragment of a page from the *Baronetage* and building from there to something which has complete utterance only at the end. It never renders the possibilities of its individual consciousnesses as comprehensively as the James novel does, but Austen is able to explore the process as it grows, from a point of inception, and can show the gradually widening set of possibilities, so that each new detail or version will do something to break the pattern previously formed: it is only when all the voices have sounded their full range that we can properly begin to seek out the more enduring patterns. *Persuasion* directs us to the analysis of the process of becoming what, in a sense, Kate Croy and Milly Theale already are when we first encounter them.

And, once we begin to comprehend this, it becomes clear that attempts to discuss the functioning of *Persuasion* in terms simply of such concepts as 'point of view' are inadequate. Wayne Booth

(1961, pp. 250–3) is interesting in this regard, just because his account, though an insufficient one, does begin to make some qualifications. He compares *Persuasion* with *Emma*, and says that Emma's point of view is much more unreliable, much more in need of correction, while Anne's is limited in only one specific way: 'her ignorance of Captain Wentworth's love'. Thus Anne's 'consciousness is sufficient, as Emma's is not, for most of the needs of the novel which she dominates'. And, apart from the narrator's interpolations at the very beginning and the very end, Booth finds only two occasions on which Anne's view is insufficient. But this oversimplifies, and the 'only' deviations that Booth finds are 'only' the most obvious ones.[17]

Actually the whole matter is rather more complicatedly that we know at the same time how important and revealing is Anne's view of things, what its limitations are, and what other possibilities exist outside her. Take the walk to Winthrop: Anne sets out on the walk not unwillingly, but primarily, she thinks, to be useful in preventing Mary from being a nuisance to the Musgrove sisters. She probably also shares, though, with the narrator, the perception that their invitation to herself is 'much more cordial' (p. 83) than that to Mary. When they are joined, at the last moment, by Charles Musgrove and Captain Wentworth, Anne acknowledges that, if she had known that this was to happen, she 'would have staid at home'; but it is the narrator, not Anne, who has the better measure of Anne's doubt and confusion, and who notes of Anne that 'from some feelings of interest and curiosity, she fancied now that it was too late to retract' (p. 84). She feels her own pleasure to be confined to a private poetic musing on the sad beauty of the autumn day, and she studies Wentworth, wondering which of the Musgrove girls he prefers, detecting an increasing preference for Louisa. At the same time, she continues to probe, in her own mind, the way she thinks Wentworth thinks about *her*, and so takes his talk of firmness and nuts to imply a rebuke to herself (p. 89); that is modified again a little later when on the return walk he perceives her to be tired and arranges for her to have a place in the Crofts' carriage:

She understood him. He could not forgive her, – but he could not be unfeeling. Though condemning her for the past, and considering it with high and unjust resentment, though perfectly careless of her, and though becoming attached to another, still he could not see her suffer, without the desire of giving her relief. It was a remainder of former sentiment; it was an impulse of pure, though unacknowledged friendship; it was proof of his own warm and amiable heart, which she could not contemplate without emotions so compounded of pleasure and pain, that she knew not which prevailed. (p. 91)

Taken as a whole the walk to Winthrop seems to bring Anne only reminders of her sorrow and her isolation, and, when she happens to ask, by way of rousing herself from a moment of especial sadness, whether they are on the path to Winthrop, it seems entirely characteristic of her situation that 'nobody heard, or, at least, nobody answered her' (p. 85).

Anne's view of the situation is both useful and understandable: but it also begins to be clear that Anne's view, on its own, is less than completely adequate; and a little reflection, a little hindsight, will bring us things that are outside the scope of her view, and that have nothing to do with her significance. Winthrop is, very much, the destination of the walk for at least three of Anne's companions, but, as their reasons are covert, it is unlikely that they would be anything but silent when Anne asks her question. The other two are unlikely to answer it anyway, since Mary is no doubt in her usual neurotically self-preoccupied state, while Wentworth will not know the answer to her question. But for Charles Musgrove and his sisters the going to Winthrop is crucial. Charles, in opposition to his wife's petty but insistent snobbery, would greet his aunt, would even try to persuade Mary to join him in going down to the farmhouse, once it comes in sight; Charles may also be party to the scheme – principally Louisa's – for the reconciling of Henrietta and Charles Hayter, the cousin who was rendered jealous and sulky by the presence of Wentworth. For, as the narrator rather laconically observes, 'young men are, sometimes, to be met with, strolling about near home' (p. 85). So the Musgroves have more than one reason, especially since Mary (who disapproves of Charles Hayter, on Elliot principles) is with them, for remaining silent about their intended destination. And it is Louisa, most active in attempting to ensure that it is her version of the events that the events fit, who, having turned her sister's thoughts away from Wentworth and back to Hayter, seizes the opportunity of the short absence of her brother and sister to take Wentworth aside and tell him what she has done, thus economically demonstrating the kind of 'firmness' that he claims to admire, and also showing him that her sister is committed to another, and is less possessed of firmness. In doing so she is, of course, overheard by Anne, overheard giving utterance, among other things, to the Musgrove version of Anne's relationship with Lady Russell (p. 81): a version which we know is less than correct, and yet one which we can see, as Anne does, will help to confirm Wentworth's own conception of Anne and her friend.

The novel, therefore, does not consist, more than partly, in what is refracted through Anne's consciousness: and her consciousness functions in a context in which the unity of what *is* is constantly being threatened and remade by the diversity of what might be; a context in which some 'versions' of the novel seem so confidently to be the novel, and then come to nothing, while other 'versions' seem to be no more than incomplete fragments, until we can see the pattern in the novel as a whole. We can only properly appreciate why Anne so dislikes Bath, we can only measure properly the irony by which Bath brings her freedom and happiness, when we remember that it was to Bath that Lady Russell took Anne just after the engagement to Wentworth was terminated – in the unfulfilled expectation that change and variety might lift her friend's spirits, might even, we can surmise, bring the consoling happiness of a 'second attachment' (perhaps one more suited to Lady Russell's own taste – p. 28). And it was to Bath, just after her mother's death, that Anne was sent to school, where she found the comfort and the kindness of the person who was to become Mrs Smith (pp. 14, 152).

The very event on which the whole novel is founded, the terminated engagement, is ambiguous not only because it is finally unresolvable, but because there are so many possible resolutions. There is the disapproval founded on the conviction, of Sir Walter and Elizabeth, of what it is to be an Elliot. There is Lady Russell, genuinely concerned for Anne, genuinely fulfilling the maternal role, yet also motivated by her notions of what Anne might become, and too rigidly certain of what Wentworth will not become. There are the conceptions and contradictions in the views of the young couple themselves: the way Anne is persuaded to terminate the engagement for, among other things, Wentworth's sake, and the speed with which she comes to regret that decision, as she and Lady Russell develop different and incompatible senses of the past and the future; there is the way that Wentworth, not without justification, but prompted also by his anger and wounded feelings, does not properly understand Anne's actions, even less the way that her view of those actions changes. Eight years after the events Anne is capable, on notably different occasions, of giving notably different accounts of her sense of them. At the beginning of the novel, when Anne's life is saddest, and her future most blank, we are told that she

> did not blame Lady Russell, she did not blame herself for having been guided by her; but she felt that were any young person, in similar circumstances, to apply to her for counsel, they would never receive any of such certain immediate wretchedness, such uncertain future good. – She was persuaded that under every disadvantage of disapprobation at home, and every anxiety attending his profession, all their probable fears, delays and disappointments, she should yet have been a happier woman in maintaining the engagement, than she had been in the sacrifice of it . . . .   (p. 29)

But in the novel's concluding sequence, when Anne knows of the happy ending of her story, she takes – can afford to take – a rather different view of the past, and the influence of Lady Russell's advice on that past:

> It was, perhaps, one of those cases in which advice is good or bad only as the event decides; and for myself, I certainly never should, in any circumstances of tolerable similarity, give such advice. But I mean, that I was right in submitting to her, and that if I had done otherwise, I should have suffered more in continuing the engagement than I did even in giving it up, because I should have suffered in my conscience.   (p. 246)

At Uppercross there is a whole new range of possibilities. At first Anne seems destined to play the role of observer–narrator of the Musgroves' story – a story in which she has herself played a minor part, as the woman to whom Charles Musgrove first proposed, and the woman his family rather wish had accepted him. Then, and most poignantly, it seems that Anne's function is to reflect on the growing attachment between Wentworth and

Louisa Musgrove: but this, too, turns out not to be the story of
Persuasion, or even of Wentworth and Louisa.

The Musgroves themselves, for all their appearance of unity,
are constantly dividing over possibilities and explanations: between Uppercross-Hall and Uppercross Cottage; between Uppercross and Winthrop; even, at one point, between that otherwise close and happy pair, Louisa and Henrietta. Wentworth,
besides linking with the complicated past and present of Anne, is
also to be seen as a potential lover or husband, a rival, a good
sportsman, a potential son-in-law, or as the brave and adventur-
ous sailor. In counterpoint to that last, there is the bathos by
which he comes, at least for Mrs Musgrove (p. 64), to represent
what worthless Dick Musgrove might have been. Surely that is
the point of this much-discussed episode: it is another vividly
dramatic instance of the way differing versions of a story can
exist together, often uneasily, and be understood in different
ways and on different levels. There is nothing that is in itself
cruel and unpleasant in the fact recorded by the narrator that
the dead son of the Musgroves was, and was generally perceived
to be, 'thick-headed, unfeeling, unprofitable' (p. 51), or in the
not-unusual circumstance by which the worthless dead are
accorded a late and sentimental mourning. But it does mean that
there will be a nicely shaded variety of ways of telling the story of
Dick Musgrove, from one that is founded on inaccuracy and the
grossest sentimentality, to one that has the thrust of an all but
brutal frankness.[18] And it is one thing, clearly, for the narrator to
reveal to us something of what we can take to be the 'truth'
about Dick Musgrove; or for Anne to perceive – or think she
perceives, founding her perception on what she feels has sur-
vived of her special relationship with Wentworth – that his view
of Dick Musgrove is not unlike what we already know to be the
narrator's (p. 67): it is quite another when it becomes a matter of
treating with the Musgroves and their grief; of doing as Wentworth does and, concealing his real feelings, offering what he can
of genuine consolation (pp. 67–8). In the novel that is Mrs
Musgrove's, it is as a genuinely consoling figure that he will
appear.

The visit to Lyme offers yet more potential stories. Harville is
a variation on the possibilities of fortitude, Benwick on grief and
poetry. But Lyme also brings the chance encounter with Mr
Elliot during which he looks admiringly at Anne, and Anne is

flattered into thinking about him, and about the way Wentworth responds to his interest in her (p. 104). Benwick also seems to find Anne unusually interesting, and for weeks after she returns from Lyme she has the expectation, never actually fulfilled, but caught also by Lady Russell, that he will 'visit' her; and Charles and Mary Musgrove come to Kellynch-Lodge partly in order to argue over their own differing accounts of Benwick, of whether he is attracted to Anne, of whether he will come to Kellynch (pp. 130–3). But, most of all at Lyme, there is the drama of the Cobb and Louisa's fall, the opportunity that brings for Anne to assert herself, the jarring shock it gives, not only to Louisa's head and ultimately to her future prospects, but also to Wentworth, his conception of himself and his understanding of Louisa and Anne.

Anne's journey to Bath brings her to the new preoccupations of her father and her sister; brings her also to her cousin, and into his schemes and devisings; brings her, before very long, to the almost offered temptation to become Lady Elliot. That is in some ways the most surprising of the possible developments, because it seems to imply that she is more like her family than she appears, and that she might have her own share of the 'Elliot pride'. But this possibility has no particular fixity: it can be grasped, even delighted in, by Anne, but is also, in 'a few moments', put appropriately in perspective. For then the 'charm of Kellynch and of "Lady Elliot" all faded away', and Anne comes to the key realisation, in part a rediscovery, that 'her feelings were still adverse to any man but one', and that, even if this were not so, then she still could not bring herself to trust her cousin.

This of course is a crucial point in the novel's development. In choosing for Wentworth and against her cousin, she is actually deciding what is not going to be a part of the story that is hers. This does not mean that no new possibilities or interpretations will be presented of the story that has become Anne's – it must be remembered that Anne makes her decision while still assuming that Wentworth will marry Louisa Musgrove – but it does mean that we can begin more clearly to rank the different possibilities in terms of their actual or potential significance to Anne. The ending of the novel is approached by a gathering coherence. Where once they seemed to be disparate stories, they now seem increasingly to be different perspectives on the same

story. Hence, for example, the story that Mrs Smith tells. Whatever one thinks of its contrived nature, or of its belatedness, it is
also a stunning revelation of the complacent, paltry, showy
world of Bath in which Anne has taken her place, stunning just
because it is the view as seen by servants and nurses, or laun-
dresses and waiters (pp. 155–6, 193). It is a point of view that
Austen had never before considered in any detail, and in using it
to reconstruct the version of the story held by Mr Elliot and his
friends the Wallises (pp. 204–5), Austen is able to shine a new
and rather harsh light on the folly and the pride of Sir Walter
and his daughter, the schemes and petty intrigues of his heir,
even – in so far as they connect with it – the doings of Anne
Elliot, because she makes this the subject of the idle gossip of the
back stairs.

And, even before we learn of this version of the way Mr Elliot
sees the world, and wants to see it, another pattern of possibilities begins to emerge. No sooner has Anne made the sure
rediscovery of her feelings for Wentworth than news comes to
Bath (pp. 164–5) of the surprising engagement of Louisa Musgrove to Benwick; almost immediately after, Wentworth himself
comes to Bath, and Anne's hopes are suddenly renewed. That is
not to say that, even here, there is a straightforward and easily
achieved resolution, since there is the halting and awkward
development of the relationship in successive chance meetings,
with the dangers of precipitance on one side, or a holding-back
on the other that might wreck the best chances. Thus it is that
Anne, desperately anxious to communicate with Wentworth,
and aware of the advantages and the disadvantages of the
jealousy he has begun to feel, is more than ready at the White
Hart to make her passionate defence of the constancy of women
to Harville: and, because by chance Wentworth overhears her,
he is compelled to the dangerous means of his letter to her.
Hence the great and resounding irony that sets off the last
chapter:

> Who can be in doubt of what followed? When any two young
> people take it into their heads to marry, they are pretty sure by
> perseverance to carry their point, be they ever so poor, or ever
> so imprudent, or ever so little likely to be necessary to each
> other's ultimate comfort.   (p. 248)

That can only be said, and with such confidence, because it is said with the knowledge that there once were two young people, who *were* Anne and Wentworth, and who somehow did not have the 'perseverance to carry their point'; that it is also perilously late before Anne can express some reasonable hope. 'Surely, if there be constant attachment on each side, our hearts must understand each other ere long. We are not boy and girl, to be captiously irritable, misled by every moment's inadvertence, and wantonly playing with our own happiness' (p. 221). And still, as she says it, she doubts.

Then at the end, we can perceive that the movement within which the differing possibilities of Anne's story are explored and ordered, the movement between bleak autumn and warm and colourful spring, is also of course a movement between tragedy and comedy. It is a link that the novel makes perpetual, for we cannot think of the very happy resolution without noticing how largely the other less happy possibilities have loomed; and we cannot remember the eight sadly wasted years, even though they do come to an end, without seeing how easily they could have turned into the waste of a lifetime, and how wonderfully they do not. If we want to invoke a late Shakespeare play then it is perhaps not the *The Tempest*, so often alluded to, that we should be thinking of, but *The Winter's Tale*. That works, one could say, in whole tones when *Persuasion* is in half-tones. There the shift is from the depths of winter to the height of summer; there the blank period lasts for sixteen years: in *Persuasion* the movement is merely from autumn to spring, and its blank is only eight years. But both show ways in which jealousy and misunderstanding can lead either to the bitterest of sorrows, or be resolved into an unexpected happiness, one that yet remembers the sorrow. And both pivot crucially on central scenes that point, at once, back to the tragedy at its grimmest, and forward to a richly enlivening comedy that even has a trace of the absurd. In *The Winter's Tale* there is the scene in which Antigonus, compelled to the task of abandoning the infant Perdita, is pursued off stage by a bear and then eaten. That could be taken as an apt conclusion to the events in Sicilia, but, since the events are also described in comic detail by a 'clown', we are prepared for the pastoral comedy of the second half of the play. And *Persuasion* has the Cobb, and Louisa's fall: dramatically and even melodramatically making a crucial and serious point, yet also finding one point of view from which the proceedings seem to be of more comic interest.

> By this time the report of the accident had spread among the workmen and boatmen about the Cobb, and many were collected near them, to be useful if wanted, at any rate, to enjoy the sight of a dead young lady, nay, two dead young ladies, for it proved twice as fine as the first report. (p. 111)

Of course Austen was always capable of finding comedy in the most unexpected places, and so of radically changing our perspectives. But nowhere is it a more fundamental or general shift than here.

In one particular respect, though, play and novel do seem to differ notably. The play ends with art being brought to life with the 'statue' of Hermione, while the novel ends in a way that has life turning into art. Here, the questions which the novel most suggests are novelistic rather than dramatic questions. As the diverse meanings of the material of the novel are successively revealed, and we move gradually to the finally achieved coherence; as Anne's life, at first peripheral, is placed more and more at the centre of our attention, so we can perceive the novel being actually formed around her. Her progress is towards the condition of a heroine, and she comes slowly to dominate over her setting, which comes to be the background to *her* novel. Increasingly, towards the end, the process becomes a conscious one. At one moment, at the concert when she is caught between the attentions of her cousin and the jealousy of Wentworth, she finds herself very anxious to give Wentworth a large opportunity to join her, and seizes the chance to 'place herself much nearer the end of the bench than she had been before, much more within the reach of a passer-by': though it is a moment of great anxiety for her, she can also see that this has, very much, the air of flirtatious opportunism, and is reminded of 'Miss Larolles, the inimitable Miss Larolles' (p. 189). Miss Larolles is an inanely chattering girl in Fanny Burney's *Cecilia*, who seems intent on bringing to life the novelistic conventions applying to flirtations, and who herself fully knows the advantage of a seat at the end of the bench, if one wants to catch the attention of a passer-by.[19] Momentarily, then, Anne is laughing at the comic literariness of her behaviour: it is a laughter in which the heroine, the narrator and the reader have joined, in complicity. It is a laughter to which we can attach even more significance if we realise that she is behaving as much like a young lady who flirts by the book in Burney's London as in Austen's Bath. The Austen character Anne most resembles at this moment is Isabella Thorpe – such is the irony by which Anne's plight reduces her to the devices much more usually employed by the merely heartless triflers who think mistakenly that they are heroines. But it must also be emphasised that the conscious complicity between heroine, narrator and reader is only momentary, since Anne's progress toward heroineship is now so far advanced that no comic challenge of a merely pseudo-heroinely nature can be sustained. By the next morning, Anne, made more happy and more anxious by the evinced jealousy of Wentworth has also become, unquestionably, a heroine in a novel, to be talked of, a little stiltedly at first (but then it is an unaccustomed form for this just-created heroine) *as a heroine in a novel*, in conventionally literary terms.

> Prettier musings of high-wrought love and eternal constancy, could never have passed along the streets of Bath, than Anne was sporting with from Camden-place to Westgate-buildings. It was almost enough to spread purification and perfume all the way.   (p. 192)

And where is she going? To hear the story of a man who is 'black at heart, hollow and black!' (p. 199), a man who looked set to play either hero or villain to her heroine, but whose potential has already been almost entirely neutralised. And, though we must still wait to know exactly what Anne's fate will be, exactly what her measure of happiness or sadness will be, it is now clear that she has, as it were, passed out of life, has become the heroine of the novel that is called *Persuasion*, and so has a story that will come to an end.

It was to be that Jane Austen, who started her first novel by emphatically asking what is a heroine, turned her last into the formal consideration of what is a novel, and so of the process by which a person called Anne Elliot becomes heroine of that novel. Both novels give us a conventionally happy ending that is at once no more than a happy ending, and a laugh at the conventions that require and achieve happy endings in novels. And in *Persuasion*, even more than in *Northanger Abbey*, there is the last irony by which, simultaneously, we have the illusion created for us that we are dealing with living, breathing life, and an active sense of the polishings and refinings necessary for the creation of what is art. In short, the novel reminds us what it is and how it works, as a novel, and it restates its relationship with us as readers, whereby it is only graspable because it is also ungraspable, just at the point when it is also terminating that relationship with us, as readers.

Notes

On the method of referencing adopted here, see 'Note on References', p. viii.

NOTES TO CHAPTER 1. INTRODUCTION: FICTIONAL METHODS AND THEIR EFFECTS

1. James, 'Gustave Flaubert' (1902) in *The House of Fiction*, ed. Edel (1957) p. 207. The *Plan of a Novel*, Austen's 'late return to the extravagance of her earliest writing', was written in 1816 (Southam, 1964, p. 79).
2. 'Jack & Alice' was probably written between 1787 and 1790 (Southam, 1964, p. 16).
3. These different approaches are all, of course, to be found in the criticism of Austen's novels. Marilyn Butler's *Jane Austen and the War of Ideas* (1975) is an obvious illustration of the first; Auden's comment is in his *Letter to Lord Byron* (1937), in *Collected Longer Poems* (1968) p. 41; Arnold Kettle (1951,I, 99) protests at the seeming ignorance of the novels on the question of 'class divisions' in the society they portray; Darrel Mansell (1973, p. ix) considers 'how the heroines become prepared to take their places in the world'; Wayne C. Booth's 'Control of Distance in Jane Austen's *Emma*' is a chapter in his *The Rhetoric of Fiction* (1961).
4. See also Iser's 'The Reading Process: A Phenomenological Approach', in *The Implied Reader* (1972; 1974).

NOTES TO CHAPTER 2. *NORTHANGER ABBEY*: SOME PROBLEMS OF ENGAGEMENT

1. Cassandra Austen's Memorandum (*Minor Works*, facing p. 242) gives some details of the composition of the novels. See also Chapman (1948, pp. 73–6). For Austen's late comment on *Northanger Abbey*, see *Letters*, p. 484.
2. Michael Sadleir (1927, pp. 3–23) has shown that the novels on

Isabella's list (*Northanger Abbey*, p. 40) make up a representative sample of the different kinds of Gothic novel. Chapman's edition of *Northanger Abbey* includes (pp. 306–12) an appendix on the links with *Udolpho*, and the even more striking similarities with Radcliffe's *The Romance of the Forest* (1791). Lascelles (1939, pp. 59–60) notes the complexity of the burlesque in *Northanger Abbey*. See also Moler (1968; 1977, pp. 17–28).

3. See Darton (1932; 1958, pp. 141–9, 158–62).
4. Sheridan, *The Rivals* (1775), in *Dramatic Works*, ed. Price (1973) I, 79–80, 78, 135.
5. Lascelles (1939, pp. 57–64) and Moler (1968; 1977, pp. 17–21, 37–41) both argue that *Northanger Abbey* is a Quixotic imitator; Litz (1965, pp. 61–2) suggests some differences between it and other imitators.
6. Barrett, *The Heroine* (1813) I, 16–18.
7. See also Tompkins (1932, pp. 113–4, 207).
8. Cervantes, *Don Quixote*, tr. Cohen (1950) pp. 434–5, 56–63.
9. Sir Walter Scott, *Waverley* (1814;1906, p. 82)
10. Yet even the incapacity is not complete. She points Catherine to the essential unreality of a Gothic novel by noticing the gross insufficiency of servants in their castles and abbeys (*Northanger Abbey*, p. 184). Ironically Catherine does not heed this one useful lesson.
11. For an account of the novel that treats it as if it *were* wholly founded on a Lockean epistemology, see De Rose (1980, pp. 15–35).
12. See also Mudrick, (1952, p. 53).
13. Litz, for example (1965, p. 69), sees incomplete competence in the way Henry is sometimes subjected to the narrator's irony. On the other hand, Howard S. Babb (1962; 1967, pp. 87, 106–11) rather too uncritically sees Henry as teacher to Catherine and assistant to the narrator.
14. This is of course one of the details in the novel that has been laboriously researched by those critics who would prove an immediate connection between the novel and its times. See Southam, (1976, pp. 122–7) and Roberts, (1979, pp. 22–33). It is surely obvious that the Tilneys are thinking of something that could actually happen in the real, contemporary world, and that their expectations are well-founded: that is what makes the contrast with what Catherine has in mind so incisive. Once this is established, it is surely unnecessary to sift through all public disturbances that Austen *might* have had in mind.
15. Lionel Trilling (1972; 1974, p. 77) is one of many to argue for Gothic possibilities in real life. Butler is one of the few to assert that the General is merely rude (1975, pp. 178–9).

NOTES TO CHAPTER 3. *SENSE AND SENSIBILITY*: IDEAS
AND ARGUMENTS

1. These are of course long-stated criticisms of the novel. See for example Lascelles (1939, pp. 157–9) and Litz (1965, pp. 72–4).
2. See Craik (1965, pp. 52–5), for instance.
3. Specific sources for *Sense and Sensibility* among contemporary didactic novelists have been suggested by Tompkins (1940, pp. 33–43), McKillop (1957, pp. 65–8) and Moler (1968; 1977, pp. 46–58).
4. The movement towards a combination goes back at least to Wright (1953; 1962, pp. 40–1), and since then it has been steadily advancing. See Wiesenfarth (1967, pp. 52–5) and Lloyd Brown (1973, pp. 22–3), for instance. Butler (1975, pp. 190–1, 194–6) wholly rejects the notion of a combination.
5. Despite Johnson's celebrated dislike of *Tom Jones* and his liking for *Clarissa*, he was said to prefer Amelia even to Clarissa, as a literary example of female virtue – Piozzi, *Anecdotes of Dr Johnson* (1786), ed. Sherbo (1974) p. 134.
6. Bate (1946; 1961, pp. 7, 160) provides a very useful introduction to eighteenth-century notions of taste. The question of Austen and taste has yet to be comprehensively treated: Martin Price (1965, p. 268) has briefly noted that Austen stresses the moral elements in taste; Lloyd Brown (1973, pp. 28–30) suggests but does not fully argue for a connection between Austen and Burke; Hermione Lee (1976, pp. 82–5) links 'taste' with 'tenderness' in Austen's novels, but is unconvincing on the eighteenth-century background to the issues.
7. Hume, *Of the Standard of Taste and Other Essays*, ed. Lenz (1965) pp. 25–8.
8. Ibid., pp. 3–24.
9. Burke, *A Philosophical Enquiry into the Origins of our Ideas of the Sublime and Beautiful*, ed. Boulton (1958) pp. 11–27.
10. For a full account of the background to Burke's 'On Taste', and its connection with Hume, see J. T. Boulton's Introduction to his edition of the *Enquiry into the Sublime and Beautiful*, pp. xxvii–xxxix. Reynolds, *Discourses on Art* (1769–90), ed. Wark (1975) pp. 117–42, 127.
11. Blair, *Lectures on Rhetoric and Belles Lettres* (1783) I, 15–33; Alison, *Essays on the Nature and Principles of Taste* (1790; 1968) pp. vii–xiii. Later still, Wordsworth, in his Preface to the 2nd edn of the *Lyrical Ballads* (1800), echoed Reynolds approvingly in stating that 'an *accurate* taste in poetry . . . is an *acquired* talent, which can only be produced by thought and a long-continued intercourse with the best models of composition' – *Poetical Works*, ed. Hutchinson

(1936) p. 741. Yet Blake, in his 'Annotations to Sir Joshua Reynolds's Discourses' (about 1808), specifically denied Reynolds's central argument about taste, asserting that 'Taste & Genius are Not Teachable or Acquirable, but are born with us' – *Complete Writings*, ed. Keynes (1966) p. 474.

12. Austen's admiration for Richardson, and for *Sir Charles Grandison* in particular, is well documented: see for instance James Edward Austen-Leigh, *Memoir of Jane Austen* (1870) p. 89. But then Austen also records the opinion, of heroines in novels, that 'pictures of perfection . . . make me sick & wicked' (*Letters*, pp. 486–7).
13. Richardson, *Sir Charles Grandison*, ed. Harris (1972) I, 465.
14. Defoe, *Moll Flanders*, ed. Starr (1971) p. 1.
15. Ibid., p. 8.
16. Though he makes some interesting points about Elinor's ambivalence, P. J. M. Scott (1982, p. 113) joins with many other critics in arguing that Austen's conception of Edward is unsuccessful.
17. Neither Edward nor Marianne is of course the neat half of one complete Wordsworthian, and Edward would probably be happier if the 'vagrant dwellers' ('Tintern Abbey', line 20) were under the proper care of the parish: the point is that aspects of Wordsworthian thinking can be traced in both.
18. Hardy (1975, pp. 72–5) treats this encounter in a way that is notably more favourable to Elinor.
19. Even those critics who smile at this point still condemn Marianne's part: see Tave (1973, pp. 92–5), for example.

NOTES TO CHAPTER 4. *PRIDE AND PREJUDICE*:
INFORMAL ARGUMENTS

1. Sterne, *The Life and Opinions of Tristram Shandy*, ed. Petrie (1967) pp. 77, 160.
2. Ibid., pp. 130–1.
3. Ibid., p. 133.
4. Some critics merely see a muddle in Austen's thinking here: see Butler (1975, p. 214).
5. As Tanner (1972, pp. 37–8) points out, 'Charlotte is only doing what the economic realities of her society – as Jane Austen makes abundantly clear – all but force her to do'.
6. Sir Walter Scott, unsigned review of *Emma* (1815, pp. 194–5). At least one critic has attempted a sophisticated defence of Scott's account: see McCann (1964, pp. 73–4).
7. Wickham and Lydia actually make an even more stark contrast with Darcy, and their income when they marry is less than half

that of Edward and Elinor: see note 17, below. Several critics have noted the great substance of Darcy's wealth: see for example Duckworth (1971, pp. 86–8).

8. The argument about the decline of the gentry was probably first given developed utterance by Joseph M. Duffy, Jr (1954b, pp. 272–89). Of the many subsequent versions, the most sustained are Duckworth's (1971) and Butler's (1975). Butler later (1981, pp. 98–109) restated her case in a way which strikingly reveals both the strengths and the weaknesses of this line of argument. Austen is declared to be 'the gentry's greatest artist', and her novels are said to have typically anti-jacobin plots: this leads to the claim that she 'is writing defensively', and that she 'never allows us to contemplate any other ideology'.

9. See also Mingay, (1976, pp. 1–17, 73–9). And see Spring (1983, pp. 53–72) for interesting thoughts on Austen and history – even if he does on occasion link Emma's views too easily with those of her author.

10. See Leavis (1941, pp. 76–8) and Southam (1964, pp. 63–78, 145–8).

11. Ronald Paulson's account (1967, p. 297) of the complex relationship between heroine and reader in this novel is perhaps closest to the truth: he detects 'the illusion of being outside Elizabeth and seeing her errors and at the same time seeing the world largely through her ironic intelligence'.

12. There is for example the argument that 'marriage is not commonly unhappy, otherwise than as life is unhappy', and mention of the 'ancient custom of the Muscovites' whereby couples did not meet until they were married, since courtship merely allows individuals 'to hinder themselves from being known, and to disguise their natural temper, and real desires, in hypocritical imitation, studied compliance, and continued affectation' – Johnson, *Works*, III (1969) 243–7.

13. Ibid., p. 192.

14. Edgeworth, *The Absentee* (1910 edn) p. 281; Sir Walter Scott, *Waverley* (1906 edn) p. 477; Wordsworth, *Poetical Works*, ed. Hutchinson, pp. 734–5; Coleridge, *Biographia Literaria* (1817), ed. Watson (1956) pp. 188–200.

15. This is counter to the vigorous arguments of a number of critics: see Brower (1951; 1962, p. 180), for example. Lloyd Brown (1973, p. 168) tentatively rejects the arguments.

16. Mr Bennet's views are generally reasonable, if we allow that he does not have the advantage of hindsight: there is nothing to suggest that Lydia would not have eloped from Longbourn, had circumstances so arisen. But many critics have been very quick to damn him: see Burgan (1975, pp. 536–43).

17. The settlement consists of an annual allowance for Lydia of £100 during the life of her father, and £50 when he is dead (*Pride and Prejudice*, p. 302). To this Darcy adds a sum 'considerably more than a thousand pounds' to pay Wickham's debts, another thousand settled on Lydia, and he buys Wickham's commission as an ensign (p. 324). At the time of the Peninsular War (1808–12) an ensign in the infantry paid £400 for his commission and drew £80 a year in pay (Halévy, 1913; 1949, p. 80). The whole affair therefore cost Darcy about £3000, and the Wickhams' annual income is £230. It is not merely because they are profligate that they are always in need of money (*Pride and Prejudice*, p. 387).

18. Mansell (1973, p. 106) notes the significance of Elizabeth's formal acknowledgement, but completely misses the meaning of Elizabeth's words before she gives Wickham her hand, and their effect, since he concludes that she 'has let her critical temper relax to keep the family together, and so has her author'.

NOTES TO CHAPTER 5.   *MANSFIELD PARK*: COMPROMISES

1. For example, Mansell (1973) finds the narrative 'leaden and witless' (p. 109), discovers 'a dismaying amount of direct or diaphanous sermonising' (p. 111) and so embarks upon a search for biographical and literary evidence that in *Mansfield Park* Austen was rejecting wit and liveliness.

2. For the history of the argument about Austen and the Evangelicals, see Garside and McDonald (1975, pp. 34–50), who affirm the influence on the novel, and Monaghan (1978, pp. 215–30), who denies it. Both studies rely heavily on the assumption that Austen was anxious to defend the gentry.

3. See Lloyd Brown (1973) for possible links with Johnson and Shaftesbury (pp. 49–50), Swift (pp. 90–1), Burke, Cowper and Addison (pp. 94–6). Duckworth (1971, pp. 38–55) places Austen on the side of Burke and Cowper, and against Repton and Godwin. On the controversy between Repton and Price, and a potential connection with *Mansfield Park*, see Butler (1979, pp. 30–7).

4. At one extreme there is Kingsley Amis (1957, p. 439), for whom Fanny is a 'monster of complacency and pride'; at the other there is Tony Tanner (1966, pp. 35–6, 20), for whom she is 'never, ever, wrong', is indeed an example of 'Anglican sainthood'. Amis claims that Austen allows Mary to exist too much as a foil for Fanny, while for Tanner she is 'frankly selfish and ambitious'. For attempts to occupy the middle ground, see Ellis (1969, pp. 107–19) and Moler (1975, pp. 172–9).

5. See Morgan (1980, pp. 133–6), for other suggested ways in which Fanny is like rather than unlike other Austen heroines.

6. See Cassandra Austen's Memorandum (*Minor Works*, facing p. 242). The process by which some letters were lost and others suppressed or edited can of course merely be guessed at: even the existence of this substantial gap can only be the subject of idle conjecture. There are several other gaps of about the same length, and one – May 1801 to September 1804 – is considerably longer.

7. The most usual explanations before Brogan's letter were either those of Chapman (1948, p. 82), who argued that Austen's statement 'cannot mean what it seems to mean', or of Trilling (1954, p. 498), who claimed that the question of ordination is crucial in the novel, but that it 'is not really a religious question . . . rather, a cultural question, having to do with the meaning and effect of a *profession*'.

8. The case for linking Austen's criticism of *Pride and Prejudice* with *Mansfield Park* has been most clearly stated by Litz (1965, pp. 112–31).

9. As at the end of the ball, when Sir Thomas approaches Fanny, 'advising her to go immediately to bed. . . .In thus sending her away, Sir Thomas perhaps might not be thinking merely of her health. It might occur to him, that Mr Crawford had been sitting by her long enough, or he might mean to recommend her as a wife by shewing her persuadability' (*Mansfield Park*, pp. 280–1).

10. Editions of Porteus's *Works* came out in 1811 and 1813; there was a new edition of Sherlock's *Several Discourses* in 1812. Some impressive-looking structures have claimed support from Austen's single favourable reference to the Evangelicals. Butler (1975, 62–3, 285–6) quotes the comment but does not give the context, declares 1814 to be 'the year of *Mansfield Park*', when it is much more properly that of *Emma*, and explains away Austen's later unfavourable reference as a rejection not of Evangelicalism but of the 'wing' of the Evangelicals influenced by Calvinism and Methodism – a 'wing' that Butler herself later denies ever existed, when the needs of her own argument have changed.

11. For a full account of the Evangelicals see Ford K. Brown (1961, esp. pp. 4–6, 26–30).

12. Wilberforce, *A Practical View of the Prevailing Religious System* (1797) pp. 7–8.

13. Gisborne, *Enquiry into the Duties of the Female Sex* (1801 edn) pp. 53–6, 71, 80–3, 183–4, 239.

14. More, *Works* (1830) V, 43–4, 123, 142–57.

15. On the popularity of More's novel, see Jones (1952, p. 193). For the Evangelicals' view of novels see Wilberforce, *A Practical View*,

pp. 383–5; Gisborne, *Enquiry*, pp. 226–30; More, *Works*, V, 22–6.
16. Ibid., VII, 45.
17. Law, *A Serious Call to a Devout and Holy Life* (1906 end) pp. 246–67.
18. Consider, for example, the efforts of some of Rousseau's English followers: Day, *The History of Sandford and Merton* (1783–9), or Maria Edgeworth's *Belinda* (1801) in *Tales and Novels* (1832–3) XI, 317–31, and XII, 131–222, with its account of false distinctions between the sexes, of the 'rights of woman', of the corruptions which life in society encourages, of alternative and more wholesome ways of bringing up children.
19. Wollstonecraft, *Vindication of the Rights of Woman*, ed. Kramnick (1975) pp. 317, 147–50. See Gisborne, *Enquiry*, pp. 239–42, 90–1, for example, on the differences between the sexes, and on rank; by contrast, see Wollstonecraft, *Vindication*, pp. 174–5.
20. Ibid., pp. 83, 269, 221, 289, 275–8, 306–9.
21. Leroy W. Smith (1983, pp. 3, 23–4) gives an outline of the critical history of this notion, and states his own version. Margaret Kirkham (1983, pp. 39–50) presents her account; she points to similarities between Wollstonecraft and More, but fails to take due account of the necessary differences between them.
22. See Tanner (1966, pp. 10–14) on Mansfield as an ideal; Lodge, (1966, pp. 96–9) on Mansfield as an ideal of which the inhabitants are unworthy.
23. Fleishman (1967, pp. 43–50) takes his model from Alfred Adler, and argues that Fanny is a 'weak woman with self-defensive and self-aggrandizing impulses' which take the form of 'moral aggressiveness'.
24. Even those who are not unaware of the difficult balance between Mary and Fanny tend to betray their prejudices here. Morgan (1980, pp. 155, 142), for example, comes down too easily on Fanny's side.
25. Mansell (1973, p. 125) makes the point about the rose-cutting. Butler (1975, p. 248) suggests that Fanny's 'feebleness' is a failed attempt by Austen to make her heroine 'more "human" and therefore more appealing'. Trilling (1954, p. 498) states that Fanny is part of a tradition of frail heroines that stretches from Clarissa Harlowe to Milly Theale.
26. Shorter, *The Brontës: Life and Letters* (1908) II, 127; and I, 388. Other responses to Brontë's claim have been made by Juliet McMaster (1974, pp. 5–24) and Barbara Hardy (1975, pp. 36–40).
27. See Moler (1968; 1977, pp. 123–7, 114–15, 147–8) and Bradbrook (1966, pp. 78, 107–8).
28. See *The Spectator* (1711–14), ed. Bond (1965) I, 86–8, on starers; I,

227–8, on peepers; II, 120–1, on giggling and ogling; II, 600, and III, 8–9, on flirting; IV, 284–7, on attention-getting. Richardson's contribution to *The Rambler*, no. 97, may be found in Johnson, *Works*, IV (1969) 153–9. Austen had already poked fun at this number of *The Rambler*, albeit not on the question of behaviour in church, in *Northanger Abbey* (p. 30).

29. Maria's career is the reverse of that of the character in the play: Agatha starts in disgrace and ends with honour. Litz (1965, p. 124) is one of the critics who traces connections between play and novel. And Mansell (1973, pp. 126–9) gives a concise indication of the many diverse interpretations which the episode of the theatricals has inspired.

30. As is D. D. Devlin (1975, pp. 104–9), for example.

31. Is Mary's letter 'remarkably indiscreet', as Lascelles (1939, p. 175) claims? Only really so if we remember the somewhat dubious use to which Fanny puts it (*Mansfield Park*, p. 459). See Fleishman (1967, pp. 79–80) for a rather sensationalised rendering of Fanny's dubiety.

32. Joel C. Weinsheimer (1974, pp. 193–4) rightly notes that this is the 'language of Gothic sensibility'.

NOTES TO CHAPTER 6. *EMMA*: MYSTERY AND IMAGINATION

1. For the pejoratively inclined accounts of *Emma* and imagination, see for instance Litz (1965, pp. 136–43), Moler (1968; 1977, pp. 155–6), and Mansell (1973, pp. 146–51), who writes of 'illusion' and 'fact'. Trilling (1957; 1967, p. 53) makes more allowance for imagination, by pointing out that its workings are not necessarily unhealthy. For more recent attempts to take a balanced view of the question see note 15, below.

2. Mudrick (1952, pp. 195–6) does so when he insists that we must see Mr Woodhouse as, among other things, an 'annoyance', an 'idiot', and a 'parasitic plant'. In the novel itself, there is John Knightley's not always amusing impatience with his father-in-law.

3. On intelligence see Julia Brown (1979, p. 125); on the interplay between the social and the moral see Schorer (1959, pp. 170–87); on emotions see Babb (1962; 1967, pp. 187–91); on sex see Duffy (1954a, p. 40); on lesbian possibilities see Wilson (1944; 1950, p. 202). Weinsheimer (1975, pp. 93–4) values Emma's love for her father; Mansell (1973, pp. 151–2) does not. For Trilling (1957; 1967, p. 53) Emma's actions are 'meant to be truly creative', and the demand she makes of life is 'in its essence, a poet's demand'; for Butler (1975, pp. 251–4) Emma's actions are to be strictly cen-

sured. Ronald Blythe (1966, pp. 16–17) praises Knightley; Wright (1953; 1962, pp. 155–9) finds minor flaws in him; J. F. Burrows (1968, pp. 9–13) finds significant flaws.

4. Booth is not, of course, incapable of conceiving of an 'unreliable' narrator, but his categories are such that they determine *when* he can form the conception – with Henry James, and in explicit contrast to what Booth sees as an earlier and much simpler state of affairs (1961, pp. 339–46).

5. Critics of *Emma* are not always as conscious of this as they might be, and it has become common to assume that Emma's errors about Mr Elton, for example, are so obvious that they should be obvious to *her*: see Litz (1965, pp. 136–7) and Tave (1973, p. 217). But Norman Page (1972, p. 43) rightly observes that Elton is often 'genuinely though unwittingly ambiguous'.

6. James, *The Portrait of a Lady* (1963 edn) pp. 408, 239–41.

7. The very location and topography of Highbury are given with an apparent precision and comprehensiveness. Yet, as Chapman notes, we cannot actually locate its position on a map of Kent, or ourselves draw a map of its streets and lanes: the picture is ambiguous and incomplete (*Emma*, p. 521).

8. Eliot, *Middlemarch*, ed. Harvey (1965) p. 312.

9. William and Richard Arthur Austen-Leigh, *Jane Austen* (1913; 1965) p. 307.

10. It is crucially a matter of timing. Had Mrs Churchill's 'seizure' happened a little earlier (she is dead within thirty-six hours of his return from Box Hill) he would not have been at Box Hill and quarrelling with Jane, and Jane would not have written to terminate the engagement. Without that spur, we can only guess at how long it would have taken Frank to mention the subject of his engagement to his uncle. It is natural, in the circumstances, for Frank to write a reply to Jane and to forget to post it, thus making Jane write the second letter, but the contents of the unposted letter and their effect on Jane can only be surmised. The timing of every detail in the sequence works directly or indirectly to Frank's advantage.

11. For the very public treatment of scandals connected with the royal family, especially the Prince Regent and the Princess, see Halévy (1913; 1949, pp. 6–8) and Watson (1960, pp. 447–8).

12. Flaubert, *Madame Bovary* (1856–7), tr. Russell (1950) pp. 48–51. 'And Emma wondered exactly what was meant in life by the words "bliss", "passion", "ecstasy", which had looked so beautiful in books' (p. 47).

13. There is a good deal of confusion about *Elegant Extracts*, and it is often assumed to be a merely 'frivolous' collection: see Nardin (1981, p. 135), for instance. In fact the *British Library Catalogue* lists

no fewer than three collections of poetry with this title, first published between 1770 and 1815, none of which are 'frivolous'. Blythe (1966, p. 467) appears rather uncertainly to opt for *Elegant Extracts in Miniature* (1796), but this is a collection largely of prose, and it is not inclined to amuse its readers with riddles. The most likely choice – it is also Chapman's – was compiled by Vicesimus Knox (1789), and by 1816 had gone through ten editions: it also has the most substantial collection of riddles and epigrams, though still only a small part of the whole.

14. Gay, *Fables* (1967 edn) p. 172.
15. Tave (1973, pp. 205–37) and Morgan (1980, pp. 23–50) illustrate a recent trend towards larger claims for imagination in *Emma*, and both stress the usefulness of an accurate intuitive understanding. Neither, though, actually makes very significant claims for imagination. Tave, for example, argues that Knightley has 'the right kind of imagination' but this is not much different from simple good sense: 'What touches him, what he will speak to, is what he has seen' (1973, pp. 232–3). Morgan argues Wordsworthian affinities, but her instancing of the 'Immortality' ode is sadly uninforming: 'Both the ode and *Emma* are centrally concerned with the growth of a person's consciousness' (1980, p. 44).
16. Locke, *An Essay Concerning Human Understanding*, ed. Nidditch (1975) pp. 104, 117.
17. She makes only one reference to Wordsworth, and that is in *Sanditon*: since it is an enthusiastic allusion by Sir Edward Denham, it is of doubtful significance (*Minor Works*, p. 397).
18. See Bullitt and Bate (1945, pp. 8–15); Addison, in *The Spectator*, II, 566–7. See also ibid., I, 54, 421 and II, 36–40, 157–60, 396; Shaftesbury, *Characteristics* (1711), ed. Robertson (1963) I, 106, 201–9. Several attempts, none more than conjectural, have been made to connect Shaftesbury with Austen: see Ryle (1966; 1968, pp. 118–22).
19. Johnson, *The Rambler*, *Works*, IV, 58; III, 318; IV, 300. See also *The Idler*, *Works*, II, 39, 181; *The Rambler*, *Works*, III, 16, 337, 356–8.
20. Johnson, *Rasselas*, ed. Tillotson and Jenkins (1971) p. 269.
21. *Shelley's Prose*, ed. Clark (1954, pp. 278–9).
22. Humphrey House (1953; 1962, p. 79) notes this similarity between Cowper and Coleridge, but observes only the immediate context of the Cowper, and so concludes that there is a significant contrast in mood between the two: that is to ignore the fact that Cowper's 'indolence' is in explicit contrast to the active venturings of the mind which he has just described.
23. *Elegant Extracts* includes a large section from book IV of *The Task*, and the first 193 lines are given complete: that of course does not include 'myself creating what I saw'.

24. See Liddell (1963; 1974, p. 111). Blythe (1966, p. 19) is less crass on the question of rank, but he does appear to think that Emma's ideas, even her worst excesses, are reflections of views actually held by Austen.
25. Cf. Burke, *Reflections on the Revolution in France* (1790), ed. O'Brien (1968) pp. 193–5, with Paine, *Rights of Man* (1791–2), ed. Collins (1969) pp. 64–5, 69–70.
26. The very words 'rights of man' were of course highly charged, and it is impossible for anyone to have used them in 1814 or 1815 without being aware of their connotations. But Austen's usage is a strange one, so strange that it probably often goes unnoticed. The possibility of holding a ball at the Crown is under discussion, and Mrs Weston's suggestion that there be 'no regular supper' is rejected as 'an infamous fraud upon the rights of men and women' (*Emma*, p. 254). Doubtless this is partly at the expense of the phrase as a cliché, but it is also at the expense of Frank and Emma.

NOTES TO CHAPTER 7. *PERSUASION*: BECOMING A NOVEL, CREATING A HEROINE

1. See for example Nina Auerbach (1972, p. 113): she tries to link with *The Tempest* on the grounds that the 'tragic motifs' in *Persuasion* are reworkings from earlier novels.
2. It is often assumed that even the choice of title for *Persuasion* was Henry Austen's rather than his sister's, but the note in Austen's hand giving the dates of composition of her last three novels (reproduced in Chapman's edition of *Plan of a Novel*, p. 36) shows her using the title *Persuasion*.
3. See Cassandra Austen's Memorandum (*Minor Works*, facing p. 242), and Southam (1964, pp. 101–2). Henry Austen managed to get *Northanger Abbey* and *Persuasion* published within six months of his sister's death; *Pride and Prejudice* came out within about three months of being sold to a publisher, but to that must be added the time taken for the preliminary negotiations (*Northanger Abbey*, p. xiii; *Pride and Prejudice*, p. xi).
4. See also the exchange of letters between Southam and Gomme on *Persuasion* (1966, pp. 480, 481); and Bradbury (1968, pp. 383–96).
5. See also Mansell (1973, pp. 191, 195–6, 198–204). For other attempts to 'explain' Mrs Smith, see Rackin (1972, pp. 52–80) and Collins (1975, pp. 383–97). Collins also notes (p. 384) the fault in Zietlow's argument for a *deus ex machina*.
6. Duckworth later qualifies his point about headships of families by claiming parsonages as the alternative reward for some of the heroines (1971, p. 184), but this ignores the insecurities that a

parsonage can imply, as the novels make clear. For other pessimistic readings of *Persuasion*, see Litz (1965, pp. 153–4) and Julia Brown (1979, p. 149).

7. Austen seems to have borrowed at least one joke from Edgeworth's novel. The Duchess of Torcaster wrongly assumes that Lord Colambre is not Irish, because of his fine 'manner' (*The Absentee*, p. 85). Austen inverts this: Lady Dalrymple has no qualms about her own Irishness, and seems actually to feel that only the best can be Irish. Thus she takes Wentworth by his fine 'air' to be Irish (p. 188).

8. Godwin, *Enquiry Concerning Political Justice* (1798), ed. Kramnick (1976) pp. 467–71; Paine, *Rights of Man*, ed. Collins, p. 105.

9. See Maria Edgeworth's letter to Mrs Ruxton, 1818, in Frances Anne Edgeworth, *A Memoir of Maria Edgeworth* (1867) II, 6; and Richard Whately, unsigned review of *Northanger Abbey* and *Persuasion* (1821, pp. 368–75). By contrast, see the anonymous review of *Northanger Abbey* and *Persuasion* (1818, p. 301).

10. On the question of who is wrong and who changes, the majority verdict points to Wentworth, and finds Anne in varying approximations to what Craik (1965, p. 167) sees as all but perfect. But some insist that there is a significant development in Anne, and some, such as Bradbury (1968, pp. 388–91), see the possibilities of Kellynch and her cousin as a significant temptation and test for Anne. On persuasion and persuadability see Rackin (1972, pp. 53–4, 77–9); on advice and evidence see Collins (1975, pp. 383–97); on growth and decay see Duffy (1954b, pp. 274–6); on dignity and duty see Wiesenfarth (1967, pp. 139–66); on reason and feeling see Morgan (1980, pp. 167, 171–6); on perception and feeling see Kroeber (1971, pp. 79–84); on memory and feeling see Ruoff (1976, p. 347).

11. *Pride and Prejudice* is an interesting comparison since Elizabeth Bennet is, after Anne, the slowest to reach the centre of the stage. But Elizabeth begins to move to the centre even in the first chapter, and Darcy snubs her only ten pages into the novel. *Mansfield Park* is also interesting, because, though Fanny Price is not central to the place, there is no doubt about her place in the novel.

12. See also Booth (1961, p. 251).

13. This line of argument goes back at least to Mudrick (1952, pp. 215–18).

14. Dickens, *Our Mutual Friend*, ed. Gill (1971) p. 53.

15. Others have touched on the way *Persuasion* is made up of many possible stories. Zietlow (1965, pp. 185–6), for example, builds too much on individual possibilities, and so does not respond to their range and variety. See also Tave (1973, pp. 280–2).

16. James, *The Wings of the Dove* (1965 edn) p. 84.
17. See also Butler (1975, pp. 278–9). Booth's two other 'occasions' on which we depart from Anne's consciousness are on p. 61 of *Persuasion*, when we see why Wentworth said he found Anne 'so altered', and on pp. 177–8, when we linger momentarily with the ladies of Wentworth's party, to hear their comments on Anne's prettiness.
18. This is of course a much-discussed episode, especially by those who wish to disapprove. See Gomme (1966, pp. 171–2) and Julia Brown (1979, p. 133).
19. Burney, *Cecilia* (1782) II, 161. It is an allusion that would probably have been caught instantly by most of Austen's contemporary readers, and is all but lost to us. Chapman does all that can be done, by giving the source and a brief quotation from the conversation of Miss Larolles, but fully to get the point it is probably necessary to have read *Cecilia*.

Bibliography

The bibliography lists only those works cited by this study. For more complete coverage see Keynes (1931), Chapman (1953), Roth and Weinsheimer (1973), and Gilson (1982), listed below.

Addison, Joseph: see *The Spectator*.

Alison, Archibald, *Essays on the Nature and Principles of Taste* (1790; Hildesheim, 1968).

Amis, Kingsley, 'What Became of Jane Austen?', *The Spectator*, 4 Oct 1957, pp. 439–40.

Anonymous, review of *Northanger Abbey* and *Persuasion*, *British Critic*, n.s. IX (Mar 1818) 293–301.

ApRoberts, Ruth, '*Sense and Sensibility*, or Growing up Dichotomous', *Nineteenth-Century Fiction*, XXX (1975) 351–65.

Auden, W. H., *Letter to Lord Byron* (1937), in *Collected Longer Poems* (London, 1968).

Auerbach, Nina, 'O Brave New World: Evolution and Revolution in *Persuasion*', *ELH*, XXXIX (1972) 112–28.

Austen-Leigh, James Edward, *Memoir of Jane Austen* (1870), ed. R. W. Chapman (Oxford, 1926).

Austen-Leigh, William and Richard Arthur, *Jane Austen* (1913; New York, 1965).

Babb, Howard S., *Jane Austen's Novels: The Fabric of Dialogue* (1962; Hamden, Conn., 1967).

Bage, Robert, *Hermsprong* (1796), ed. Vaughan Wilkins (London, 1951).

Barrett, Eaton Stannard, *The Heroine*, 3 vols (London, 1813).

Bate, Walter Jackson, 'Distinctions between Fancy and Imagination in Eighteenth-century English Criticism': see Bullitt.

——, *From Classic to Romantic* (1946; New York, 1961).

Blair, Hugh, *Lectures on Rhetoric and Belles Lettres* (London, 1783).

Blake, William, *Complete Writings*, ed. Geoffrey Keynes (London, 1966).

Bloom, Harold (ed.), *From Sensibility to Romanticism*: see Hilles.

Blythe, Ronald, Introduction to *Emma* (Harmondsworth, 1966).

Booth, Wayne C., *The Rhetoric of Fiction* (Chicago, 1961).

Bradbrook, Frank W., *Jane Austen and her Predecessors* (Cambridge, 1966).

Bradbury, Malcolm, '*Persuasion* Again', *Essays in Criticism*, XVIII (1968) 383–96.

Brogan, Hugh, letter on *Mansfield Park*, *The Times Literary Supplement*, 19 Dec 1968, p. 1440.

Brontë, Charlotte, *Jane Eyre* (1847), ed. Q. D. Leavis (Harmondsworth, 1966).

Brower, Reuben A., 'Light and Bright and Sparkling: Irony and Fiction in *Pride and Prejudice*', in *The Fields of Light* (1951; New York, 1962).

Brown, Ford K., *Fathers of the Victorians: The Age of Wilberforce* (Cambridge, 1961).

Brown, Julia, *Jane Austen's Novels: Social Change and Literary Form* (Cambridge, Mass., 1979).

Brown, Lloyd W., *Bits of Ivory* (Baton Rouge, La., 1973).

Browning, Robert, *The Ring and the Book* (1868–9), ed. Richard D. Altick (Harmondsworth, 1971).

Bullitt, John, and Walter Jackson Bate, 'Distinctions between Fancy and Imagination in Eighteenth-century English Criticism', *Modern Language Notes*, LX (1945) 8–15.

Burgan, Mary A., 'Mr Bennet and the Failures of Fatherhood in Jane Austen's Novels', *JEGP*, LXXIV (1975) 536–52.

Burke, Edmund, *A Philosophical Enquiry into the Origins of our Ideas of the Sublime and Beautiful* (1757–9), ed. J. T. Boulton (London, 1958).

——, *Reflections on the Revolution in France* (1790), ed. Conor Cruise O'Brien (Harmondsworth, 1968).

Burlin, Katrin Ristkok, ' "The Pen of the Contriver": The Four Fictions of *Northanger Abbey*', in *Jane Austen: Bicentenary Essays*, ed. John Halperin (Cambridge, 1975).

Burney, Fanny, *Evelina* (1778), ed. Edward A. Bloom (London, 1970).

——, *Cecilia*, 5 vols (London, 1782).

Burrows, J. F., *Jane Austen's 'Emma'* (Sydney, 1968).

Butler, Marilyn, *Jane Austen and the War of Ideas* (Oxford, 1975).

——, *Peacock Displayed* (London, 1979).

——, *Romantics, Rebels and Reactionaries* (Oxford, 1981).

Byron, George Gordon, Lord, *Don Juan*, ed. T. G. Steffan, E. Steffan and W. W. Pratt (Harmondsworth, 1977).

Cervantes Saavedra, Miguel de, *Don Quixote*, tr. J. M. Cohen (Harmondsworth, 1950).

Chapman, R. W., *Jane Austen: Facts and Problems* (Oxford, 1948).

——, *Jane Austen: A Critical Bibliography* (1953; Oxford, 1955).

——, 'A Reply to Mr Duffy on *Persuasion*', *Nineteenth-Century Fiction*, IX (1954) 154.

Coleridge, Samuel Taylor, *Poetical Works*, ed. Ernest Hartley Coleridge (London, 1967).

____, *Biographia Literaria* (1817), ed. George Watson (London, 1956).

Collins, K. K., 'Mrs Smith and the Morality of *Persuasion*', *Nineteenth-Century Fiction*, XXX (1975) 383–97.

Congreve, William, *The Way of the World* (1700), ed. Brian Gibbons (London, 1971).

Cowper, William, *The Poetical Works*, ed. H. S. Milford (London, 1934).

Craik, W. A., *Jane Austen: The Six Novels* (London, 1965).

Crane, R. S., *The Idea of the Humanities*, 2 vols (Chicago, 1967).

Darton, F. J. Harvey, *Children's Books in England* (1932; Cambridge, 1958).

Day, Thomas, *The History of Sandford and Merton* (1783–9; London, 1878).

Defoe, Daniel, *Moll Flanders* (1722), ed. G. A. Starr (London, 1971).

de Genlis, Stéphanie Félicite Brulart, *Adéle et Théodore*, 3 vols (Paris, 1782): tr. anonymously as *Adelaide and Theodore*, 3 vols (London, 1783).

De Rose, Peter L., *Jane Austen and Samuel Johnson* (Washington, DC, 1980).

Devlin, D. D., *Jane Austen and Education* (London, 1975).

Dickens, Charles, *Our Mutual Friend* (1865), ed. Stephen Gill (Harmondsworth, 1971).

Duckworth, Alistair M., *The Improvement of the Estate* (Baltimore, 1971).

Duffy, Joseph M., Jr, '*Emma*: The Awakening from Innocence', *ELH*, XXI (1954a) 39–53.

____, 'Structure and Idea in Jane Austen's *Persuasion*', *Nineteenth-Century Fiction*, VIII (1954b) 272–89.

Edgeworth, Maria, *Angelina: or, L'Amie Inconnue* (1801), vol. III of *Tales and Novels* (London, 1832–3).

____, *Belinda* (1801), vols XI and XII of *Tales and Novels* (London, 1832–3).

____, *The Absentee* (1812), in *'Castle Rackrent' and 'The Absentee'* (London, 1910).

____, letter to Mrs Ruxton, 21 Feb 1818, in Frances Anne Edgeworth, *A Memoir of Maria Edgeworth*, 3 vols (London, 1867).

Elegant Extracts: see Knox.

Eliot, George, *Middlemarch* (1871–2), ed. W. J. Harvey (Harmondsworth, 1965).

Ellis, David, 'The Irony of *Mansfield Park*', *Critical Review*, XII (1969) 107–19.

Farrer, Reginald, 'Jane Austen, *ob.* July 18, 1817', *Quarterly Review*, CCXXVIII (1917) 1–30.

Fergus, Jan, *Jane Austen and the Didactic Novel: 'Northanger Abbey', 'Sense and Sensibility' and 'Pride and Prejudice'* (London, 1983).

Fielding, Henry, *'Joseph Andrews' and 'Shamela'* (1742, 1741), ed. A. R. Humphreys (London, 1973).

——, *Tom Jones* (1749), ed. R. P. C. Mutter (Harmondsworth, 1966).

——, *Amelia* (1751), ed. A. R. Humphreys (London, 1974).

Flaubert, Gustave, *Madame Bovary* (1856–7). tr. Alan Russell (Harmondsworth, 1950).

Fleishman, Avrom, *A Reading of 'Mansfield Park'* (Minneapolis, 1967).

Garside, Peter, and McDonald, Elizabeth, 'Evangelicalism and *Mansfield Park*', *Trivium*, X (1975) 34–49.

Gay, John, *Fables* (1727, 1738; Los Angeles, 1967).

Gilson, David, *A Bibliography of Jane Austen* (Oxford, 1982).

Gisborne, Thomas, *Enquiry into the Duties of the Female Sex* (1797; London, 1801).

Godwin, William, *Enquiry Concerning Political Justice* (1798), ed. Isaac Kramnik (Harmondsworth, 1976).

Gomme, Andor, 'On Not Being Persuaded', *Essays in Criticism*, XVI (1966) 170–84.

——, letter on *Persuasion*, *Essays in Criticism*, XVI (1966) 481.

Goodin, George (ed.), *The English Novel in the Nineteenth Century* (Urbana, Ill., 1972).

Graves, Richard, *The Spiritual Quixote* (1773), ed. Clarence Tracy (London, 1967).

Greene, Donald, 'Jane Austen and the Peerage', *PMLA*, LXVIII (1953) 1017–31.

Halévy, Elie, *England in 1815* (1913), tr. E. I. Watkin and D. A. Barker (London, 1949).

Halperin, John (ed.), *Jane Austen: Bicentenary Essays* (Cambridge, 1975).

Harding, D. W., Introduction to *Persuasion* (Harmondsworth, 1965).

——, 'Two Aspects of Jane Austen's Development', *Theoria*, XXXV (1970) 1–16.

Hardy, Barbara, *A Reading of Jane Austen* (London, 1975).

Harvey, W. J., 'The Plot of *Emma*', *Essays in Criticism*, XVII (1967) 48–63.

Hilles, Frederick W., and Bloom, Harold (eds), *From Sensibility to Romanticism* (New York, 1965).

House, Humphrey, *Coleridge* (1953; London, 1962).

Hume, David, *A Treatise of Human Nature* (1739–40), ed. L. A. Selby-Bigge, rev. P. H. Nidditch (Oxford, 1978).

——, 'Of the Delicacy of Taste and Passion' (1741), in *Of the Standard of Taste and Other Essays*, ed. John W. Lenz (Indianapolis, 1965).

——, 'Of the Standard of Taste' (1757), in *Of the Standard and Other Essays*, ed. John W. Lenz (Indianapolis, 1965).

Inchbald, Elizabeth (tr.), *Lovers' Vows*: see Kotzebue.

Iser, Wolfgang, *The Implied Reader* (1972; Baltimore, 1974).

——, *The Act of Reading* (1976; London, 1978).

James, Henry, *The Portrait of a Lady* (1880–1; Harmondsworth, 1963).

_____, 'Gustave Flaubert' (1902), in *The House of Fiction*, ed. Leon Edel (London, 1957).

_____, *The Wings of the Dove* (1902; Harmondsworth, 1965).

Johnson, Samuel, *The Rambler* (1750–2), 3 vols, ed. W. J. Bate and Albrecht B. Strauss (New Haven, Conn., 1969): vols III–V of *The Yale Edition of the Works of Samuel Johnson*.

_____, *'The Idler'* and *'The Adventurer'* (1758–60, 1753–4), ed. W. J. Bate, John M. Bullitt and L. F. Powell (New Haven, Conn., 1963): vol. II of *The Yale Edition of the Works of Samuel Johnson*.

_____, *Rasselas* (1759), ed. Geoffrey Tillotson and Brian Jenkins (London, 1971).

Jones, M. G., *Hannah More* (Cambridge, 1952).

Kearful, Frank J., 'Satire and the Form of the Novel: The Problem of Aesthetic Unity in *Northanger Abbey*', *ELH*, XXXII (1965) 511–27.

Kettle, Arnold, *An Introduction to the English Novel*, I (London, 1951).

Keynes, Geoffrey, *Jane Austen: A Bibliography* (London, 1931).

Kirkham, Margaret, *Jane Austen, Feminism and Fiction* (Brighton, 1983).

Kliger, Samuel, 'Jane Austen's *Pride and Prejudice* in the Eighteenth-century Mode', *University of Toronto Quarterly*, XVI (1947) 357–71.

Knox, Vicesimus (compiler), *Elegant Extracts, or Useful and Entertaining Pieces of Poetry* (London, 1789).

Kotzebue, August von, *Lovers' Vows*, tr. Elizabeth Inchbald, in *Mansfield Park*, ed. Chapman, pp. 475–538.

Kroeber, Karl, *Styles in Fictional Structure* (Princeton, NJ, 1971).

_____, *'Pride and Prejudice*: Fiction's Lasting Novelty', in *Jane Austen: Bicentenary Essays*, ed. John Halperin (Cambridge, 1975).

Lascelles, Mary, *Jane Austen and her Art* (London, 1939).

Law, William, *A Serious Call to a Devout and Holy Life* (1728; London, 1906).

Leavis, Q. D., 'A Critical Theory of Jane Austen's Writings', *Scrutiny* (1941–4) X, 61–87, 114–42, 272–94, and XII, 104–19.

Lee, Hermione, ' "Taste" and "Tenderness" as Moral Values in the Novels of Jane Austen', in *Literature of the Romantic Period*, ed. R. T. Davies and B. G. Beatty (Liverpool, 1976).

Lennox, Charlotte, *The Female Quixote* (1752), ed. Margaret Dalziel (London, 1970).

Lewis, Michael, *A Social History of the Navy 1793–1815* (London, 1960).

Liddell, Robert, *The Novels of Jane Austen* (1963; London, 1974).

Litz, A. Walton, *Jane Austen: A Study of Her Artistic Development* (London, 1965).

Locke, John, *An Essay Concerning Human Understanding* (1690), ed. Peter H. Nidditch (Oxford, 1975).

Lodge, David, *Language of Fiction* (London, 1966).

_____, (ed.), *Jane Austen: 'Emma'* (London, 1968).

McCann, Charles J., 'Setting and Character in *Pride and Prejudice*', *Nineteenth-Century Fiction*, XIX (1964) 65–75.

McDonald, Elizabeth, 'Evangelicalism and *Mansfield Park*': see Garside.

McKillop, Alan D., 'The Context of *Sense and Sensibility*', *Rice Institute Pamphlet*, XLIV (1957) 65–78.

McMaster, Juliet, 'Surface and Subsurface in Jane Austen's Novels', *Ariel*, V, no. 2 (1974) 5–24.

Mansell, Darrel, *The Novels of Jane Austen* (London, 1973).

Mingay, G. E., *English Landed Society in the Eighteenth Century* (London, 1963).

——, *The Gentry: The Rise and Fall of a Ruling Class* (London, 1976).

Moler, Kenneth L., *Jane Austen's Art of Allusion* (1968; Lincoln, Neb., 1977).

——, 'The Two Voices of Fanny Price', in *Jane Austen: Bicentenary Essays*, ed. John Halperin (Cambridge, 1975).

Monaghan, David, '*Mansfield Park* and Evangelicalism: A Reassessment', *Nineteenth-Century Fiction*, XXXIII (1978) 215–30.

——, *Jane Austen: Structure and Social Vision* (London, 1980).

——, (ed.), *Jane Austen in a Social Context* (London, 1981).

More, Hannah, *Poems, Tragedies*, vol. II of *The Works of Hannah More* (London, 1830).

——, *Strictures on the Modern System of Female Education* (1799), vol. V. of *The Works of Hannah More* (London, 1830).

——, *Coelebs in Search of a Wife* (1808), vol. VII of *The Works of Hannah More* (London, 1830).

Morgan, Susan, 'Intelligence in *Pride and Prejudice*', *Modern Philology*, LXXIII (1975) 54–68.

——, 'Polite Lies: The Veiled Heroine of *Sense and Sensibility*', *Nineteenth-Century Fiction*, XXXI (1976) 188–205.

——, *In the Meantime* (Chicago, 1980).

Mudrick, Marvin, *Jane Austen: Irony as Defense and Discovery* (1952; Berkeley, Calif., 1974).

Nardin, Jane, 'Jane Austen and the Problem of Leisure', in *Jane Austen in a Social Context*, ed. David Monaghan (London, 1981).

Odmark, John, *An Understanding of Jane Austen's Novels* (Oxford, 1981).

Page, Norman, *The Language of Jane Austen* (Oxford, 1972).

Paine, Tom, *Rights of Man* (1791–2), ed. Henry Collins (Harmondsworth, 1969).

Paulson, Ronald, *Satire and the Novel in Eighteenth-Century England* (New Haven, Conn., 1967).

Perkin, Harold, *The Origins of Modern English Society 1780–1880* (London, 1969).

Piozzi, Hester Lynch, *Anecdotes of the Late Samuel Johnson* (1786), ed. Arthur Sherbo (London, 1974).

Pope, Alexander, *The Poems of Alexander Pope*, ed. John Butt (London, 1963).

Porteus, Beilby, *The Works* (?1808), 6 vols (London, 1811).

Price, Martin, 'The Picturesque Moment', in *From Sensibility to Romanticism*, ed. Frederick W. Hilles and Harold Bloom (New York, 1965).

Rackin, Donald, 'Jane Austen's Anatomy of Persuasion', in *The English Novel in the Nineteenth Century*, ed. George Goodin (Urbana, Ill., 1972).

Radcliffe, Ann, *The Romance of the Forest*, 3 vols (London, 1791).

——, *The Mysteries of Udolpho* (1794), ed. Bonamy Dobrée (London, 1966).

Reynolds, Sir Joshua, *Discourses on Art* (1769–90), ed. Robert R. Wark (New Haven, Conn., 1975).

Richardson, Samuel, *Clarissa* (1747–8; London, 1932).

——, *Sir Charles Grandison* (1753–4), 3 vols, ed. Jocelyn Harris (London, 1972).

Roberts, Warren, *Jane Austen and the French Revolution* (London, 1979).

Roth, Barry, and Joel Weinsheimer, *An Annotated Bibliography of Jane Austen Studies 1952–1972* (Charlottesville, Va., 1973).

Rothstein, Eric, 'The Lessons of *Northanger Abbey*', *University of Toronto Quarterly*, XLVI (1974) 14–30.

Ruoff, Gene W., 'Anne Elliot's Dowry: Reflections on the Ending of *Persuasion*', *The Wordsworth Circle*, VII (1976) 342–51.

Ryle, Gilbert, 'Jane Austen and the Moralists' (1966), in *Critical Essays on Jane Austen*, ed. B. C. Southam (London, 1968).

Sacks, Sheldon, 'Golden Birds and Dying Generations', *Comparative Literature Studies*, VI (1969) 274–91.

Sadleir, Michael, 'The Northanger Novels: A Footnote to Jane Austen', *English Association Pamphlet*, LXVIII (1927).

Schorer, Mark, 'The Humiliation of Emma Woodhouse' (1959), in *Jane Austen: 'Emma'*, ed. David Lodge (London, 1968).

Scott, P. J. M., *Jane Austen: A Reassessment* (London, 1982).

Scott, Sir Walter, *Waverley* (1814; London, 1906).

——, unsigned review of *Emma*, *Quarterly Review*, XIV (1815) 188–201.

Shaftesbury, Antony Ashley Cooper, 3rd Earl of, *Characteristics* (1711), ed. John M. Robertson, 2 vols (Gloucester, Mass., 1963).

Shelley, Percy Bysshe, *A Defence of Poetry*, in *Shelley's Prose*, ed. David Lee Clark (Albuquerque, 1954).

Sheridan, Richard Brinsley *The Rivals* (1775), in *The Dramatic Works of Richard Brinsley Sheridan*, I, ed. Cecil Price (Oxford, 1973).

Sherlock, Thomas, *Several Discourses Preached at the Temple Church* (London, 1754–8).

Shorter, Clement, *The Brontës: Life and Letters*, 2 vols (London, 1908).

Smith, Charlotte, *Emmeline* (1788), ed. Anne Henry Ehrenpreis (London, 1971).

Smith, Leroy W., *Jane Austen and the Drama of Woman* (London, 1983).
Southam, B. C., *Jane Austen's Literary Manuscripts* (London, 1964).
——, letter on *Persuasion*, *Essays in Criticism*, XVI (1966) 480.
——, (ed.), *Critical Essays on Jane Austen* (London, 1968).
——, '"Regulated Hatred" Revisited', in *Jane Austen: 'Northanger Abbey' and 'Persuasion'*, ed. B. C. Southam (London, 1976).
Southam, B. C. (ed.), *Jane Austen: 'Northanger Abbey' and 'Persuasion'* (London, 1976).
The Spectator (1711–14), 5 vols, ed. Donald F. Bond (Oxford, 1965).
Spring, David, 'Interpreters of Jane Austen's Social World: Literary Critics and Historians', in *Jane Austen: New Perspectives*, ed. Janet Todd (New York, 1983).
Steele, Sir Richard: see *The Spectator*.
Sternberg, Meir, *Expositional Modes and Temporal Ordering in Fiction* (Baltimore, 1978).
Sterne, Laurence, *The Life and Opinions of Tristram Shandy* (1759–67), ed. Graham Petrie (Harmondsworth, 1967).
Swift, Jonathan, *Gulliver's Travels* (1726), ed. Herbert Davis (Oxford, 1959).
Tanner, Tony, Introduction to *Mansfield Park* (Harmondsworth, 1966).
——, Introduction to *Sense and Sensibility* (Harmondsworth, 1969).
——, Introduction to *Pride and Prejudice* (Harmondsworth, 1972).
——, 'In Between: Anne Elliot Marries a Sailor and Charlotte Heywood Goes to the Seaside', in *Jane Austen in a Social Context*, ed. David Monaghan (London, 1981).
Tave, Stuart M., *Some Words of Jane Austen* (Chicago, 1973).
Thompson, E. P., *The Making of the English Working Class* (1963; Harmondsworth, 1968).
Thompson, F. M. L., *English Landed Society in the Nineteenth Century* (London, 1963).
Todd, Janet (ed.), *Jane Austen: New Perspectives*, Women and Literature, n.s. III (New York, 1983).
Tompkins, J. M. S., *The Popular Novel in England 1700–1800* (London, 1932).
——, 'Elinor and Marianne: A Note on Jane Austen', *Review of English Studies*, XVI (1940) 33–43.
Trilling, Lionel, '*Mansfield Park*', *Partisan Review*, XXI (1954) 492–511.
——, 'Emma and the Legend of Jane Austen' (1957), in *Beyond Culture* (1965; Harmondsworth, 1967).
——, *Sincerity and Authenticity* (1972; London, 1974).
Trimmer, Sarah, *Fabulous Histories* (London, 1786).
Van Ghent, Dorothy, *The English Novel: Form and Function* (1953; New York, 1967).
Warnock, Mary, *Imagination* (London, 1976).

Watson, J. Steven, *The Reign of George III 1760–1815* (Oxford, 1960).

Weinsheimer, Joel C., *An Annotated Bibliography of Jane Austen Studies 1952–1972*: see Roth.

——, '*Mansfield Park*: Three Problems', *Nineteenth Century Fiction*, XXIX (1974) 185–205.

——, 'In Praise of Mr Woodhouse: Duty and Desire in *Emma*', *Ariel*, VI, no. 1 (1975) 81–95.

Whately, Richard, unsigned review of *Northanger Abbey* and *Persuasion*, *Quarterly Review*, XXIV (1821) 352–76.

Wiesenfarth, Joseph, *The Errand of Form: An Assay of Jane Austen's Art* (New York, 1967).

Wilberforce, William, *A Practical View of the Prevailing Religious System* (London, 1797).

Wilson, Edmund, 'A Long Talk about Jane Austen' (1944), in *Classics and Commercials* (New York, 1950).

Wollstonecraft, Mary, *Vindication of the Rights of Woman* (1792), ed. Miriam Kramnick (Harmondsworth, 1975).

Woolf, Virginia, *The Common Reader*, 1st ser. (London, 1925).

Wordsworth, William, *Poetical Works*, ed. Thomas Hutchinson, rev. Ernest de Selincourt (London, 1936).

Wright, Andrew, H., *Jane Austen's Novels: A Study in Structure* (1953; Harmondsworth, 1962).

Zietlow, Paul N., 'Luck and Fortuitous Circumstance in *Persuasion*: Two Interpretations', *ELH*, XXXII (1965) 179–95.

Zimmerman, Everett, 'Pride and Prejudice in *Pride and Prejudice*', *Nineteenth-Century Fiction*, XXIII (1968) 64–73.

Index